Yul Brynner

Yul Brynner

A Biography

Michelangelo Capua

McFarland & Company, Inc., Publishers
Jefferson, North Carolina, and London

LIBRARY OF CONGRESS CATALOGUING-IN-PUBLICATION DATA

Capua, Michelangelo, 1966–
    Yul Brynner : a biography / Michelangelo Capua.
        p.   cm.
    Includes bibliographical references and index.

    ISBN-13: 978-0-7864-2461-0
    (softcover : 50# alkaline paper) ∞

    1. Brynner, Yul.   2. Actors— United States— Biography.
I. Title.
PN2287.B74C37   2006
792.02'8092 — dc22   2006013607

British Library cataloguing data are available

On the cover: Yul Brynner in an undated publicity shot

Manufactured in the United States of America

McFarland & Company, Inc., Publishers
    Box 611, Jefferson, North Carolina 28640
    www.mcfarlandpub.com

To Yaakov

Acknowledgments

For their assistance and support, I am indebted to many friends, without whom the completion of this project would have been impossible. I would like to thank Irma Galente, Yaakov Perry, Walter Federico Salazar, Massimo Ranieri, Christine Kruger from Margaret Herrick Library of the Academy of Motion Picture Arts and Sciences, Beverly Hills; the staff of the New York Public Library for the Performing Arts at Lincoln Center; the Museum of Television and Radio of New York; the staff of the British Library's Humanity Reading Room, St. Pancras, London; the staff of Vancouver Public Library, Vancouver, British Columbia; Rock Brynner, author of the memoir *Yul: The Man Who Would Be King*; and Jerry Ohlinger's Movie Material Store, New York.

Most of all, my great gratitude goes to my sister Roberta for her precious help and immeasurable generosity and to my editor Stuart Williams for his invaluable work and patience.

Contents

Acknowledgments   vi

A Note on Yul Brynner's Name   viii

Introduction   1

  1. Past Imperfect   3

  2. Gypsy King   10

  3. Television Debut   25

  4. I'm the King! Etc., Etc., Etc.   30

  5. Dietrich and Crawford   42

  6. Cecil B. DeMille   49

  7. Once Upon a Time in Hollywood   56

  8. A Bastard with a Heart of Gold   75

  9. *The Magnificent Seven*   93

10. Surprise Flops   108

11. Terrible Choices   123

12. *Westworld*   136

13. Long Live the King!   145

Filmography   161

Stage Appearances   172

Documentaries, Music and Soundtracks,
  Radio Programs and Television Appearances   175

Brynner as Director   177

Notes   179

Bibliography   187

Index   195

A Note on
Yul Brynner's Name

Yul Brynner was named Youl Bryner by his parents, but for professional reasons he later changed the spelling of his first and last name from Youl Bryner to Yul Brynner. The spelling change is explained on page 19, after which the book uses the spelling "Yul Brynner" throughout.

Introduction

"Who was Yul Brynner?" A simple-sounding question, but a difficult one to answer. "He is the hairless cowboy, all dressed in black with a cigar in his mouth, from *The Magnificent Seven* and *Westworld*," men usually answer. "That bald, sexy actor who played in *The King and I* and *Anastasia*," women often reply. Yul Brynner was indeed a very handsome man, but with a different type of beauty, in stark contrast to the other Hollywood stars of the 1950s. He represented the antithesis of the myth of Samson, discovering his power only after *losing* his hair. Some Hollywood stars are born with special qualities, others have to invent them. Yul had the amazing capacity to transform his baldness from a common blemish into an outstanding trademark. Suddenly, after a razor cut, Yul Brynner became one of the sexiest actors in film history, representing the most authentic and irresistible image of masculinity.

"Who was Yul Brynner in private life?" For many years his origins were shrouded in mystery. His exotic past, which he created himself by inventing different versions of his childhood, became a fascinating question solved only after his death.

Yul was one of the very few actors of his generation who was not tormented or introverted. He showed a complete disinterest in psychoanalysis, and was quoted as saying, "The day anyone stretches me out on a couch, I'll be either drunk or dead."

Although he always showed great self-confidence and determination, many remember him sitting by himself in a corner, absorbed in his thoughts, sometimes with eyes bright with tears. He rarely spoke about his childhood but it was clear that something or someone in his past had hurt him and he was not able to completely forget the pain he suffered.

Once, while he was in Madrid shooting a movie, a girl approached him in a bar and asked, "Are you Yul Brynner?" He was sitting on a stool at the counter with a glass in his hand and, without turning or looking

1

at her, he replied, "No, I'm his double." It was an unkind lie to get rid of an intrusive fan, but also an answer that subconsciously hid an odd truth.

Only those who knew Yul in his private life knew that his personality was completely different from the characters he played on the screen and on the stage. He was neither as cold or as tough as he appeared in his pictures, but a true gentleman — cosmopolitan, intelligent, learned, sophisticated, womanizing, gifted with a rare sensitivity and a great sense of humor. Moreover, Yul was a man with a deep social commitment toward needy children. His life was ended by an incurable disease that he fought with a superhuman strength until he breathed his last breath.

1

Past Imperfect

"Ordinary mortals need but one birthday."
— Yul Brynner

It is extraordinary to note, after reading hundreds of articles and listening to numerous interviews, that no two versions of Yul Brynner's origins are alike. The exact dates and locations are unknown.

Respectable sources such as *Current Biography, Who's Who* and many periodicals include fabrications or imprecise information that came from Yul himself. Beginning when Yul added five years to his age to find a job, and then throughout his life, he always misinformed others about his past. Part of the reason was his huge ego, part was akin to playing a game, and part was because he really wanted to maintain some privacy in his life.

It was also his belief that reporters would never write about his family's amazing saga accurately. He preferred to let his own fervid imagination create sensational and often contradictory tales, rather than leaving it to the journalists.

Yul loved to surround himself with an aura of mystery. Some of his intimate friends recalled that Yul would love to accurately speak about the present and the future but rarely would discuss the past, trying to dispel the demons of some unhappy childhood memories. Inventing conflicting stories seemed to be the best solution to exorcise a haunting past which he was desperately trying to forget.

In the early 1960s, when astute journalist Pete Martin pointed out the inconsistencies in the circulating information Yul provided about his past, Yul tried to justify it by saying: "I think that as a human being I am entitled to keep that part of my life private. I believe the public is entitled to information about the past of me which is an entertainer, not about my wife and child, not about my childhood. My life in show business has been in my own hands; I am responsible for it. I'm willing to answer for it. My childhood was not in my hands. I am not responsible for it. Usually I refuse to discuss it. In spite of this, there are 10 or 12 stories in circulation about my early life.

"In one I was born in Sakhalin, an island lying off the coast of Siberia. In another my father was a Mongolian who chanced to be born in Switzerland. There is still another story that my father borrowed the Swiss name Bryner and substituted it for his real name, which was Taidje Khan. Some of the stories have it that my name at birth was Taidje Khan, too, although they do not make it clear whether I am supposed to be Taidje Khan, Jr.

"Another story runs that my mother was a Romanian gypsy, that in my eighth year my mother's mother took me with her to live in Europe and not long after our arrival there she died.... If you took the trouble to trace those stories, you'd find none of them was really told by me. They came out of conversations someone is *supposed* to have had with me, and when writers come to me to verify them, I tell each of them, 'Yes, that's true.' Because, no matter what story I tell them, writers invent things about me. Once they've invented them, they believe them. They tell these tales at a dinner party and they become part of the Brynner story. I don't want to embarrass anyone, so who am I to deny their fictions? I enjoy them."[1]

Until his very last interview, released shortly before his death, Yul would continue to add and remove false autobiographical details. Many years after his death, his son Rock wrote a book about his father that cleared up some of the mystery.

During the early years of his life, Rock Brynner did not know the truth about the origins of the paternal side of his family. Only after a rare moment of intimacy in a long, poignant conversation with his father was he able to finally piece together the complicated puzzle of Yul's family history.[2]

It all began in the early 1840s in Möriken-Wildegg, a small Swiss village not far from Zurich, when local doctor Johannes Bruner married the young and beautiful Marie Huber Von Windisch. Within several years, the couple had six children. Bruner tried to give them the best education available, despite struggling with economic difficulties. The only child not interested in going to school was Julius, their youngest son, whose undisciplined behavior and infrequent classroom attendance became a problem for his teachers.

Julius was 14 when he ran away, driven by a rebellious spirit and a strong desire to travel around the world and make his fortune abroad. His travels brought him to the coast of North Africa, where he befriended a captain whose ship was bound for Japan. The captain offered to take him aboard if he would work as the ship's boy. Julius accepted the job, unaware that it was a pirate ship on which he would be traveling for the next few months. During the long voyage, the pirates would attack cargo ships returning from the Orient with valuable goods. Julius was locked in the galley during these battles, and released only after the raids were over. The ship finally docked in a little Japanese port near the town of Yokohama, where the young Bruner found a job as a clerk at an import company. He became close to the company's owner, who considered him almost like a son. When the old man died, Julius (now called Yulius Bryner) inherited a business that had become one of the Far East's most successful import-export operations. He renamed it Bryner & Company.[3]

A few years later, Yulius, then married with children, was dissatisfied with his wealthy life. He abandoned his family and moved to Vladivostok in the Russian Orient, about 70 miles from the Chinese border, where he expanded his company.

In Russia, ignoring his previous marriage, he wedded Natalya Kurkutova, a very stern woman with a strong, cold character. Natalya was the daughter of a Mongolian prince whose descendants were said to go back to Genghis Khan. The couple had six children — three boys and three girls. Natalia's favorite was handsome and outgoing Boris, who became a mineralogical engineering student at the University of St. Petersburg, where Yulius had sent all three sons.

In St. Petersburg, Boris fell in love with Marousia Blagovidova, the daughter of a doctor from Vladivostok. A statuesque Russian beauty, blue-eyed and slender, she was studying voice and acting at the St. Petersburg Conservatory. Not tolerating his future wife's desire for an artistic career, Boris pressured Marousia into marriage during her final year at the conservatory. The couple got married in St. Petersburg in 1914, only two and a half months after their first meeting. They lived there until Vera, their first child, was born. The Bryners then moved to Vladivostok, where they settled with Boris' mother — who detested Marousia and considered her unfit for her favorite son. Natalya pestered her daughter-in-law even more when Marousia's sister Vera married Felix, another of

Natalia's sons. On July 11, 1920, Marousia gave birth to her first baby boy, who was christened in the Russian Orthodox Church as Youl Borisovitch, honoring the memory of his paternal grandfather Yulius.

In these years after the 1917 Revolution, terrible economic conditions existed throughout Russia, even in the remote city of Vladivostok. Unlike many members of the well-off local bourgeoisie, the Bryners decided not to flee abroad, even though Brynner & Co. had branches in several towns in Northern China.

In 1924, Boris Bryner followed his father's example and abandoned his family, leaving only a brief goodbye letter in which he explained that he had fallen madly in love with an actress of the Russian Art Theatre. Boris moved to Harbin, Manchuria, and married his lover a few months later.

Although Youl was still very young, the trauma of abandonment had strong, painful effects on him that he carried forever inside him, greatly influencing his own life. But the greatest shock was for Marousia, who suddenly found herself alone with two small children to support. The desperate mother moved first to her sister's country house outside Vladivostock. Then she decided to take the children to Harbin, closer to their father, hoping to receive better financial support.

While in Harbin, Youl was enrolled in an excellent Russian-speaking school.[4] A beautiful child, with a distinct personality, Youl was not only active and outgoing but also loved reading and watching ants for hours and hours.

Often Youl would wear different colored socks or shoes just to attract the attention of his schoolmates. Once, his mother bought him some very large swimming trunks (that was the current fashion). Youl, not happy with that style, shortened them with a pair of scissors, making them a pair of bathing briefs. When Marousia gave him his first guitar as a present, he played it in school recitals, making up melodies that he would claim were old gypsy songs.

One funny anecdote demonstrates that Youl had a narcissistic personality even as a young boy. One day while he was having a hot bowl of porridge for breakfast, he began coughing and could not stop. The coughing spell was so intense that he was almost choking, so Marousia rushed him to the hospital. The coughing stopped the first night, but the doctors kept him for observation for almost a week. They were unable to find the cause of the problem. When it seemed that he had recovered completely and the attention of the doctors was not concentrated on him any more, Youl pretended that the cough had returned. The following day, he also claimed that he was losing his sight. His acting was so convincing that a doctor gave him a walking cane, which he took back when Youl told him that he miraculously could see again.[5]

During his first year of life, Youl came in contact with the entertainment world. He once told an interviewer, "A neighbor was the famous Chinese actor called Mai Long Thang. He played only feminine roles, in the classical Chinese opera. And I think that his being a neighbor had something, some influence, because he would invite me and he'd show me costumes and so forth. But he lived, dressed entirely as a woman, although he was a man, married and everything.... He always dressed as a woman and walked as a woman.... He was an extraordinary man ... a very courageous man, in fact. And I think that it had some influence on me."[6]

Youl also remembered that someone once took him to the theater to see Mai Long Thang in a show called *Pe Pai Ke*. Its American version, *Lute Song*, would mark Yul's Broadway debut several years later.

Living with his mother and his sister, Youl would wait anxiously for a visit from his estranged father, who, in a rare prior meeting, had told Youl that he would visit him at home. Boris did not keep his promise, greatly disappointing his son, who would develop a deep hatred for him.

Boris' despicable behavior toward his family is probably a good explanation of Yul's refusal, as an adult, to discuss his childhood and his family, making up multiple, imaginative tales of his early days.

Marousia wanted to move, and tried to decide between the U.S. and France before choosing the latter. For one reason, American officials viewed her and her offspring as Russian (despite the Swiss passports she obtained by marrying Boris), and would not admit her under the Swiss quota. For another, she felt that France might provide an easier transition. At the time, Paris had one of the largest Russian communities in Western Europe, and Marousia thought that her daughter Vera would have had a better chance to pursue her budding career as a professional opera singer, and that Youl, now 14, would receive a better education.

The Bryners arrived in Paris with very little money and changed their address frequently until they finally settled in an apartment in Rue Catulle-Mendès. Thanks to the help of some Russian friends, Youl was able to attend the exclusive Lycée Moncelle, outside Paris. There he immediately showed his sharp intelligence and an energetic, stubborn character.

Youl's exuberance soon became the despair of his teachers and schoolmates, with whom he often would pick fights.

Worried by the teachers' continuous complaints, Marousia decided to consult a psychiatrist about Youl. The specialist did not find anything wrong with Youl's vivacious behavior.

Youl attended school in Paris for only two years. At the time, Youl was speaking only Russian and some Chinese, but was struggling to learn French. His difficulty with French probably contributed to his lack of interest in studying. He seemed interested only in participating in individual sport competitions.

One evening a friend of Marousia's took Vera and Youl to a restaurant in Montmartre where The Dimitrievitches, a group of Russian gypsies, performed dances and songs from the Tzigan repertoire. It was love at first sight for Youl. Only a few days later, he acquired a seven-string guitar and began to take lessons, learning the songs of the tziganes. He would tell his mother he was going to the movies and then sneak off to see the gypsies night after night.

In several nocturnal escapes, Youl returned to the Dimitrievitches and became acquainted with them. The family patriarch Ivan had performed for Rasputin in the 1920s before moving to Paris with his three children, Valentina, Aliosha and Marukha.

Valentina, the eldest daughter, had long pitch-black hair and a very distinctive voice. Aliosha, the only son, was a gifted guitarist with a powerful deep voice, while Marukha was the beauty of the family. Her sexy voice and feminine sensuality attracted Youl, who developed a huge crush on her. Before long, the Dimitrievitches became Youl's second family; their invaluable professional advice was crucial to his fledgling musical career.

On June 15, 1935, Youl made his debut playing the guitar in a Parisian nightclub with a gypsy orchestra of 30 guitarists. A few days later, he went with his mother to Deauville in Normandy where she had rented a cottage for the summer. On the beaches of the resort city, Youl was able to find work as lifeguard thanks to his well-built body. During that summer he broke the hearts of many girls vacationing in that area. One girl got pregnant and Youl's family financially helped her get an abortion.

Once he returned to Paris, Youl did not go back to school, but kept this hidden from his mother. He changed many jobs until one day, by chance, he came in contact with a new world—the circus—which suddenly changed his life.[7]

2

Gypsy King

"I have no respect for money at all, I piss on it."
— Yul Brynner

In Paris, Youl would regularly sing with a group of gypsy musicians in several nightclubs, earning only the tips left by customers.

One day in Place Pigalle, in a small café not far from a cabaret where he would work until dawn, Youl met some circus performers who were having an early breakfast before their daily training. A group of trapeze artists invited him to watch their rehearsals. Youl was so impressed by their acrobatic performances that he lied shamelessly, telling them that he had been on a trapeze once. The artists pushed him to try it again and Youl, without any hesitation, climbed up to the pedestal from which they were swinging. At that point, he discovered he had a fear of heights, but his reckless pride was stronger than his fright. He pushed off and within seconds found himself in the hands of the catcher. His bravado caused him serious physical pain, however. This stunt required incredible arm and hand strength, which is normally gained from extensive professional training. He went back to the pedestal with everyone laughing and telling him, "You can practice with us, if you want to. We think you have the build and eventually there'll be an opening and you'll come in."[1] Three months later, *Cirque d'Hiver* officially hired Youl.

The *Cirque d'Hiver* was one of the oldest established circuses in Europe that had the unique characteristic of performing in a theater in the center of Paris rather than a less-permanent structure. Youl spent a great deal of time with the acrobats and the clowns. As he recalled in an interview many years later, "There were some very old [clowns], and one of them was a great mime, a marvelous mime, a very silent clown, and I started studying pantomime with him. I developed a character of a very sad clown, who flew around on the trapeze and made terrible mistakes, caught himself at the last moment, saved himself at the last moment, grabbed for empty air, and suddenly would catch this trapeze coming from nowhere. And that flying clown was really quite success-ful."[2]

For the curtain call, the trapeze artists used to do a few specialties. Youl was always the last of them to jump off. He would bounce up from the net and try to reach for the trapeze again, and did a kind of run-ning-in-the-air act. His performance was indeed original, because he was the only trapeze artist wearing a clown costume and making a flashy dive (like a triple somersault).

Youl's exotic look and his charm quickly gained him the reputation of a Don Juan with the ladies in the audience. A few of his colleagues remember episodes (some probably fictional) in which a couple of infu-riated men were looking to teach him a lesson at the end of the show when they learned that he had been intimate with their girlfriends.

One tragic night, Youl's promising circus career was suddenly com-promised by a terrible accident during the curtain call. "The man who jumped just before me was our catcher," Youl recalled. "He was a much heavier man than any of us.... And somehow it dislodged one of the side cords when I rebounded on the net, trying to jump up.... I used to rebound and then jump up and try to reach the trapeze once again ... pretending to, or running in the air.... Well, I found myself doing that comedy routine going completely sideways. And I went into a corridor, into an exit, out of the arena and fell on my left side on a set of paral-lel bars from a Japanese parallel bar act that preceded us and cracked up my whole left side. I had 49 fractures."[3]

In a later interview, Youl explained that he developed a phobia of whistling after the accident. "When I cracked up in the circus, I was 17. In circuses, people turn their back and move away from you when you're badly hurt because it puts fear into them. So they just let me lie there until the ambulance arrived. And, in the corridor behind the seats, some-one was whistling. And I didn't have the strength to yell, 'Don't whis-tle.' And somehow, these things come to haunt you."[4]

Youl wore a plaster cast for several months. The doctors told him he would probably walk with a limp for the rest of his life and would not regain the use of his left arm because the shoulder was badly smashed. When they finally took off the plaster cast, he immediately started rehabilitation, beginning with very simple movements like open-ing and closing his hands three minutes in the morning and three minutes in the afternoon. This ritual gradually increased to three hours a day at the end of the tenth day.

His great determination (and fierce rage over what the doctors told him) gave him incredible strength, miraculously contributing to an almost full recuperation of his arm. The recovery was so extraordinary that after nine months of being out of the cast, he ended up playing jai alai professionally as a therapeutic sport. With eight to nine hours of daily physical work, Youl developed a stronger right arm and stronger legs, the latter being an underdeveloped part of the body for trapeze acrobats. "What it did to my life," Youl pointed out, "was that I decided that I would not contemplate any kind of acting career which had been kind of in the back of my mind, eventually to leave the circus and become an actor or have a pantomime company of my own.... It turned my mind toward other things. I decided to cover a lot more ground in the theater, train myself eventually to become a director ... a director can limp. I did have a limp, although I was covering it up and nobody noticed it. I still have it, although you don't see it on stage. But when I'm tired, I limp on my good leg — not the one that was so badly broken."[5]

Seventeen-year-old Youl had a capacity to maintain a positive attitude even in tragic moments, showing not only physical strength, but also an inner power. He later explained this power was coming out of a strong instinct of self-preservation. However, Youl's return to work at the *Cirque d'Hiver*, now only as a clown, was heartbreaking. Each time he would watch the trapeze acrobats flying over his head, he cried. For that reason, he quit.

During his recuperation, Youl began smoking opium. Imported from the French colony, Indochina, opium was very fashionable in Paris during the '20s and '30s. At first he started using it as a painkiller for his recurrent backaches and joint pain. Later it became an addiction that he tried to keep secret.

After leaving the circus, Youl performed in the Russian *boites* of Paris, even though playing the guitar had became extremely difficult for him. In fact, his hands had acquired the tendency to close; his long, strenuous training as a trapeze artist had increased fibrous growth in his fingers.

At the time, the Moscow Art Theater was touring France under the direction of Michael Chekhov, nephew of the famous playwright. Chekhov was a disciple of Stanislavsky, who had developed one of the most famous acting techniques. Youl watched many of the plays performed by the Russian company and was impressed by the personal variations Chekhov had brought to the original acting method. That experience gave him the deep conviction that only through Chekhov would he find what he was looking for—"a concrete and tangible way to reach a mastery of the elusive thing that one calls the technique of acting."[6]

Chekhov's company was on its way to Devon, England, where the director planned to seek political asylum and establish an acting school. To Chekhov, Russia's political regime had become intolerable.

Youl's opium dependence had become so strong that he had to postpone following Chekhov to England and ask for help from his aunt Vera, who lived in Switzerland. In order not to alarm his mother and sister, Youl lied about his health and told them he was going simply to visit his aunt. He left for Lausanne, where he was first hospitalized and then transferred to a private sanatorium. His long period of recovery continued at his aunt's home. After a year he was able to return to Paris in perfect shape.

With the help of a friend, Youl got work as an apprentice at the Theâtre des Mathurins with Georges and Ludmilla Pitoëff. There, the repertory of dramas by Strindberg, Pirandello, Shaw and Ibsen was performed in both Russian and French. "I worked without being paid as an apprentice ... and I did about everything you can do in the theater. I worked as a carpenter ... as a rigging man. I worked with ropes. I worked as a stagehand, I worked as an electrician.... And the Russian actors always insisted an actor must know how to do makeup. That is why so many of them later on became makeup artists. And one curious incident that happened was that one of them said, 'Look, you can pick up some money by helping me. I have to make something like 300 and 400 mustaches.' I said, 'Fine.'"[7] That was the way Youl learned how to apply makeup, which later became useful to him when he performed in *The King and I.*

After a few months of sweeping the stage, cleaning the dressing rooms and putting the props in order, Youl was finally given some minor roles. He played parts like the lover in the play *Camille,* but without much success.

Youl claimed that during that time he also attended the Sorbonne. This seems very unlikely, not only because of his dislike of studying, but also because he wouldn't have had the time to work and study simultaneously. Moreover, the university in Paris does not have any sort of documentation of his graduation. It is more likely that he only audited some classes for a limited period of time and later, when he became a star, embellished the truth to make his *curriculum vitae* more interesting.

In those days, Europe was in a state of political turmoil with the looming threat of war. Youl's sister, now a fairly successful soprano, married a Russian pianist and moved to the United States. Youl wanted to enlist in the French army, but due to his trapeze injuries he was rejected. His mother decided to go back to China, this time to the city of Dalian, where her former husband Boris had settled with his new wife Katya Kornakova and their adopted daughter.[8]

Youl decided to travel together with his mother. The trip was an occasion to get to know his father, who left him when he was four years old. When they finally reunited, things did not go as Youl had imagined. Boris was, in fact, a complete disappointment. Physically he looked much older than Youl remembered and in the photographs he had seen. But what really overwhelmed him was Boris' arrogant and authoritative behavior, causing many arguments. As Victoria Brynner (Yul's daughter) pointed out years later, "Yul never talked about his father much, but when he did it wasn't with great tenderness. It was with quite a bit of rejection."[9] Youl found Katya more interesting than his father. Years before, she had been a student of Michael Chekhov at the Moscow Art Theater. She shared with Youl her memories of her experience with Chekhov, co-founder and director of that acting school. His father's new wife told him how important it would have been for Youl to study acting with Chekhov. Youl revealed that, before going into rehab in Switzerland, he had sent an application to Chekhov's theater at Dartington Hall in England, which was rejected. Katya informed him that, after the beginning of the war, Chekhov had moved to the United States and started a new acting company in Ridgefield, Connecticut.

During his stay in China, Marousia was diagnosed with leukemia. With the hope of receiving more advanced treatments, she decided to join her daughter Vera in America. Youl decided to accompany her on the long journey. He also obtained a letter of recommendation from Katya in hopes of gaining admittance to Chekhov's acting school again.

Youl remembered the trip to the United States as very tortuous. He and his mother had to wait a month in Kobe, Japan, until they could get on a boat headed for San Francisco. Because of the war, all the American citizens were ordered to immediately evacuate Japan and therefore had priority to board all the ships going to the U.S. Youl and Marousia were finally able to leave, and after a four-month crossing arrived in California, just a month before the bombing at Pearl Harbor.[10] They continued the trip to New York by train.

Speaking his native Russian, a flawless French and virtually no English, Youl headed at once for Ridgefield, Connecticut, where he was admitted to the Chekhov Theatre Studio run by "The Professor" (Youl's nickname for Chekhov) and his assistant George Shdanoff.

"All we knew was that a Chinaman was coming to join our group," recalled one student. "He came from China and we expected someone on an order of a Chinese laundryman. We were all amazed when he arrived. No one had ever seen anyone like him. He was very young, but he had done so much. His stories about his experiences in France and China seemed fantastic, but we never caught him in an out-and-out lie, although we tried."[11]

"The Professor" was crazy about Youl from the beginning because he was energetic, charming and capable. Chekhov wanted his new pupil to go on tour with the company, playing one-night engagements of Shakespeare's *Twelfth Night*. Although he was playing the small role of Fabian the servant, Youl worried about his accent. His presence on stage and his fencing ability hid his mediocre acting. The company toured little towns across America performing in local small theaters or auditoriums. Youl drove the company truck with the show's props and costumes. In Louisiana he was stopped by the police, who arrested him for not having a valid license. Youl could not explain himself in English and spent a night in jail with black prisoners, since the "white" jail was full.[12] The unsanitary conditions made it a traumatizing experience. The following day, some members of the company were able to rescue him.

On December 2, 1941, *Twelfth Night* opened at Broadway's Little Theater. The reviewers utterly panned the show without mentioning Youl's name. *The New York Times* praised some of the performers but deeply disliked Chekhov and Shdanoff's adaptation of Shakespeare's comedy.[13] This Broadway fiasco would later convince Chekhov to move the Theatre Studio from Connecticut to 56th Street in New York in order to teach special classes for professional actors.

Life with Chekhov's group was very strict in some respects. The dedicated actors polished their art from early morning until late at night, studying different subjects including psychology, occultism and hypnosis. Youl lived at the dorm where his room on the men's floor had an original tent-like Oriental décor with rugs hung on the walls and drapes looped down from the ceiling. He would often go to visit his mother, with whom he shared part of his earnings to help pay her costly medical bills.

In New York, Youl frequently posed nude for art classes and photographers for $5 or $10 a session. "It was for money, eatin' money. I did it three, four times a week.... I don't see anything wrong with it morally," he explained in 1977, when one of his nude photographs (taken by George Platt Lynes) was published in Andy Warhol's *Interview*. "It was done in a studio with 50 people around. I didn't do it for art. I did it from hunger." That particular photograph was part of a full-frontal nude series in which Youl had a full head of hair and showed his statuesque, athletic body. "I needed the money. It would only be surprising if I did it now that I am a star."[14]

To supplement his income, Youl performed as a guitarist and singer at the Blue Angel and the Monte Carlo, the trendiest nightclubs in New York, and entertaining at exclusive parties. He never refused any part-time job offered to him. "I have done everything to earn a buck and I hated every minute of it," he once said.[15]

Vera Brynner explained that her brother worked very hard in those days to help pay for their mother's medical expenses. He made sure that Marousia received the best treatments by the best doctors with the best nurses. He also made sure to spend as much time as he could by her side and to read every new publication or book on leukemia to see what things could be done to improve her health.

When America entered the war, Youl tried to enlist in the U.S. army, but he was declared unfit because of tubercular spots in one of his lungs. In the summer of 1942, Youl obtained a job at the French Desk in the Office of War Information. He worked as a French-language announcer and commentator on the *Voice of America*, sending short-wave broadcasts beamed at Nazi-occupied France. Despite French not being his mother tongue, his pronunciation was perfect and without any trace of an accent. Youl would spend time between broadcasts reading detective pulp magazines. His part-time job allowed him to attend Chekhov's classes, and lasted two years, until the invasion in Normandy in June 1944.

Ludmilla Pitoëff, Youl's former acting teacher in France, planned a United States tour with her company and cast him in a leading role in Paul Claudel's drama *L'Annonce fait à Marie*. The play debuted at the Barbizon Plaza Theatre in New York on May 20, 1942, as a benefit performance for the scholarship fund of the Lycée Français in New York.

L'Annonce fait à Marie was a dramatic medieval allegory in which Youl played two parts—one of them Pierre de Craon, a leper appearing only in the prologue. Both were ignored by the *New York Times* critic who lukewarmly reviewed the show.

One night, at a party given by his agent Margaret Lindley, Youl met Virginia Gilmore. Gilmore, whose real name was Sherman Poole, was only one year older than Youl but already a known actress in Hollywood, where she lived. She had appeared in several films, some very successful, like *The Pride of the Yankees* with Gary Cooper. During the party, Youl performed with the guitar while Gilmore listened to the Gypsy lyrics and was enchanted. He was struck by her beauty and charm. They ended up chatting for the entire evening. When the party was over, Gilmore (who was in New York working in a play) invited him to her place, a little pied-a-terre which a friend had sublet her. During her five-week stay in the Big Apple, they saw each other almost every day. Finally Gilmore returned to Hollywood, where she was under contract with 20th Century-Fox. The relationship continued over the telephone.

In a 1949 interview, Youl revealed a curious anecdote: One of his friends had seen Virginia on stage and took Youl to the opening night, telling him he was about to see just the right girl for him. Youl was very skeptical and did not pay much attention. A few weeks later, when he met Virginia at the agent's party, he did not realize that she was the same girl his friend wanted to match him with. He became aware of it a few days into dating her.[16]

Nineteen hundred forty-three was a year of many events in Youl's life. The saddest event was the loss of his mother on February 4. He had done the impossible with the help of his sister, keeping his mother alive as long as he could without her suffering. But in the last months of her life, Marousia had to be hospitalized at New York Presbyterian Medical Center, a facility specializing in the treatment of leukemia. The week following his mother's death, Youl played in *The Moon Vine*, an unsuccessful play presented at the Morosco Theatre. For the first time he received a small mention in the bad review written by *The New York Sun*: "Among the cast members are Youl Bryner whose Southern accent is as believable as hominy served to an Eskimo."[17]

Youl spent part of his earnings in endless long-distance calls to Virginia in California. One night he was sentimentally nostalgic and proposed over the telephone. She immediately accepted and a few weeks later Youl made his first trip to Los Angeles.

After four long days crossing the country by train, Youl arrived in Hollywood, where the news of the wedding was already the talk of the town thanks to gossip columnist Louella Parsons. She wrote in her column, "Virginia Gilmore and some gypsy she met in New York will be married on September 6th." On that very date, Youl Bryner and Virginia Gilmore married at the Los Angeles County Courthouse. 20th Century-Fox did not favorably view the union; some studio executives had threatened that she would never get another part if she went through with the wedding. They would have preferred Gilmore marrying someone more famous rather than an "unknown gypsy," so that they (Fox) could make good use of the publicity. Youl never forgot that intimidation and, when he worked with Fox years later, gave them a very hard time.

At the end of 1943, the newlyweds went back to New York, where Virginia was cast in *Those Endearing Young Charms* on Broadway and Youl returned to performing at the nightclubs. A couple of weeks before the end of the year, Youl got a part with Ludmilla Pitoëff's company, which was presenting for the first time on an American stage the play *The House in Paris*, based on a novel by Elizabeth Bowen. The play premiered at Toronto's Royal Alexandra Theatre on January 17, 1944. Despite the mixed reviews, the show was a big hit. Youl was briefly mentioned by a critic of *The Toronto Daily Star*: "Yone Bryner [sic] effectively plays the tragic Jewish banker."[18] When the play was presented in Boston, the company was having serious financial problems. A new producer was found to back the show, but he did not like Youl's performance and wanted to fire him. When a production assistant tried to deliver the bad news to Youl, he did not even let him open his mouth, shouting, "I quit. I won't tolerate any money man telling me how to perform!"[19]

Upon his return to New York, Youl became ill — the tubercular spots found in his lungs during the Army medical examination had dramatically worsened. Many years later, Youl imaginatively explained to Italian writer Nantas Salvalaggio how he got that illness. "Once a beautiful actress, who was ill with tuberculosis, happened to be in my house. She maintained that the orgasm reached by people with tuberculosis had a very high and strong intensity and that Thomas Mann had said it as well.... Yes, tell me: I'm crazy, but I wanted to try it and that's how I got it. I wanted to make sure my friend was right"[20]

The doctor told Youl to go away to Arizona for at least three years, but Youl's dire financial situation and Virginia's work would not allow him to do so. Instead, he borrowed a friend's house in upstate Mount Kisco, New York, and stayed there for three months. Then he returned to work for the Office of War Information.

When Youl again went to see the doctor, he examined him and found his lungs healed and that all the scars had disappeared. When the physician asked him where he went, Youl teased him at first. He answered "the Himalayas" before telling the truth, explaining that he had learned an inner discipline that filled him with great positive energy which helped him to recover and gave him a more muscled, toned body.[21]

During that time, Youl became a naturalized American citizen and had the opportunity of changing his name into one more easily pronounced. He dropped the *o* from the first name and added an *n* to his last name. Youl Bryner finally became Yul Brynner.

After Yul's recovery from tuberculosis, Virginia's Broadway show closed and the Brynners found themselves living on her unemployment insurance. For a long period of time they ate nothing but rice. When someone invited them out, they would stuff themselves on big, rich meals after not eating right for days, and then get horribly sick. Yul, however, seemed not to worry too much about his financial situation.

Finally a colleague from the Office of War Information told Yul that the CBS television network was looking for an entertainer in a new comedy show called *Mr. Jones and His Neighbors*. Yul auditioned and got the job. The producers liked his accent and thought it could add a funnier touch to the show. Unfortunately, the program was canceled after only a week.

Years later, in a long interview with journalist Pete Martin, Yul explained what happened after his disastrous television debut. "It began in the winter of 1942–43, when CBS-TV was on the air only twice a week,

Tuesday and Friday afternoons from two to four. We had only one television studio. That one was way up under the roof on top of Grand Central Station. I got into TV first as a performer. Soon I became a TV director. The possibility of telling with pictures had great appeal to me. In those days the pay was extraordinary low. For performing in TV as well as directing I was paid $25 a week. It was the usual approach to an experimental job. Nobody was supposed to be out to make any money. CBS was hoping to make it in the future, but there were no profits on sight then, since there were no sponsors no commercials. Our only interruptions were stations breaks."[22]

When CBS started to hire directors, Yul applied and got a position as assistant director. However, his financial condition did not improve, forcing him to often borrow money from his sister Vera, now a successful lyric soprano. Every penny Yul earned he would immediately spend irresponsibly, like paying for a dinner in one of the most expensive restaurants in New York and then starving for two days. This extravagant lifestyle caused numerous arguments with Virginia, who could not understand his behavior.

At the end of 1945, Yul heard that Michael Myerberg, a Broadway impresario, was looking for a financial partner to produce a musical. The producer did not find any other backer and decided to finance the show himself. Myerberg hired John Houseman to direct the show and cast Mary Martin as the leading lady. He was only missing the right actor for the leading role of Tsai-Yong, a provincial young student who leaves his wife and his elderly parents to make his mark in the world, eventually falling in love with a princess from another village. *Lute Song*, originally titled *Pi Pa-Ki*, was adapted from an ancient Chinese legend and made into an 8-hour show.

As Mary Martin remembered in an interview, "Michael had seen Yul socially somewhere and asked me to audition him. He showed up at our house in New Canaan [Connecticut]. With no trace of stage fright he sat down yogi-fashion on the living room floor with his guitar and started playing and singing like a gypsy. His voice had such an excitement, such poise. I loved him and we signed him right away."[23]

Myerberg said to Yul, "Yes, I have a job for you. I'm going to give you the lead."[24] It took Myerberg two weeks to convince Yul that he was serious. The proof was the salary of $400 a week, which Yul received in advance.

Raymond Scott, who wrote the music of the show, was not very enthusiastic about Yul's untrained and wavering voice, but he was satisfied by Yul's other qualities: a sexy, vaguely Oriental look with an interesting speech.[25] To play the princess, the producer engaged an attractive unknown young actress by the name of Nancy Davis, who years later would marry Ronald Reagan. In her 1980 autobiography, Davis remembered Yul's charm and "how all the ladies in the company had crushes on him."[26]

Houseman, the director, was dissatisfied by Davis' acting and sought to fire her, but Mary Martin would not have it, threatening to quit if he dared. Davis' father was one of the country's most illustrious orthopedic surgeons and Martin had chronic back trouble. So Nancy stayed on.[27]

Rehearsals began early in October in the ballroom of the Beaux Arts Building on 67th Street and Central Park West. The show was rehearsed in three parts: the personal scenes on which Houseman worked alone with the actors; the musical numbers, mostly solos and duets for Yul and Martin (often rehearsed at Martins' home); and the group numbers.

On stage, Yul, who was not totally bald, wore a black toupee to emphasize his Oriental look.

Myerberg and Houseman had several quarrels before the show opened on Broadway. Once, according to Houseman, Myerberg called the entire company to rehearsal because he was completely dissatisfied with the production. The producer began to restage *Lute Song* beginning with scene one while the director was away for the weekend and unaware of the situation. The cast was too stunned to object and the new rehearsals lasted for hours, during which Yul almost fainted. Equity rules, which required that actors to have a 90-minute dinner break before their performance, had to put a stop to this maniacal activity. But Myerberg called another rehearsal for the following morning, increasing the general tension. Houseman arrived to find out that the producer, who had been in and out of a hospital several times for health problems, had a sudden relapse and was once again hospitalized. When he was finally released, he seemed completely pleased with the director's work and never mentioned that episode of "madness."[28]

Wanting to celebrate Yul's debut on Broadway, actress and producer Haila Stoddard threw a party. Yul and Martin sang some show tunes, making this gathering one of the unforgettable soirées of the season.

On February 6, 1946, after opening in New Haven and Boston, *Lute*

Song debuted at New York's Plymouth Theatre, where it ran for about six months before going on tour all over the United States.

Yul considered this show his real Broadway debut (the role he played previously in *Twelfth Night* was too small to be counted). Although *Lute Song* always had a special place in Yul's memory, he completely disliked his part, which he considered very difficult. "I had no skill as an actor — none at all. I was very, very untrained.... So I tried to hide my shyness, because I really felt shy on the stage playing this, this very weak young man.... I went back to what I knew of pantomime and I hid behind a very stylized performance that many people wrongly remember as quite remarkable, because I know it was not.... I was ashamed of myself playing that character. It was terribly awkward and terribly painful. Every performance was very painful for me and I hated my acting."[29]

Despite Yul's self-criticism, *Lute Song* received some good reviews. *Herald Tribune* editor Howard Barnes wrote, "Yul Brynner gives an extraordinarily honest and restrained characterization. His is not an easy role to play, since he is the unwitting villain of a piece which has death and destruction as a leitmotiv."[30]

After 142 performances on the New York stage, Yul proceeded to tour the United States with the show for one year. Mary Martin was replaced by German actress Dolly Haas, whose better characterization made *Lute Song* a hit.

Even though the musical received critical acclaim in New York, it was in Chicago, after Claudia Cassidy's enthusiastic review (she called the show a "sublime" experience), that it sold out all the performances. For his performance as the errant Tsai-Yong, Yul won the Donaldson Award as the most promising new star of the 1945–46 Broadway season.

In some of his first interviews, Brynner was already coming up with bizarre inventions about his past. One of the most bizarre and absurd was the explanation given about his baldness, which incredibly was included in the Broadway playbill of the show. He claimed that his hair was receding as the result of an incident that occurred while he served in the International Brigade during the Spanish Civil War. He was driving a truck for the Spanish Loyalists near Madrid when he was captured and imprisoned for two months, and the stress of his detention brought on his baldness. Yul, of course, had never been to Spain. When he repeated this fictional tale to a shrewd reporter, he gave too many implausible, contradictory details, and when confronted, he finally admitted that he had lied. "I planned to go, but I got sick," he alibied. "Doesn't that count for anything? The trouble with the world today is that it has become too exact-fact conscious!"[31] Afterward, when *Lute Song* toured, the "Spanish military experience" was removed from his playbill biography. In 1953, the story backfired on him again: Yul's name appeared on a list of Actor Equity members accused of Communist activity.[32] Luckily, he was able to disprove the allegation.

Although his financial situation improved drastically, Yul kept spending more money than he was actually earning. He even hired a personal assistant, Don Lawson, a patient man who stayed by his side almost 20 years, addressing him as Mr. B.

When *Lute Song* opened in New York, Virginia had a leading role in *Truckline Café*, produced by Elia Kazan. The cast included Karl Malden and Marlon Brando in one of his earliest roles on stage. The play closed after only 13 performances, just in time for Virginia to discover she was pregnant. She reluctantly decided to stay home, finding herself very lonely now that Yul was on tour. She was also tormented by persistent rumors about her husband's reputation as an unrepentant seducer of his female colleagues.

In fact, Yul was having an affair with Judy Garland, who saw him on stage and developed a crush on him after a meeting behind the scenes. Garland was married at the time to Vincent Minnelli. According to Rock Brynner. Yul fell madly in love with her. The lovers tried their best to keep their brief but intense romance a secret. But the gossip reached Hollywood columnist Louella Parsons, who reported in an article how Garland longed to make a movie of *Lute Song* with Yul. Apparently Vincent Minnelli knew what was going on and in his memoirs mentioned Judy's "intense infatuations."[33] When Virginia became aware of her husband's affair, she acted with great discretion, feigning ignorance. During her marriage, she would always handle Yul's numerous escapades with great dignity.

In December 1946, Virginia gave birth to a beautiful baby. When the contractions started, she unsuccessfully tried to reach Yul, who was in San Francisco. With the help of Vera Bryner, Virginia was able to pay the hospital expenses. Once Yul returned home, he was so excited about the birth of his son that he insisted to Virginia that they pass on the name Jules (Yul) to him. On the baby's birth certificate was written "Yul Brynner Junior," but they changed their minds shortly after. They then called him Rocky after Italian-American boxer Rocky Graziano.[34]

Yul returned to his tour, leaving wife and son at home. When *Lute Song* was performed in Chicago, Virginia went to visit him. While there, the actress playing Princess Nieou-Chi all suddenly left the cast. Myerberg, who happened to be visiting the production at the time, encouraged Virginia to take over the role. She accepted, despite the new baby keeping her busy, and played the part for three weeks at the National Theatre in Washington, D.C.

3

Television Debut

"I never sleep more than five hours a night. That gives me twice as much living time as most people have."
— Yul Brynner

When the *Lute Song* tour was over, Yul went back to work for CBS. Producer Worthington Miner had seen him on stage and offered him a part as a singer in a television musical program. Yul performed with great confidence in front of the cameras and it was a smash! Suddenly thousands of women were swooning over him, not only for his vocal ability but for his exotic, charismatic and telegenic look.

In March 1948, CBS permitted him to travel to London, accompanied by Virginia and Rocky, to perform at the Strand Theatre in *Dark Eyes*, a musical comedy written by Elena Miramova and Eugenie Leontovich.

British theatergoers and drama critics gave a warm reception to Yul's performance and to the play. In England the Brynners lived comfortably for the first time since their marriage. However, by the time the play closed, Yul was broke again. While Virginia and Rocky flew back to New York, Yul, who had lost his ticket playing poker, decided to go to Paris. There, he found a job through the manager of the famous restaurant, Chez Maxim's, singing and playing the guitar in the club Chez Carrere.

Yul returned home a few months later to find that Myerberg wanted him to play Tsai-Yong in *Lute Song* once again — this time at the Winter Garden Theater in London. In desperate need of money, Yul accepted and returned to England in October 1948. The show was damned by faint praise from critics. *The Daily Mail*, however, did describe Dolly Haas and Yul in their leading roles as a "rare feast for the eye."

In London, Yul stayed at a small bed and breakfast and sent part of his salary to Virginia, who had moved with Rocky into a modest Third

Avenue apartment. When Yul returned to the U.S., he worked for CBS in a late-afternoon talk show called *Mr. and Mrs.* that he had created with Virginia. The first American TV program hosted by husband and wife, it ran for 13 weeks. Yul recalled, "Virginia and I were the producers, writers, directors and performers…. We paid our guests' taxi fare. The budget didn't allow more than that. But we obtained some startling effects. We went on the air; we'd chat with our guests for 10 or 12 minutes. Then the floor manager would snap his finger and yell, 'You're on!' Virginia would turn to me and say with a surprised air, 'We're on!'"[1] Among the famous guests invited to appear on the show was Salvador Dalí, who became one of Yul's dearest friends when he (Yul) moved to Europe.

Virginia often would bring along Rocky to the TV studios because she could not afford a babysitter. Once *Mr. and Mrs.* ended, Yul was offered a position as director, marking the beginning of a brilliant career. As film director John Frankenheimer remembered, "When I first met Yul, I was an assistant director at CBS in New York television and I was working with Sidney Lumet, who had been Yul's assistant director. Yul was a myth to me because Sidney kept telling me these great stories what it was like to work with him in live TV in the programs he directed."[2] Frankenheimer recalled Yul as non-conformist. For instance, in many of Yul's CBS projects, he was not credited with the standard format "Directed by Yul Brynner"—rather, "Yul Brynner Directed."[3]

Working as a TV director was a satisfactory profession for Yul. He revealed in an interview a few years later that he even briefly thought of abandoning his acting career. "I worked 14 hours a day, made over $1000 a week and, frankly, felt very comfortable."[4]

Among Yul's colleagues were future Hollywood directors Martin Ritt and Sidney Lumet, with whom he co-directed segments of such prestigious programs as *Starlight Theatre, Danger, Omnibus* and *Studio One.* The latter is now considered a classic of American television. A whole generation of future stars got their first taste of acting in front of the camera in CBS's *Studio One*: Anne Bancroft, Charlton Heston, Jack Lemmon, Grace Kelly, James Dean, John Forsythe, Walter Matthau and Leslie Nielsen.

For some time, Yul and longtime friend Martin Ritt jointly directed and acted in CBS's *Starlight Theater* from a studio on New York's Ninth Avenue. Ritt and Yul would alternate the weekly chores: One week Yul

Smoking a cigarette with his wife, actress Virginia Gilmore.

directed while Ritt acted, and the next week Yul acted while Ritt directed. Cameraman Hamilton Morgan said years later that, at the beginning of each week, Ritt would storm into the studio and tell everybody what a "lousy" job Yul had done the preceding week. Then Yul would arrive a while later and pronounce his "negative" judgments on Ritt's performance from the prior week.[5] They were making fun of each other just to see the reaction of the people in the studio. In fact, they had great respect for each other.

Comedienne Carol Channing wrote in her autobiography that at that time Yul asked her to join him for one of his TV shows. "He wanted me to do a duet with him.... We had to wear brown lipstick because the red went white on the receiver.... We went to an apartment building way up on the West Side. We broadcast out of a small room that was about ten stories up. Yul grabbed his guitar for Tziganka, and we shrieked up a storm. We were wild. But only a few people had TV sets in 1947, so we never knew if it appealed to anyone.... I was always, along with many other women, crazy about Yul. He was married at the time to Virginia Gilmore, a movie star, and I was married to a pro football player on the Ottawa Rough Riders, but I don't think either of those people crossed our minds while we were televising this song.... Nothing ever came out of it, with only seven TV viewers, but this is what cemented our friendship."[6]

Channing also remembered that, years later, she inquired about Yul's mysterious origins. "I said: 'Now, Yul, I read in an interview with you that you were born in Shanghai and raised in Indonesia. The last time I saw you, you told me your mother was a Bessarabian Gypsy and your father was from Outer Mongolia.' Yul: 'Whatever I last said, that's what I am!' ... I know this sounds as if there were a romance between Yul and me. There wasn't. We were just crazy about each other, that's all."[7]

In 1948, Yul's father arrived in New York with his wife Katya for a brief visit. Boris had been in ill health for the past several months and wanted to see his children, who had been estranged from him for such a long time. Because Yul was always busy working at CBS, Boris spent most of his days with Virginia and Rocky. In the rare moments when father and son were together, it was still hard for Yul to forget that Boris had once abandoned him, his sister and his mother. He could not avoid reacting to him in a distant and cold manner. That was the last time Yul saw his father alive. A few weeks later, Boris returned to Asia, where he died the following year.

At the end of 1949, Yul did a screen test for a B-movie called *Port of New York*. It was the first American film directed by recent Hungarian émigré Lazlo Benedek (who would attain success directing major films like *Death of a Salesman* and *The Wild One*). Yul, screen-debuting with his own hair, was cast in the part of Paul Vicola, a cold and unforgiving racketeer involved in a plan to hijack a ship loaded with opium for medical needs.

Shot using a documentary approach (a narrator explains time and action) and employing interesting black-and-white, "neo-realistic" cinematography of New York in the '40s, *Port of New York* was a complete flop. *The New York Times* dismissed all the performances as "methodical"[8]; other critics considered Yul the only convincing actor in a forgettable film.

Between 1950 and 1951, Yul directed two successful TV series: *Danger*, a murder mystery series, and *The Stork Club Show*, a talk program. Via the latter, Yul became adept at introducing a commercial break when the guests became tongue-tied. One day after an episode of *The Stork Club Show*, he announced to the entire studio, "Wish me luck, kids, I'm going to an audition for *The King and I*."[9]

Sidney Lumet always remembered Yul's professionalism and generosity. "We'd had some rough days together, were good buddies; he called up and said, 'Listen, come on in, nobody knows what the hell they're doing, it's a ball,' and so I went in as Yul's A.D. and then when Yul left to do *The King and I*, I took over *Danger* from him."[10]

4

I'm the King!
Etc., Etc., Etc.

"Shaving my head, I suddenly was free of all that nonsense of young actors of being concerned with my looks."
— Yul Brynner

In 1950, composer Richard Rodgers and lyricist Oscar Hammerstein received a call from Fanny Holtzmann, Gertrude Lawrence's lawyer, asking if they would be interested in writing and producing a musical adaptation of Margaret Landon's best-selling novel *Anna and the King of Siam*.

The book had been already made into a successful 1946 film starring Rex Harrison and Irene Dunne. The story was based on the real adventures of Victorian English governess Anna Leonowens, who went to the court of the king of Siam in the 1860s to teach the king's many children English. The clash between Eastern and Western cultures is seen in the king and Anna, who ultimately found some values in common without falling in love with each other.

Gertrude Lawrence, who became a star after playing in Noël Coward's *Private Lives*, had acquired the rights to Landon's novel for the stage adaptation after literary agent Helen Strauss first brought the idea to her attention. Lawrence was convinced that the character of Anna was the perfect role for her to play in a musical.

Lawrence originally wanted Cole Porter to write the score, but the composer was not available. A chance encounter between Lawrence's lawyer and Dorothy Hammerstein led to an offer to the duo Rodgers and Hammerstein, the most successful creative team in American musical theater history at the time. Their musicals *Oklahoma!*, *Carousel* and *South Pacific* were all Broadway hits.

"At first," Rodgers recalled in his autobiography, "our feelings were decidedly mixed ... we had never before written a musical specifically with one actor or actress in mind, and we were concerned that such an arrangement might not give us the freedom to write what we wanted the way we wanted. What also bothered us was that while we both admired Gertrude tremendously, we felt that her vocal range was minimal and that she had never been able to overcome an unfortunate tendency to sing flat."[1]

After a private viewing of the original film *Anna and the King of Siam* in a screening room at 20th Century-Fox , the duo decided to do it. They were eagerly ready to go to work, but they informed Lawrence that they could not promise a production before the spring of 1951. Hammerstein immediately asked his friend Josh Logan, who skillfully directed *South Pacific* on Broadway, to collaborate with him. Since Logan showed little interest in the project, Hammerstein approached John Van Druten, who agreed to stage the musical despite never before having directed a show he had not written.

In November 1950, the agent Leland Hayward, who was involved in producing the musical, wrote to Rodgers and Hammerstein from Paris that he had discussed the project with choreographer Jerome Robbins and that he was eager to create the perfect sequences for that show.[2]

Meanwhile, in New York, Rodgers and Hammerstein hired costume designer Irene Sharaff. Sharaff started her research without delay, examining hundreds of pictures from the Royal Archives in Bangkok. She sketched her first costumes based on the fashion in Siam in the mid–1800s and later ordered many yards of Thai silks and brocades to make her first prototypes.

Slowly, *The King and I* was taking shape as a sumptuous and expensive production. The $360,000 budget was an incredible amount of money for a musical at the time.

By Christmas, Rodgers had written about six songs and expected to write another dozen by the following spring.

The most difficult task was casting the musical, especially the problematic role of the king. Since Rex Harrison had skillfully played that role in the film version, he seemed to the authors to be the first and best choice for the musical, despite the actor's non-existent musical background. When Harrison received a call from the production, he was already involved in another project, but agreed to audition for the part because of the great respect he had for the two writers. "That was the last thing I wanted to do. Go and sing for Rodgers and Hammerstein," remembered the actor. "So I said: 'Yes, all right. What theater do you want me to go to?' And they told me what theater, Her Majesty's I think, and there they were sitting in the stalls, and I can't even think what I sang. Anyway I sang something and they said, 'Oh, very nice. That's very nice, Rex. Thank you.'—'We'll let you know later,' sort of thing!—Well, thank God, of course, I never heard a word, because if by any mischance they had liked what I did, which they obviously didn't, and offered me *The King and I*, I might have been tempted to do it, and what a mess that would have been. I mean, I might have missed an even greater opportunity, and a much more suitable triumph, of Higgins in *My Fair Lady* than ever an Oriental potentate could be."[3]

Other actors who were considered for the part were José Ferrer, Ezio Pinza, Macdonald Carey, Noël Coward and Alfred Drake. The latter had become a star since appearing in *Oklahoma!* and asked for too high a salary. (Eventually, Drake played the role as Yul's summer replacement.)

Discouraged after the unfruitful meeting with Drake, Rodgers and Hammerstein went directly to the Majestic Theatre, where casting director John Fearnly was holding auditions for the part of the king. In his autobiography, Rodgers recalled, "The first candidate who walked from the wings was a bald, muscular fellow with a bony, Oriental face. He was dressed casually and carried a guitar. His name, we were told, was Yul Brynner, which meant nothing to us. He scowled in our direction, sat down on the stage and crossed his legs, tailor-fashion, then plunked one whacking chord on his guitar and began to howl in a strange language that no one could understand. He looked savage, he sounded savage, and there was no denying that he projected a feeling of controlled ferocity. When he read for us, we were again impressed by his authority and conviction. Oscar and I looked at each other and nodded. It was no more than half an hour after we had left Drake, and now, out of nowhere, we had our king."[4]

Yul's version of the story was in line with his narcissist and egocentric personality. He maintained that when his agent told him they were looking for the lead in a Broadway musical, he showed no interest. "I was making such an amazing amount of money as a television director, I didn't need an acting job. For three and a half months I wouldn't answer telephone calls from their casting director, John Ferarnly [sic]. I was fed up with acting. I was afraid I'd have to play a lover, and to me that was a horrible idea.... There was a plot to persuade me to change my mind. Mary Martin and my wife were both in on it, also an agent, William Liebling. He had such love and respect for the theater that to him the thought that someone would turn down a leading part on Broadway because of a television involvement was nothing short of sacrilege.... The deep conviction of this dear friend had a lot to do with my canceling a TV rehearsal and calling on Rodgers and Hammerstein, who said, 'All we have on a paper is the first act. Would you read it and tell us if you're interested?' I read it. The character of the king carried me away. He was irresistible. There was nothing mawkish about his love life."[5]

The truth was that Mary Martin, after reading the script, suggested Yul to the casting director, thinking he was just perfect for that role.[6]

Nevertheless, Yul still seemed uninterested. A few weeks later, Martin contacted him asking him to come to the Majestic Theatre, where she was playing in *South Pacific*. When he entered her dressing room, the actress was not there, but there was the first act of the play *The King and I* with a request to sit down and read it. As Yul explained in an interview, "[Reading it] I saw for the first time in my life the possibility of playing something and truly enjoying it, which I never seen before in anything that was offered to me."[7]

Yul signed a contract for seven months and was able to keep his job as a television director. In the beginning, he took a leave of absence from directing, but when the musical opened on Broadway, he spent his daytime at CBS. Rodgers advised Yul not to read the book on which the show was based so that he would not be confused by the differences between the book and the musical. He disobeyed and adapted his character's personality to resemble the king in the novel.

Gertrude Lawrence had wanted Yul for the role since the day she arrived early to rehearse a broadcast. Inadvertently opening a studio door, she heard a commanding masculine voice say, "Come here." The command was not addressed to her, but to an actor in a play being rehearsed. Lawrence, however, chose to obey it. She recognized Yul—she had seen him in *Lute Song*—and remained to watch him work.[8] She was impressed by his ability and she immediately thought he could be the perfect king.

During the rehearsals of *The King and I*, director Van Druten had trouble handling Lawrence's difficult behavior. Although she was an experienced professional actress, once she started working on *The King and I*, all her insecurities about her vocal qualities came to the surface. Many times Yul had to calm her down, using his ability as a television director. With his patience and strength he was always able to get Lawrence to listen to him.

Years later Yul admitted, "She was not known to be easy to work with. She was a taskmaster. I used to criticize her severely, send her notes on her performance every day. Even on stage if necessary. Once I went to her and said, 'How can you take all this from me?' She said, 'Because I'm so grateful for the fact that there is somebody who takes full responsibility.'"[9]

The most difficult problems became evident as soon as the show opened in New Haven. Lawrence's vocal performance was flat and shaky, and the plot did not include a love story between the main characters — a first for a musical. There was nothing but conflict in the show, which lasted almost five hours. Lawrence had missed the dress rehearsal on account of laryngitis, and on opening night she had to deal with a score that was set in a key too high for her.

As Yul recalled in an interview, "The show was obviously a flop. I remember New York friends coming backstage and saying, 'Well, it doesn't matter, you'll find yourself another one.'"[10] But Yul saw to it with great determination that all the needed changes were made, including a love story between Anna and the king.

The day following opening night, Yul took Lawrence to dinner alone and said, "Darling, from now on, from the moment you come on, come into my palace, from the moment we are together on the stage, we're going to play a great love story — through conflict, through everything. If that is what is the underlying thing, we will have a hit." She said, "Well, we'll try. I don't see how, but we'll try."

"She could not believe that she could do that in acting. She was mostly a performer … and not that much of an actress, although she had all the instincts to be the best of actresses, of course. And she found a way to do it, same as I did."[11] Yul also explained that *The King and I* became a hit thanks to the incredible tenacity of the extraordinary team of Rodgers and Hammerstein, who cut the show from the endless five hours to under two hours, taking out everything that was superfluous. The changes were all made before the musical finished its first week in New Haven. "We already opened in Boston with something that was

Yul and Gertrude Lawrence in an early (1951) performance of *The King and I* (before he shaved off his hair).

much more presentable. It wasn't complete, but it was already very presentable," Yul recalled. "With the name of Gertrude Lawrence on top and Rodgers and Hammerstein, we were sold out. And in Boston they started writing new numbers, new scenes. Hammerstein had an extraordinary eye and he saw that what was, what we were doing — Gertrude Lawrence and I — we were playing a love story, and he wrote right into it. And out of that came his writing of that whole section that surrounds *Shall We Dance*.... And it was marvelous to see how these things happen, how Rodgers could write *Shall We Dance* in something like three or four minutes. That's the length of time it takes to play it! That's how fast he wrote it."[12]

Costume designer Irene Sharaff remembers that her first meeting with Yul happened on Madison Avenue. While talking briefly about the show, suddenly Yul asked her, "What shall I do about my hair?" He was bald with one or two strands across the top of his head and a fringe of dark hair around the back. "Shave it!" Sharaff replied impulsively.

Horrified, Yul said, "Oh no! I can't do that. I have a dip on the top of my head. With nothing covering it, I'd look dreadful."[13] But right up to the opening in New Haven, the costume designer urged him to try shaving his head, assuring him that if he did not like it, it would be simple to get him a wig. In her long research, Sharaff learned that the king of Siam had indeed spent about 17 years in a monastery, studying with monks. She logically assumed that if he studied with monks, he must have dressed like them and therefore he must have been bald.[14]

During the rehearsals in Boston, Yul finally shaved his head close. He then covered his head with the same furniture polish he applied to his body to look brownish-yellow. Later he replaced the polish with a more natural, non-toxic walnut makeup that did not easily run with sweat. His new look was a hit with audiences. His shaved head became his trademark, his logo, and soon a number of bald men were emulating him.

On March 29, 1951, *The King and I* opened at Broadway's St. James Theatre. It was a gala evening, despite the general tension in the theater of all involved and the heavy rain that paralyzed Times Square's traffic, delaying the arrival of limousines and taxis. Among the many celebrities present was First Lady Bess Truman. Critics were unanimously mesmerized by the music, the sets and the exotic costumes as well as by Yul and Lawrence's extraordinary performances. In the *Herald Tribune*, Otis L. Guernsey, Jr., enthusiastically wrote, "Musicals and leading men will never be the same after last night ... Brynner set an example that will be hard to follow.... Probably the best show of the decade."[15]

Yul stole the show and became an overnight star. The role of the king was perfect for him. It involved several aspects of his own personality and his experiences as an artist, such as the mystery about his Oriental origins, his ability to sing and play the guitar, his exotic look and his magnetic charisma. On stage these combined elements transformed him into a real monarch. He delivered the lines with an accent that was a mix of all the languages he knew. Oddly, a show that began as a vehicle for Gertrude Lawrence eventually became a vehicle for Yul.

In the play, the king of Siam showed his lack of confidence in the political choices of Anna; in real life, Yul had his own insecurity, which he hated to show publicly. He suffered intense stage fright before every performance. Since his first dress rehearsal in New Haven, he would vomit for about an hour before curtain, trembling incessantly on his way to stage. But once the curtain opened, his fear magically disappeared and his concentration and imagination took command.[16] In order to calm his stress, Yul would practice a relaxation technique that required him to spread his legs wide and push his arms wide against a wall, often surprising those who caught him in that strange posture.

Several years later, Yul humbly admitted his problem: "I suffered so much from stage fright that it was terrible, for all four years of *The King and I* on stage. And it was not the king who had stage fright because once I was on stage I was all right. It was me. I would be sitting in my dressing room, hearing over that little loudspeaker the audience beginning to come in, and the overture beginning to play, and sometimes I threw up, just from fear how to face it. Just not being able to face stepping on the stage and starting. Once I was on, then it was all over."[17]

The day after the premiere of *The King and I*, Yul received many telegrams congratulating him on his performance. Among them was one sent by Rex Harrison saying, "The King is dead, long live the King." Lawrence told him to pin it on his dressing room wall as a lucky charm.

An intercom connected the Brynner and Lawrence dressing rooms. Yul could hear anything occurring in his colleague's dressing room, while she could talk with him only if he pressed a button. Every day, Yul would arrive at the theater around noon and, with the help of his personal assistant Don Lawson, begin his makeup session in preparation for the show. After removing a gray flannel suit, he would change into a hand-woven silk robe. Then Lawson would put on rubber gloves and, with a rubber sponge, he would carefully apply the walnut juice all over Yul's body. With a pair of poodle clippers the assistant would make sure that Yul's head was as smooth as an egg and later cover it with the same tint.[1]

Yul briefly considered the idea of taking injections of melenine to give him the desired tint and avoid the necessity for daily makeup. His doctor mixed it, as well as the idea of swallowing atabrine, a malaria repressor, which had the tendency to turn the body yellow. Yul was left with no other choice but to have a daily two-hour makeup routine.

After that, Yul would put the makeup on his face, using a technique he learned at *Le Cirque d'Hiver*, accentuating the bones of his face by rubbing off a bit of the walnut makeup above his eyes and deftly painting a pair of fierce eyebrows. At that time Yul was a 31-year-old playing a 55-year-old King Mongkut; in order to look that age, he would draw on his cheeks several vertical lines like long wrinkles making him appear sterner and more mature.

Throughout the run of *The King and I*, Yul often gave acting tips to the children in the cast playing the king's offspring. The youngsters sat around him and learned how to improve their acting skills. Yul always had a special bond with children, a tie that later became a real mission when in 1960 he became part of the United Nations Office of the High Commissioner for Refugees to help refugee children from all over the world.

One curious fact about the casting of the children in *The King and I*: When the casting call was made for the king's large family, crowds of children — Chinese, Japanese, Filipinos and some from the Middle East — showed up, but none were Siamese. Therefore kids from varied nationalities were chosen, even Puerto Rican and Italian.[18] Among those cast was young Sal Mineo, who later would reach fame starring opposite James Dean and Natalie Wood in the 1955 film *Rebel Without a Cause*. Mineo was initially hired as an extra, and later became the understudy for the actor playing the role of the Crown Prince of Siam. He was frightened of playing in scenes with Yul. "I had watched him from the wings for over a year," Mineo said in a movie fan magazine interview. "He was so very stern as the King with his Oriental makeup, his broad, unrestrained gestures, his very loud voice, that I thought he must be that way off stage, too. I had heard he had a good sense of humor but I couldn't believe it. I couldn't see how anyone who played the King as ruthlessly as Yul Brynner could have a sense of humor!"[19]

Mineo did not dare to speak to the man everyone referred to as "Mr. B," though he very much wanted to on many occasions. The young actor was forced to speak with Yul when he was asked to play opposite him. Mineo realized he had never been shown how to apply the prince's makeup, so he sought help from Yul's assistant. "Why don't you ask Mr. B?" Lawson responded. "I'm sure he'll be glad to teach you." Sal hesitated. "An important actor like Mr. Brynner," he reportedly thought, "would never be bothered with such trifles as telling a 13-year-old kid how to put on greasepaint."[20]

Finally trembling with fear, he went to Yul's dressing room, knocked on the door and entered. Yul was seated in front of his makeup table, looking at the mirror, when he saw Mineo standing by the door and greeted him, "Hiya, Sal!" The child was surprised that "the King" knew his name, but that gave him the courage to lay out his problem.

Yul listened with attention and kindly taught him how to put on his makeup. One hour later, Mineo was on stage standing in front of the king of Siam. As Mineo lowered his head, Yul whispered, "Relax, kid." After the show, Yul shook Mineo's hand and congratulated him. That friendly sign marked the beginning of a long-lasting professional and personal friendship.[21]

"Every night, we would meet in the wings before we went on. He would talk to a 13-year-old boy as an equal," Mineo recalled. "We discussed acting and one day he presented me with several books on the subject."[22] Yul taught him acting technique, explaining timing and how to listen to the other actor's lines and react to them.

During one of these conversations, Yul mentioned the recent purchase of a motorboat to practice water-skiing, his favorite sport. When Mineo told him he loved swimming, Yul gave him as a gift a pair of water skis he had personally made. Yul also invited him to spend a weekend at the summer house he rented by a lake in Darien, Connecticut.

Yul had never left his job at CBS, continuing to direct TV programs during the day before going to the theater. In 1953 he directed the episode "The Capital of the World" for the Sunday afternoon series *Omnibus*. Starring Anne Bancroft and Leslie Nielsen, it was a 33-minute adaptation of a Hemingway short story. About that television experience, Mineo said, "As a director, Yul gives the actor a feeling of security. You know you're going to be good if he's guiding you."[23]

Yul's respect for Mineo was so high that in 1962 he persuaded director Ronald Neame to cast him in *Escape from Zahrain*, in which he (Yul) was starring.

Ronnie Lee, the young actor who played Anna's son in the musical, remembers how fond Yul was of him. "In the final scene of *The King and I*, Yul Brynner would lie on the deathbed, and I would kneel beside him. The bed was toward stage left, I was to the left of the bed, and the traveler, the curtain that goes in one direction, would be moving stage right to open stage left. As that was happening, Yul would whisper dirty jokes to me. I was supposed to be weeping, but instead I would be shaking with hysterical laughter."[24]

With The *King and I*, Yul attained a sensational, unexpected success. Every night at the end of the show, he and Gertrude Lawrence had to be escorted by policemen through the crowd of fans waiting outside the theater. For his performance, Yul won three of the most prestigious stage awards, the Donaldson, the Critics' Circle and the Antoinette Perry (the Tony). The most flattering compliment was paid to him by Prince Suksawat of Thailand, the great-grandson of the king Yul portrayed in the show. At the end of one performance, the prince visited him in his dressing room and congratulated Yul on his superb performance. The monarch said that he felt that Yul's portrayal of his great-grandfather was surprisingly accurate, and that he hoped that his relative had acted in life as regally as Yul did on stage.[25]

In each performance, Yul added something different to the personality of his character. "I played a man," he admitted. "You never act like a king when you are playing a king. The people around you act as if you are a king."[26]

He also revealed that he learned how to maximize the audience's reaction. "I am a great one for stepping on laughs. The moment they would start to laugh I would rush on, not letting then laugh when they wanted to. You can get an audience helpless that way and do what you please with them."[27]

Throughout his career, Yul was always very superstitious. "I remember a sad incident when I had to get rid of a man who worked backstage in *The King and I*, because he whistled. There is superstition that to sing backstage is bad luck. Well, it was much more than that, because one of the things that you bring on the stage when you work is utter concentration. What you're showing is a condensation, a distillation of life, and so the concentration must be enormous. And a man who whistles is a man who is distracting. Also, just from purely a practical point of view, it's like flushing toilets, it's the only thing the audience can hear. That's why backstage, an actor always pees in a sink."[28]

During the first year's run of *The King and I*, Gertrude Lawrence was plagued by poor health. She had been suffering for some time from cancer that had been misdiagnosed as hepatitis. She took off six weeks in the summer of 1952, resting in her house in Cape Cod. Yul recalled, "She came back in wonderful shape, in wonderful spirit. She had asked me before she left on vacation not to take my vacation immediately upon her return, to give her two weeks to get back into it ... so that she could then do it with my understudy while I went off for a week.... Two weeks after she came back I went on my vacation. Played Saturday night show and I got on a friend's boat and we were steaming toward Cape Cod and on Sunday we got contacted by ship to shore communication saying that I must return to New York. There was an emergency, that Gertrude Lawrence was taken to the hospital. I came back, and I found out she was very, very, very ill, gravely ill. I went back into the show and she died four weeks later. She lost consciousness, I believe, two weeks after she was taken to the hospital … and never regained it, just died. It was cancer of the liver. Apparently [she] had been on a U.S.O. tour and they were given anti-malaria shots and the whole company got hepatitis from this shot … or something similar to hepatitis. And as a result of that she developed cirrhosis of the liver.… It was a terrible, terrible loss."[29]

Gertrude Lawrence died on September 7, 1952; she was buried in the ball gown that she wore in *The King and I*. Yul was so upset that after the funeral he got drunk and cried. In her honor the show closed for one day, and the lights of all of Broadway's theater marquees were briefly turned off. For several weeks following Lawrence's death, Yul would remain alone in his dressing room before his call on the stage, avoiding everybody. "When Gertie died," he said, "some of me died, too."[30]

Constance Carpenter substituted for Gertrude Lawrence and later other fine actresses played the role of Anna.

The King and I ran on Broadway for more than three years (1,246 performances), followed by an 18-month tour across America.

5

Dietrich and Crawford

"Girls have an unfair advantage over men. If they can't get what they want by being smart, they get it by being dumb."
— Yul Brynner

Thanks to the unbelievable success of *The King and I*, the Brynners were able to afford an apartment on 104th Street with a view of Central Park. Yul enjoyed a very high standard of living now that his financial situation had improved. He did not hesitate to buy a luxurious new car, a motorboat and many custom-made suits matched with expensive shoes. He also rented a summer house by a lake in Connecticut where every weekend he practiced water skiing, his favorite sport.

At that time, Yul's marriage was in trouble because of his infidelity. After Rocky's birth, Virginia decided to leave the entertainment world to be a full-time mother, although she felt abandoned by her husband and took up drinking.

Yul was constantly besieged by female fans who were crazy about him. It was during the first-year Broadway run of *The King and I* that he started a blazing affair with Marlene Dietrich, who was 19 years his senior. Many details of Dietrich's obsessive and secretive four-year relationship with Yul were revealed by her daughter Maria Riva in the biography she wrote about her mother. Yul terminated the affair when Dietrich's morbid and possessive jealousy was no longer endurable. As a result of Yul's decision, her love for him suddenly transformed into profound loathing that she bore until his death.

Thirty-four years after the end of their affair, Dietrich sent her daughter a newspaper photo of Yul in a wheelchair, returning from a session of radiotherapy. Across his face, she had written with a big silver marker: "Goody-goody — he has cancer! Serves him right!"[1]

In 1950, Yul met Maria Riva after she was cast in *Sure as Fate*, a CBS television series he was directing. He met her mother a few years later

Yul Brynner and wife Virginia Gilmore water-skiing in Connecticut (ca. 1956).

when Dietrich visited him backstage after a *King and I* performance. The fact that Yul was married was not an obstacle for Dietrich, who often had affairs with married men and fell in love with him at first sight. Her feelings toward him soon became so strong that she developed hatred toward Virginia, urging Yul to divorce his wife and marry her. Dietrich even tried to get pregnant, a nearly impossible task for a 50-year-old woman!

Yul's son, who remembered meeting Dietrich often in his father's dressing room, recalled, "She was the most determined, passionate and possessive lover he had ever known, not the least concerned about discretion since, after all, she was not married. It would have suited her fine if Yul's marriage to Virginia collapsed ... it was up to him to enforce discretion."[2]

He rented a studio for their romantic encounters and Dietrich furnished it. But their relationship wasn't only physical. She was attracted by Yul's intelligence and culture as well. Together they visited flea markets, museums and art galleries, often conversing in French. Dietrich would spend entire days waiting for his phone calls. Yul would call her the instant he arrived in his dressing room, then during the intermission and again as soon the curtain went down. Afterwards he would avoid his friends and admirers who waited for him backstage and would run to her still in his makeup.

Yul's assistant Don Lawson became their confidant and go-between, as Riva revealed in her book. "As neither could use their distinctive first names in messages, to escape detection Yul invented monikers for them: He, of shaved head, became Curly, my mother he christened Crowd."[3]

When Dietrich left for a singing tour in Europe, she almost lost her mind, obsessed by the passion and distressed by the separation. "The difference in time, her performance schedule, and Yul being only reachable in his dressing room made phoning practically impossible. So they had worked out a letter system: He wrote on Tuesdays, Thursdays, and between shows on Saturdays, she on all the others."[4] Yul also kept urging her to return to the stage, possibly co-starring with him in *Samarkand,* a play by Jacques Deval. But Dietrich withdrew from the project, unsure of her own ability to sustain regular nightly performances.[5]

It became impossible for Yul to spend any free time with his family. Sometimes he would go home for a quick dinner between shows in his makeup. Little Rocky got used to seeing his father as the king of Siam. (Early on, Yul did not permit Rocky to see the show, fearing Rocky might be frightened by some of the king's violent on-stage reactions.[6])

If Yul's fame and success were on the rise, Virginia's unhappiness and sadness were too. She had to cope with an army of ladies always around her husband, who was at the same time cheating on her not only with Dietrich but with many other women. In an article she wrote for

Good Housekeeping during the tour of *The King and I*, Virginia expressed her feelings:

> I have noticed one thing that all women who come backstage to see my husband after the show seem to have in common, and that is a distinct envy of what they assume to be "my glamorous life." After congratulating Yul on his thrilling performance, they invariably glance at me and, in a suppressed, breathless whisper, say, "My, your life must be exciting!" or, with a smiling insistence that dares me deny it, "I'll bet it is pretty thrilling to be married to a famous actor!" Mumbling agreement, I secretly add to myself, yes—but not the way you think.[7]

In fact, Virginia was not very happy about Yul's decision to tour with the show. She knew from experience how hard it was to follow her husband all over America, lodging in crummy hotels, packing and unpacking trunks every week, and waiting until late at night for her husband's return. The situation made it impossible to have a quiet domestic life and prevented her from normally raising their eight-year-old child—being in a different city every week, unable to attend school, no friends to play with and educated only by a tutor. Virginia's solitude and discontent grew every day. She fought her depression by drinking, which made her extremely moody and more miserable.

Yul Brynner

Among the countless celebrities who saw *The King and I* on Broadway was Joan Crawford. According to one of her biographers, Crawford, mesmerized by Yul's performance, said to herself, "I want him." Once she returned to California, she wrote him an anonymous letter with the return address a post office box in Beverly Hills. At first she planned the whole thing as a joke. In her letter she wrote that he was the most glorious-looking man she had ever seen in her life and that she could understand any woman wanting to get her hands on him and falling desperately in love.

Yul wrote her back, curious to discover the true identity of Madame X (as Crawford signed her letter). She eventually identified herself and invited him to spend a weekend in her Beverly Hills home. Yul accepted the invitation, taking a flight right after the show. The actress was so excited that she did her best to make that short weekend perfect for her dream man, who could only stay for one night before taking a morning flight back to New York for his performance on Monday. She ordered her assistant to keep her adopted children quiet and out of the way. Finally, after a 12-hour flight, Yul arrived at Crawford's estate, where she welcomed him in a sexy transparent gown. After a dinner and a brief walk in the garden, they laid themselves down on a sofa and Yul fell into a deep sleep caused by the long, exhausting trip and the jet lag. At one point, he was only able to ask for his bed, where he collapsed once again. Crawford was greatly disappointed that nothing happened that night. Then while he was still asleep, all hell broke loose — she took it out on the kids![8] Yul left for the airport very early the next morning, just in time to catch his flight back to New York.

A few years later, when Yul was in Hollywood shooting the film version of *The King and I*, Crawford was finally able to seduce him. Cristina Crawford remembers in her memoir *Mommie Dearest,*

> One night the doorbell rang and Mother told me to answer it as usual. She said the man's name was Brenner and that I'd never met him before. I skipped down the stairs, knowing the entire routine by heart. I opened the front door and gasped. A bald-headed gypsy man wearing yellow pantaloons, sandals, a necklace, and nothing else was standing at our front door. Except for the necklace he was naked from the waist up. I slammed the door in his face, locked it, and dashed upstairs in a panic insisting that Mother call the police immediately! Instead of being upset, she asked me to calm down and tried to explain. The man at the door was an actor named Yul Brynner. He was making a picture called *The King and I*, and he must have come from the studio in his costume. I stared at her and thought: the fights with Uncle Greg [one of Crawford's lovers] are one thing but a half-naked, bald-headed gypsy man at the front door that I'm supposed to entertain is something else altogether. Against my protestations, I found myself headed back downstairs to the front door again. I tried to be polite

to this Mr. Brynner but it was very embarrassing. I fixed him a whooper of a drink and left the room immediately.[9]

Yul had several dates with Crawford. When he went to pick her up at her house, he was always ushered into the bedroom, where cocktails were served while Crawford greeted him wearing only sheer undergarments.[10]

Yul often boasted about never missing a performance during the long tour of *The King and I.* Again, the truth was slightly different. The first time he missed a show was in June 1954, after a backstage accident at the Philharmonic Auditorium in Los Angeles. While he was standing in the wings, two young actors in a ballet number ran on stage with a bolt of blue cloth, used to give the effect of a river in the Thunder and Storm number. The narrow, four-foot-long box carrying the cloth struck the bridge of Yul's nose as they went by. His nose bleeding, Yul was given first aid and later rushed to the hospital as his understudy took over for the second half of the show. He resumed his role the next day.[11] But as a result of that incident, Yul began to suffer from excruciating headaches and pain all the time during the rest of the tour. Three months later, he had to fly from Denver to Los Angeles and immediately enter the Good Samaritan Hospital, where he underwent surgery to remove splintered wood in his nose. A few weeks later, an acute attack of appendicitis forced him to again undergo surgery, and he again missed several performances.

When *The King and I* arrived in Chicago, Yul received an invitation from Northwestern University to be a guest speaker in an acting class. Two years earlier he had written the preface of the book *To the Actor,* a reference manual for actors about technique, training and preparation, published by his master Michael Chekhov. The book had quickly become an essential textbook for all acting students and Yul was pleased to talk about it in an academic environment. The conference room where he gave the lecture was overcrowded not only with acting students but also with fans and onlookers.

During his stay in Chicago, Yul studied philosophy under Prof. Paul Arthur Schlipp at Northwestern University. Schlipp said in a magazine interview about his famous student, "Mr. Brynner was a student in my ethics class in the winter of 1955 ... he not only did all the required reading for classes, but a great deal more. It is my deliberate judgment that he is one of the most brilliant students I ever had."[12]

At Northwestern, Yul also brilliantly passed courses in photographic laboratory techniques. When *The King and I* was on stage, he used to sneak a camera under his robes to photograph the audiences. He also won a local prize for a series of shots from a tumor operation on a woman's hand.[13] Photography was a hobby he took up while working at CBS and he became so skilled that he created a little darkroom in his temporary apartment in Evanston, Illinois.

In his spare time, Yul practiced water skiing; his assistant Don drove the speedboat while he and Virginia took turns on the skis. Yul also enjoyed water ski jumping, and made an 85-foot jump attempting to beat the world record of 125 feet. Rock Brynner remembers how passionate his father was for that sport. After a matinee performance, Yul drove with Rocky and Don straight to the lake in Connecticut where his speedboat was located. Once they were out in open water, Yul jumped into the lake, ready to begin. Don tossed him the tow handle, which hit him on his head, wounding him. Yul became incredibly upset, not by the accident itself, but by the fact that his day was ruined and that they had to go back ashore to look for an emergency room. Then an idea suddenly struck him. He took two small fishhooks and a nylon thread out of a tool kit and, while Don held a mirror, he closed the wound with stitches. Half an hour later he was water-ski–jumping as if nothing had happened.[14]

When *The King and I* was about to close in Chicago, Yul announced that he would not renew his contract. His decision generated an unexpected rise in ticket sales for the last performances. The producers of the show decided not to go on with it because they believed they would never find someone as perfect as Yul for that role. On the other hand, Yul was ready to begin a new adventure with one of the greatest directors in film history: Cecil B. DeMille.

6

Cecil B. DeMille

"Along with his great acting abilities, Yul has the pure knack of appealing to women at the same time he commands the respect of men."

Cecil B. DeMille

"I had a rule when I was doing *The King and I*, that I never allowed anybody backstage, except after the show, because all this work went into creating an illusion and would be destroyed by a visit backstage. I really had rather stark makeup, because I was 30 years old then and I was playing a man of 55, and I used stain instead of real makeup, and looked ghastly. So I never wanted anybody to see me in this condition. And one day, during the intermission, the stage doorman came in and said, 'I don't know what to do, Mr. Brynner, there's a man who says he's Cecil B. DeMille and he has to see you immediately about a matter of life and death.' I said, 'Well, show him in, if he doesn't mind I'm almost stark naked, but I don't mind. Ask him in.' So he came in, shook my hand and said, 'Mr. Brynner, how'd you like to make a picture that your grandchildren will see in the theaters around the world?' I said, 'I think I'd like that.' He said, 'Then will you play Rameses in *The Ten Commandments* for me?' I said, 'Certainly.' We shook hands, and that was the deal. It was as firm a deal as I've ever had in this business. I was the first actor engaged for the movie."[1]

This was the first meeting Yul had with Hollywood director DeMille, as Yul described it to British journalist Michael Parkinson during a 1975 television interview.

DeMille had previous contact with Yul in 1950, when DeMille tried to produce a TV program called *Lux Theatre of the Air* based on the popular airwave program *Lux Radio Theatre* that he directed from 1936 to 1945. DeMille wanted a team of directors with Yul at the head of it. So, while Yul would establish the overall style in which these shows would be made, *and* direct, DeMille would supervise the making of the series. But the project remained unrealized and Yul was cast in *The King and I.*

During DeMille's meeting with Yul, DeMille went into so many details of the complex personality of Rameses that Yul was very impressed. DeMille wrote in his autobiography that after the meeting, "I went back to my seat in the theater, Yul became the King of Siam once more; and I did not see him again until we were ready for him to become King of Egypt."[2] In 1954, after four long years of pre-production, DeMille was ready to shoot.

In the meantime, Yul committed to star opposite Audrey Hepburn in *A New Kind of Love*, a film directed and produced by Billy Wilder. However, Hepburn backed off due to previous engagements and the film was put on hold. Eventually the project was cancelled and Yul kept his $15,000 advance but remained under contract to Paramount for one film, which only by coincidence was *The Ten Commandments* that DeMille distributed through that studio.

In March 1955, before shooting *The Ten Commandments*, Yul got a chest X-ray at L.A.'s Stanford University Hospital to help the American Cancer Society dramatize the importance of annual chest check-ups. Thirty years later, Yul would die of lung cancer.

Most of Yul's scenes in *The Ten Commandments* were shot in Hollywood; only a few were filmed on location. Yul traveled to Egypt together with Max Jacobson, personal doctor to DeMille; the director's frail health had to be constantly watched.

Although Yul was the first actor to be cast, he was not the first to be considered for the role of Pharaoh Rameses. DeMille and his assistants had previously considered Jeff Chandler and William Holden (both were dismissed because they were too American-looking), Stewart Granger, Michael Rennie (both dismissed because they were too British), Mel Ferrer, Anthony Dexter and Michael Wilding (all dismissed because they were not exotic enough). In addition to the task of finding someone "exotic," DeMille needed to convince the chosen star to shave his head completely — something that not too many actors were willing to do in those days, not even for a master director like DeMille. Bald, exotic-looking Yul seemed the perfect choice. Yul would laughingly explain, "It's my gypsy mother! The word 'gypsy' is slang for 'Egyptian.' We all know that the gypsy tribes originated in the Near East."[3]

In addition, DeMille always carefully cast actors who could direct themselves and assembled a crew that could run itself. The fact that Yul was an experienced TV director was another good reason to give him the part. Usually DeMille did not tolerate any interference when he was behind the camera, but with Yul he made an exception. DeMille highly respected Yul's intelligence and his ability as an actor and always listened attentively to his advice. During the course of *The Ten Commandments,* DeMille and Yul became very close. The director was considerate of him and took him under his wing, perhaps to satisfy a paternalistic desire which was part of his own personality. Yul was in need of a paternal figure that he never had. In the past it had been Michael Chekhov; now DeMille with his experience and self-confidence seemed to be another perfect father-figure.

Yul was the only cast member allowed to see the first rushes and to sit at DeMille's staff table for lunch, a privilege the director granted to very few. "I learned more things from him," explained Yul, "than almost anyone in the motion picture business. He was [a] truly extraordinary showman. He himself thought that he was not a good director.... He would often re-shoot things because he was simply ashamed with the way he directed it."[4]

Yul got along perfectly with all his colleagues. Charlton Heston, who played Moses, met Yul for the first time on the set. In his autobiography, Heston defined Yul's "transcendent performance" as "a superb incarnation of Rameses."[5] Heston also remembered how Yul was always polite to him, but also how difficult he could be at times. "[His] disdainful arrogance was exactly right for Pharaoh. All our scenes together were confrontations; perhaps he was using that. It certainly worked for the film, which is what counts."[6]

Eugene Mazzola, who played the Pharaoh's son, was only six years old at the time, but he still cherishes the memories of the friendship he established with Yul on the set. Often between takes, Yul would patiently take him on his lap, read an illustrated children's book about a circus and tell him his own stories of working at *Cirque d'Hiver.* "When he held me, he did it with passion," recalls Mazzola. "When you looked into his eyes, there was somebody there. He was warm, he was strong. He was working the character all the time.... Anne Baxter (who played the Pharaoh's wife) did not relate to me as her son ... she seemed distracted."[7] Baxter, whose character's name was changed from Nefertiti to

Nefertiri because DeMille was afraid people would make "boob" jokes, remembered Yul as "expressionlessly arrogant, thrusting out his arm with first and second fingers open in a victory sign, into which his trembling body servant slid a lighted cigarette. Regal Yul never, ever looked around. That used to really impress DeMille."[8]

Under DeMille's tutelage, Yul became almost an extension of the older man's mind. After a scene was shot, if the director liked it he would nod at Yul with a little twinkle in his eyes. If he did not like it, he would merely turn to the crew and ask for a retake. Then Yul would look at him in a questioning way and DeMille would look back and say a particular word in the dialogue he wanted changed. Then Yul would go through it again, with the change that DeMille wanted.

Yul spent his spare time photographing the director and fellow actors at work. As he explained in an on-set interview, "My greatest problem was finding something to do in long waits between takes. So I hid my camera behind the throne or in my chariot and during rehearsals or while waiting for a scene to begin, I would bring it out and start shooting."[9] *Collier's* magazine published Yul's beautiful photographs a few months before *The Ten Commandments* debuted. According to Yul, DeMille maintained an inspired feeling throughout the long weeks of shooting. The set was enveloped in an almost religious atmosphere that made the actors believe that what they were doing was really happening.[10]

On another occasion, Yul said that DeMille's only regret was that he (DeMille) did not die as he finished the film. "I had finished my part … a couple of months before they were finishing shooting. And I went back East, and I was very, very fond of him, and his birthday coincided with the last day of shooting the movie. And I flew back here to spend that day and that evening with him to have dinner, his birthday dinner…. And I could see he just didn't want to get off that boom. He wanted to stay behind that camera and die sitting behind it. He was so sad. He was trying to think of another shot to get when it was really over, and it was only four o'clock in the afternoon. He said, 'Yul, can't you think of another shot that I need?' It was wonderful…. He was a gorgeous man, really a wonderful man of enormous size."[11]

Once he finished his scenes, Yul went on holiday with his family to his house in Connecticut. "My first real vacation in 11 years," he said to columnist Hedda Hopper. "I'll water ski, fish, and spend some time with my son. I'll have two whole months of no make-believe before I return here in September for *The King and I* [the film version]."[12]

After undergoing a long editing process, supervised by DeMille, the final cut of *The Ten Commandments* ran 221 minutes. The film previewed in Salt Lake City, on October 5, 1956, followed by a gala evening in Los Angeles and one in New York a month later. The final cost amounted to over $13.5 million, making *The Ten Commandments* the most expensive film ever made until 1963, when *Cleopatra* reached $20 million.

Yul as Pharaoh Rameses II in *The Ten Commandments.*

Although *The Ten Commandments* was nominated for seven Oscars, it only won one (for Special Effects). All the reviews praised the film for its spectacular cinematography, along with Yul's performance as Pharaoh Rameses II. The few critics who disliked the film criticized Yul's characterization, calling it too similar to the monarch of Siam in *The King and I*. In his autobiography, DeMille advised those who believed that Yul, in any role, was still playing the king of Siam to watch the two films again carefully in quick succession and "see the subtle differences in characterization between the barbaric, puzzled, arrogantly defensive king of Siam, and the no less arrogant but sophisticated, self-assured Pharaoh in *The Ten Commandments*. There are similarities in the two performances for Yul Brynner, after all, he is only one man; but it is the subtle differences which show his great artistic competence."[13]

The night Yul went to see *The Ten Commandments* was the first

Mr. and Mrs. Charlton Heston and Yul at the premiere of *The Ten Command-ments.*

time he saw himself on a screen in a movie theater. He disliked his per-formance so much that he left the theater before the end of the film. Years later, he explained his reaction. "I kept thinking I could have done it bet-ter. If I make a picture in, say January and February, it doesn't appear on the screen for months. In those months I have learned more about

54

motion pictures. I have new standards. I am dismayed at the 'me' of ten months ago. I want desperately to do the job again."[14]

Yul's busy working schedule was still having a negative effect on his private life, including his shaky marriage. At the end of that year, Yul terminated his affair with Dietrich; as the actress' daughter remembered, "Yul slowly began to fade from the pages of her diary. She had once said that if she could hate him, she could then stand the pain of losing him. With her Teutonic discipline, she was now true to her word."[15] It took another three years for Dietrich to completely forget Yul, changing her obsessive love into deep hatred. Ernest Hemingway, a dear friend of Dietrich, responded to her complaints about her problems with Yul by inviting her to his home in Cuba, where he could free her mind from her unhealthy obsession.[16]

According to Rock Brynner, Yul also had a little romance with Marilyn Monroe, who was at the peak of her career. Nine-year-old Rocky remembered an unexpected meeting with Monroe when Yul brought her home one night. The following morning, Rocky found her clothes scattered around the house. When he later questioned his father, Yul told him, "That will be *our* secret, laddie."[17] Virginia, in fact, never knew it.

7

Once Upon a Time in Hollywood

"I never feud with actors, I feud with studios."
Yul Brynner

When 20th Century-Fox considered producing a film based on the musical *The King and I*, Yul wanted to direct it and to offer the part of the king to Marlon Brando, the only actor he considered right for that role. After Brando turned it down, Yul decided to perform the role himself, once again elaborating on his Broadway performance.

Charles Brackett, the film's producer, asked Ernest Lehman if he was interested in writing a script based on the play. Lehman, who wrote screenplays for big hits like *Sabrina* and *Sweet Smell of Success*, had not seen the play. He traveled from Los Angeles to New York to watch the show and then accepted the job. The screenwriter was one of the few people to get along with Yul, who proved difficult to work with on the set. His short temper and petulance were faults which often affected his work and his private life. Nevertheless, this inner anger had helped him show the rage present in the character of Rameses II and in the king of Siam.

English actress Deborah Kerr was cast as Mrs. Anna. Vivien Leigh was first considered for that part, but she was uninsurable since she suffered from manic-depressive attacks. One of Kerr's closest friends, singer Dinah Shore, waged a heavy campaign for that role, but the studio did not find her convincing enough and preferred to cast Kerr.

Yul particularly wanted Kerr to do the part in the film, having met her briefly when he went to see her in *Tea and Sympathy* on Broadway. "It was Yul who was the solid inspiration behind the movie," she said. "He knew and loved every line of the story and every note of the music, and it came out so well due to his insistence that this and that had to be done the way *he* wanted. He could be difficult, but only because he knew he was right."[1]

Yul was indeed not very easy to work with. He detested 20th Century-Fox and nicknamed it *16th Century Fuck* because of the changes they insisted on making in the film. For example, 20th Century-Fox insisted on putting in a scene where he would fight an elephant, believing that would explain why the king dies. Yul was outraged and, in a special meeting with Fox's executives, he had to explain that the king dies of a broken heart because he cannot fulfill his desire to become a modern king and modernize his country in a way

As King Mongkut of Siam in the 1956 film of *The King and I.*

that will make it better for his son. Under the tutelage of Mrs. Anna, he hopes his son can do the job for him. Moreover, he dies because he cannot have the love he has for Anna. Although the executive laughed at his explanations, Yul fought like a tiger and won them over.

During the filming, Yul became so exasperated with producer Charles Brackett that he told him in a burst of rage, "You don't know but you died several years ago."[2] Yul's frustration was caused by his belief that the film looked like something made ten years earlier. According to him, neither the producer nor the director Walter Lang had truly grasped the real spirit of the story, considering it more a fairy tale, and making all the set designs look fake.

Actress Rita Moreno, who played Tuptim in the film, says that she cannot remember seeing Walter Lang actually directing Yul beyond instructions concerning the correct angle for the best shot.[3]

Yul would often deeply offend the director when they disagreed. Yul considered Lang's presence totally unnecessary since he could direct the movie himself. Sometimes Yul's outbursts of uncontrolled rage were so intense that he resorted to oxygen to calm him down. Deborah Kerr later recalled, "When it came to filming the famous polka, I tried [the oxygen] too. I felt completely drunk.... Obviously, I don't need that."[4]

Kerr's voice wasn't considered good enough to handle the lead-ins to most of the Rodgers and Hammerstein songs, so she was dubbed by Marni Nixon. "Marni was so brilliant at adapting her voice to mine," Kerr reportedly said. "I could never be entirely sure whether it was she helping me on high notes — with the help of the experts of sound mixers, of course — or whether I myself was responsible for the sounds which came out in the completed version."[5]

"Fortunately ... I had my Deborah Kerr," Yul said years later. "She was heaven. She was the perfect Mrs. Anna. She understood Mrs. Anna completely. She understood the relationship between the two. And this is really what made the picture work."

Of her co-star, Kerr said, "Yul helped me so much, taught me so much. He rehearsed with me — not to tell me how to play the role, but to show how others had done it, so I could play it better in my own way.... He was so wonderful. I'll be forever his slave."[6]

20th Century-Fox hired Irene Scharaff to design the costumes for the film, aware that her outstanding work contributed greatly to the play's success. About Scharaff's lavish creations, Yul enthusiastically said, "She outdid herself in costumes. It's the most gorgeous costume design I've seen on almost any picture."

The film version of *The King and I* was made on a bigger scale than the original play, including more opulent costumes, more sumptuous set design and more creative choreography. According to rumor, one of the greatest musical numbers in the film, "Small House of Uncle Thomas," was directed by an unaccredited Vincente Minnelli (Walter Lang did not have any experience directing a musical[7]).

Although Yul worked with his usual perfectionism, he did not notice while he sang "It's a Puzzlement" that he was wearing an earring in some shots and not in others. As a consequence, the earring disappears and reappears throughout the sequence.

Despite numerous complaints, Yul wore a lighter makeup than in the play. On the stage it was essential that his exotic features were visible to all the spectators, but on film excessive makeup was unnecessary.

Once again Yul proved to be masterful not only as monarch, but

Deborah Kerr and Yul in *The King and I*.

also as photographer. He shot with his Leica a series of beautiful candid photographs which appeared on the cover of *Life* and in an interior spread one month before the film opened.

The King and I was completed in seven months. The first six weeks were only rehearsals, followed by six months of filming at the 20th Century-Fox studios. Despite Yul's conflicts with the director and the producers, the cast became like a family. To celebrate the end of the production, a Christmas party was organized and gifts were presented to all the children in the cast. Yul was paid $300,000 and a percentage of the profits, allowing him to purchase a house in Los Angeles and a Mercedes.

The King and I opened in June 1956 and met with immediate popular success and critical acclaim. *New York Times* critic Bosley Crowther wrote, "Mr. Brynner, whose original performance of the volatile King of Siam was *so* utterly virile and commanding that he took possession of the role, repeats it here in a manner that the close-in camera finds fresh with pride and power. Mr. Brynner has a handsomeness of feature and a subtlety of expression that were not so evident on the stage.... The king is the heart of this story and Mr. Brynner makes him vigorous and big."[8]

On the screen, the eccentric arrogance of Yul's character seemed in perfect harmony with his exotic look. His shaved head in fact emphasized his Oriental features more than on the stage.

Despite its unbelievable success, Yul detested the movie, criticizing it severely. "I don't like the film," he revealed years later. "I say it loud in spite of the fact that I'm very grately [sic] for the fact that I've got an Oscar for it. I did not like the film when we made it. I did not like the making of it and still get quick [sic] sick when I see it.... The shame of it is that the picture really should have been ten times better, because the play was ten times better. Whenever people say, 'But it's such a marvelous movie ...,' I said, 'If you haven't seen it on the stage, you cannot imagine what you are seeing. It is not even ten percent of the power and of the fascination and of the charm and glorious joy that it was on the stage."[9]

On March 22, 1956, three months before the movie opened nationwide, Yul and Deborah Kerr placed their handprints in cement for the Hollywood Chinese Theatre. The ceremony, for reasons unknown, took place on a 20th Century-Fox stage housing one of the movie's interior sets. Yul, in full costume for his role, made his footprints with sandals, signed his name and wrote THE KING. On his square is also a faint imprint of what appears to be a failed first attempt at his signature above the finished version. Yul's square was later placed alongside Kerr's (which says AND I) in front of the Chinese Theatre.[10]

Once completed *The King and I*, Yul accepted another role at 20th Century-Fox, this time in a film produced by Buddy Adler. Fox paid $400,000 for the rights to *Anastasia*, a French play by Marcelle Marette, adapted in English by Guy Bolton. The story was based on real events involving a drowning woman pulled out of a Berlin canal by a policeman. The woman appeared to be Anastasia Romanov, the last daughter of the Czar of Russia, Nicholas II. If so, then she miraculously survived the Romanovs' execution in July 1918 during the Russian Revolution.

Director Anatole Litvak was a Russian émigré with a deep interest in the Romanov culture. From the beginning, both Yul and Litvak had in mind Ingrid Bergman for the leading role. At the time, this was a controversial choice, since Bergman had been ostracized from Hollywood after having a child with Italian director Roberto Rossellini while still married to another man. Litvak met with Bergman in Paris and, without the approval of Fox, offered her the role. The Swedish actress immediately accepted. Only after long, exhausting meetings between the director and the studio did Fox agree to cast her.

In May 1956, Yul flew to London where costume fittings and rehearsals were to begin. *Anastasia* had a high budget of $3.5 million and was to be filmed in Technicolor and CinemaScope. Except for a few exteriors shot in Paris, it was entirely made at the Borehamwood Studios outside London.

The opening scenes were to be shot in Paris, around a Greek Orthodox church. At the last moment the ecclesiastical authorities wavered about granting the necessary permission, leaving the moviemakers with no other choice but to build a copy of the church on the Borehamwood back lot. Meanwhile, screenwriter Arthur Laurents worked day after day on the script, constantly modifying it.

Yul played the role of Bounine, an authoritarian general who persuades Anna Anderson to pretend to be Grand Duchess Anastasia in order to claim the fabulous Romanov inheritance saved in the Bank of England. Gradually Bounine starts to wonder if Anderson really *is* the surviving daughter of the czar, and falls in love with her.

Akim Tamiroff, Yul Brynner and Ingrid Bergman in *Anastasia.*

Litvak cast Helen Hayes as the Dowager Empress Marie, whose recognition and acceptance of Anna as her granddaughter Anastasia is essential. The producers cast Hayes not only for her extraordinary acting skills, but also because they wanted someone with a moral and upright reputation to co-star with the once-banned Bergman.[11]

Hayes was hesitant to accept the part since she was still mourning her late husband, but eventually agreed. Outside the set she did not mix much with the other actors, except for Yul — who seemed to be the only one to make her smile with his jokes.

Yul pressed the producers to cast Sacha Pitoëff, the son of his former drama teacher, and some gypsy musicians from the Dimitrievich family. The musicians performed a tzigan song with him in a scene at the Parisian nightclub managed by Bonine.

During the entire shoot, Bergman and Hayes had a Russian coach to help them speak with believable Russian accents. Yul, whose mother tongue was Russian, would use the excuse of helping Bergman with the language and be in her dressing room for hours. They began a secret romance that lasted during filming.

That summer, Yul rented a house for his family in Saint-Jean de Luz, about 300 miles from Paris. However, Virginia and Rocky did not see much of him. He occasionally visited on the weekends but, with the excuse of a frantic working schedule, he preferred to spend most of his free time with Bergman. In her autobiography, Bergman never mentioned her brief affair with Yul, merely writing, "[H]e was so helpful and understanding, such a wonderful friend."[12] But Yul's son, a visitor to the set, quickly noticed how his father would change the tone of his voice when he switched from English (when talking to Virginia) to soft-spoken French (when left alone with Bergman).[13]

The rumor of the romance between the *Anastasia* co-stars quickly crossed the Atlantic and reached Marlene Dietrich in Hollywood. Dietrich was also told the false gossip that Yul was about to divorce his wife to marry Bergman — something she had hoped Yul would do during their relationship. Wildly jealous, Dietrich developed a deep hatred for "the Swedish horse," as she would call Bergman, and tried to forget Yul after this terrible insult.[14] To better understand the story of the film, Yul carefully watched the filming of every scene he wasn't in. "By that time," Helen Hayes recalled, "he was living in a state of absolute infallibility. He could not make a mistake."[15]

Yul Brynner with Martita Hunt in a scene from *Anastasia* (1956).

Variety TV show host Ed Sullivan sent a TV crew from New York to London to shoot behind-the-scenes footage on *Anastasia* to air on his popular Sunday night program. The idea was to bring a new image of Bergman back to the United States. Sullivan also asked his viewers (via a national survey) if the Swedish actress should be allowed to visit the country again. The majority disapproved of her return; therefore the program never aired.

Anastasia wrapped by the end of August 1956, and was quickly edited for a Christmas release.

The film premiered at Radio City Music Hall in New York, but none of the three stars participated at the event. *Anastasia* received immediate international acclaim and marked Bergman triumphal re-entry. As Yul stated during a press conference, "It was about time she returned to the American screens!" The *New York Times* critic commented how in the film Yul "appears oddly youthful for a former Russian general, some ten years out of circulation, but he sure has the vigor for the role."[16]

When Yul heard that Bergman decided to travel to New York to accept an award from the American critics, he called her in Paris and advised her to take some tranquilizers with her because of the possible nasty reactions by some of the journalists. Although her return was a triumph, Bergman later admitted that she followed his advice and even took one pill.[17]

With three major films presented one after another, Yul was incredibly popular in 1956. The American press called him "the magnetic barbarian" and "the sexiest bald actor in Hollywood," putting his photograph on the cover of many magazines. *Motion Picture Herald* added him to the list of the ten most promising Hollywood stars of 1956. His fame reached its peak when Yul won the National Board of Review Award for all three performances (*The King and I*, *The Ten Commandments* and *Anastasia*), a Golden Globe nomination as Best Actor in the category of musical-comedy and an Oscar nomination as Best Actor for *The King and I*.

That same year, a group of 14 Des Moines, Iowa, high school students shaved their heads to make themselves look like Yul, assuming that looking like the "hot movie star" would improve their popularity among girls. Their gesture just got them a suspension by the school principal. A picture of the bald students appeared in several magazines all over the country.[18]

According to his agent, Yul earned almost a half million dollars in 1956 — a real record considering that those were his first three films in Hollywood.

During an appearance on *The Tonight Show* in the early '80s, Yul told a funny anecdote dating back to those days. Academy Award–winning Italian actress Anna Magnani was working on a set not far from Yul's and would often chat with him in French between takes. A few days before the Oscar ceremony at which Magnani was a presenter, she asked him to listen to her rehearse the names of the five nominees for Best Actor, including Yul's. When the actress read Laurence Olivier's name and his nomination for *Richard III*, Yul burst into laughter and warned her to be very careful pronouncing "third." With her thick Italian accent, Magnani had announced, "*Richard the Turd!*"[19] Several weeks later, Magnani gave the precious statuette to Yul.

After the success of *The King and I*, Yul was exclusively offered roles in which his masculinity, physical strength or invulnerability were emphasized. His muscular body and exotic accent were unique but at the same time limiting. In time, his baldness would become a handicap. He was not "an average clean-cut Mongolian kid" as he often joked. In fact, producers and directors never thought to cast him in conventional roles.

He had an atypical part with great psychological profundity when he played Dmitri Karamazov in *The Brothers Karamazov*. The film was based on Fyodor Dostoyevsky's masterpiece; Yul accepted the role with great enthusiasm.

For ten years, Metro-Goldwyn-Mayer producer Dore Schary had planned to make *The Brothers Karamazov* with Marilyn Monroe as Grushenka and Marlon Brando as Dmitri. Schary commissioned Julius J. and Philip G. Epstein to write a screenplay with those two stars in mind. Monroe was under an exclusive contract with Fox, whose executives did not believe in her dramatic acting skills; they refused to lend her to MGM. At the beginning, Monroe seemed interested in playing a part different from her usual comedic roles, but when she discovered she was pregnant by husband Arthur Miller, and later suffered a miscarriage, she lost interest in the project. The film was postponed.

After a long delay, producer Pandro S. Berman and director Richard Brooks got involved on the project. Brooks chose a cosmopolitan cast: Opposite Yul the director cast Austrian actress Maria Schell, who had just starred in *White Nights*, another Dostoyevsky screen adaptation. British actress Claire Bloom was cast as Kathya, Canadian William Shatner as Alexei Karamazov, and Americans Lee J. Cobb as Fedor Karamazov and Albert Salmi as Smerdjakov. Many were skeptical about the realization of a picture which would retain the grandiosity of the 1000-page Russian novel. Before writing the script, Brooks re-read the novel several times and studied 19 volumes of literary criticism on it.

From the very beginning, Yul and Brooks got along. The director agreed to go on a Mexican fishing trip with him to discuss several changes to the final script. Everybody was aware of the risks involved in making and performing in a screen adaptation of such a literary masterpiece. Brooks relied on the universal romanticism present in the story, which potentially could appeal to all kinds of audiences. As he explained, "In writing the screenplay of *The Brothers Karamazov*, it was not primarily a question of what to omit, change or add. The major problem was one of finding an approach to a condensation of so rich and complex a novel within the framework of a motion picture, while still retaining the meaning, essence and spirit of Fyodor Dostoyevsky's greatest work."[20] Once the script was completed, the director had problems finding the right locations to shoot the film. "The Russians wanted me to shoot the picture in Russia, but MGM alleged that shooting there I would end up making a Communist film. I replied saying: 'Dostoyevsky lived way before Communism. How do you possibly want me to recreate Russia in a studio? I should film only by night or indoor. That's impossible.' They answered me, 'You'll make the film and it won't have anything to do with the Russians.'"[21] Having no choice but to shoot at MGM studios, Brooks and cinematographer John Alton decided to film using particular lenses and lightning with different shades of colors to fit the mood of the story and its setting. For instance, the rich use of red symbolized Dmitri's death wish. These unusual chromatic choices were dismissed by many critics as pretentious, but its visual effect created a better Russian environment and added a dramatic dimension to the story.

Before and during the shoot, Yul demanded that he be coached by a Russian historian, Prof. Count Andrei Tolstoy, nephew of the famous writer. Tolstoy's job was to help improve Yul's knowledge of Russian culture as it related to his character.

Principal photography began in summer 1957 at MGM, where the film was shot using tons of artificial snow. The torrid summer season made it difficult for the cast to wear the heavy costumes.

Yul rented a house by the beach in Malibu for himself and his family. On the set he bombarded Brooks with questions with an eye toward improving his performance and understanding the psychology of his character. He even kept a journal (written as Dmitri would) in order to better understand the part.

A few days after the start of filming, Yul was involved in a terrible accident in which he badly hurt his back; the injury afflicted him for the rest of his life.

"I had to shoot a scene which demanded that I do trick riding," explained Yul. "It was a gay scene in which two young officers were competing for the attention of a lady. There was talk of a [stunt] double, but I felt I could do it myself. It is always better if you do things yourself before a camera. A lot of characterization goes into the way you walk or

Yul and Maria Schell in a lively scene from *The Brotherss Karamazov*.

talk, even the way you sit a horse. If you do it in character, it's one thing. If you let Joe Blow do it for you, it doesn't fit your role. My accident was simple. I didn't fall off my horse. He was at full gallop. I was leaning over to touch the ground. As I did so, he changed the position of his front feet. There was a jarring jerk. I felt as if my breath was cut off. When the scene was finished, I got into a car and was driven to my dressing room for a second breakfast before I went on with the rest of the day. Once more I could hardly breathe. X-rays were taken. They showed two fractured vertebrae. That was on a Friday. That afternoon they made me a brace. They told me I'd have to wear it for seven months. I devoted what was left of that afternoon and Saturday and Sunday to adjusting myself to my hurt back and to my brace. On Monday I went before the camera once more. My big problem was sleep. None of those pain killers reached the agony. In such an accident, the pain is intense because so many nerves are involved with the vertebrae. Mine was so incredible that I called up my doctor and said there must be something wrong with me. He only said, 'That's the way it is with your injury.'"[22]

Yul, Lee J. Cobb and Richard Basehart in *The Brothers Karamazov*.

Driven by his great strength and discipline, Yul bore the excruciating pain in such a stoic manner that no one on the set knew of his agony. As he finished his scenes. For 11 weeks Yul suffered from agonizing back pain with cramps that did not let him sleep more than a few hours per night and causing him to lose his usual voracious appetite, costing him 14 pounds.

Despite his acute physical pain, Yul still had the energy to start an affair with co-star Claire Bloom. The British actress wrote in her memoir that she vainly tried not to fall in love with him. She also remembered that he "needed to be surrounded by an adoring harem of women. Toward the close of filming, after a relationship of three months, Yul's visits to my apartment became less frequent, then finally stopped altogether. I felt enormously let down…. I wasn't naïve enough to suppose this relationship could have ended any differently; Yul had never promised me more, and I never expected anything else."[23] Yul had in fact quickly replaced Bloom with blonde Kim Novak.

Italian journalist Oriana Fallaci, in Hollywood reporting on the

American cinema, visited the *Karamazov* set and interviewed Yul. Fallaci was influenced by comments she had read or heard about Yul's charisma and the inconsistencies in his stories about his past. With tongue in cheek she described her first meeting with him: "He was all withdrawn in a corner with his shiny bald pate, smoking a cigarette, long like a conductor's baton while he was staring at the tip of the boots with his magnetic gaze. The director Richard Brooks introduced me to him. Yul stopped hypnotizing those lucky boots and asked me what I was doing in that awful place. He had a husky voice, a little cavernous like those who have a cough. I replied that I wanted to meet him. It seemed that he liked the idea. His round face suddenly relaxed with a smile. He offered me one of his cigarettes. His dark eyes kept staring at me almost as if they were trying to worm a secret. His silky, curvy and mascara looking eyelashes trembled insistently. He lighted me a cigarette with a studied slow motion, his full lips blew over the match. The blow was strong and delicate at the same time. I would disappoint Mr. Brynner if I wrote that he did not provoke in me a delightful shiver. He did not."[24]

Yul told Fallaci the story of his childhood (described as "terrible"), about his circus career, about his experiences on stage, about the Pitoëff, and about his longtime friendship with Jean Cocteau. "I want to reveal to you something important. I'm not bald as some people insinuate. If I want, I could grow my hair long up to my knees." Fallaci recalled, "He said it with great confidence, without smiling, all of a sudden I remembered I never saw Yul Brynner have a real good laugh and I asked him why. Yul said, '*Ma chère,* laughing upsets me as much as crying. Life is too sad to make us laugh.' I frowned. I remembered I read those sentences. It was said by Greta Garbo 20 years ago.... 'I want to give you a present. I want to tell you the truth. I don't laugh because I'm shy. If I could, I'd hide under a table like a child.' He said it with so much sadness that not for a moment I doubted he was sincere. Suddenly he appeared to me for what he was: just a good man who struggles not to say the truth."[25]

Elvis Presley, who was shooting another MGM film visited Yul on the *Karamazov* set. The singer knew Yul and was eager to introduce him to an old friend visiting from Memphis. After shaking Yul's hand, the friend all of a sudden cried out, "You're a short little mother, aren't you?"[26] Elvis, visibly embarrassed, immediately apologized for his friend's behavior, which had touched one of Yul's weak spots: He was always very sensitive about his height. Although he claimed to be six feet tall, in reality he barely measured five-nine.

The Brothers Karamazov opened in February 1958 and ran at the Cannes Film Festival, where Yul introduced it. Public and critics gave it a lukewarm reception; the American press falsely described the reception as "hostile." The truth was that an American reporter made up the news of a bad audience reaction for the benefit of his readers.[27]

Most of the American reviews praised Yul's performance, which *The New York Times* described as "excitingly haughty and intense."[28]

Yul always considered that performance one of his best and *The Brothers Karamazov* one of his favorite films. As he admitted in an interview, "Richard Brooks did an extraordinary job with it. Of course it's inevitable that everybody will be in disagreement over it. Out of that book you could make 15 pictures, depending on the story you chose."[29]

That year, Alfred Hitchcock was casting *North by Northwest*. Yul was the director's original choice for the evil Vandamm, an importer and exporter of government secrets and the lover of Eve Kendall, played by Eva Marie Saint. Yul did not like the character and the minor role and Hitchcock went for James Mason.[30] French director Gabriel Pascal was interested in casting Yul as Gandhi in a film about the Indian pacifist. Pascal's sudden death put an end to the project.

David Lean was also interested in making a film on Gandhi with an all-star cast including Alec Guinness in the leading role, Cary Grant as a British policeman in the Indian force, William Holden as an American doctor, Laurence Olivier as Lord Mountbatten, John Gielgud as John Irwin and Yul as cultivated Pandit Nehru. But producer Sam Spiegel convinced Lean to make *Lawrence of Arabia* instead.[31]

One of Yul's greatest ambitions was to direct a film produced by DeMille, with whom Yul was still very close. It was his idea to make a musical version of DeMille's 1938 film *The Buccaneer*, which had starred Fredric March. De Mille, who didn't particularly like musicals and was not "sold" on Yul's idea, was persuaded to wait until the completion of the script. Producer Henry Wilcoxon remembered Yul's assuring words: "[DeMille] will like this one. It will be different, fresh. I have all sorts of ideas, Harry, and the Old Man has told me that he's looking forward to my treatment. I'll make sure to consult him every step of the way.

But first I want to present my ideas in the best possible light."[32] Since Yul had never written a screenplay, Wilcoxon suggested that he look for a real writer, preferably someone who knew DeMille's tastes and whims. Yul took his advice and asked Jesse Lasky, Jr., to collaborate. Lasky recalled that Yul invited him to lunch, where he explained his project. The screenwriter was baffled by the idea and reminded Yul that DeMille already made that film 20 years earlier; Yul assured him, "This won't be anything like that. It will

A publicity shot on the set of *The Brothers Karamazov.*

be a musical — or rather a film with music — songs that come in naturally. I have a lot of ideas to make this original. Do things that have never been done before. DeMille will give us a free hand."[33] Lasky had not planned on doing any more scripts for DeMille, but when Yul stressed that this was *his* film and not the "Old Man's," Lasky accepted the challenge.

The first three months went by with no problems. DeMille stayed away from the project; occasionally, without pressure, he would ask if the duo had something ready to show him. Lasky knew that the "Old Man" would have loved to have been consulted, but "Yul and I continued to avoid him like the plague."[34] When Lasky grew concerned, Yul relaxed him by saying, "Don't worry, Jesse. I will tell him the story. The Old Man will listen to me. I'm like — his son."

Yul was too optimistic. The day of their meeting with DeMille, Lasky felt some storm signals. "[Yul's] storytelling was super," remembered Lasky in his autobiography. "It would have thrilled any audience. Except one. Yul could see DeMille's growing anger. It burned slow at first. The gentle sabotage of polite interruptions, delicately seasoned with sarcasm, at crucial points in the story. 'I'm curious as to when we will hear the presence of a woman. I take it, you do have—a love story? Somewhere in your'—too long a pause—'drama?' ... DeMille interruptions became quicker, sharper, more insulting. And suddenly he was citing every weakness of the story we had scarcely begun to tell.... I saw the cold rage mounting in Yul. More than a story had fallen to bits. A relationship had crumbled."[35] Yul resigned as director.

Since his heart attack in Egypt on the set of *The Ten Commandments*, DeMille felt he was not able to direct the film himself. Although Yul moved out of writing and directing the picture, contractually he was still bound to play the lead.

DeMille asked his son-in-law Anthony Quinn (married to his daughter Katherine) who had a tiny role in the original *The Buccaneer*, if he was interested in directing the remake. The night DeMille asked that question, Quinn was having dinner in a restaurant with Anna Magnani, his co-star in *Wild Is the Wind*. The actor was taken by surprise. He knew only that DeMille and Yul had had a quarrel, and did not expect his father-in law to trust him to direct a film with Yul Brynner. In his autobiography, Quinn wrote, "I had known Brynner since my days on the New York stage, and found him to be one of the most pretentious people in show business. He had a thing for brown rooms. During every production, he had to have his dressing room painted over in a deep, depressing brown, and I had a constant image of him, sitting backstage, wallowing in a room full of shit. He was such a dreary man that I sometimes thought they painted over his soul."[36]

Although full of doubts, Quinn accepted the offer to direct *The Buccaneer* and hired, with DeMille's authorization, Oscar-winning screenwriter Abby Mann to rewrite the script. The result was again unsatisfactory to DeMille, who found it "too dark and too political." Finally the film was shot according to DeMille grand style: an updated, dull version of the first picture.

Along with Yul, the cast included Charlton Heston, Claire Bloom, Charles Boyer and Inger Stevens. The film retained most of the 1938 original plot. Yul was pirate Jean Lafitte (this time in "dandy version" thanks to Edith Head's lavish costumes), who helped Gen. Andrew Jackson, played by Heston, win the war against the British in 1812.

Yul signed a 250-page contract, which included a list of "prima donna" demands such as a large dressing room with a hammock on which he could lie when he suffered from his recurring backache and a great number of other perks.

The shooting of *The Buccaneer* began in a very tense atmosphere. Yul quarreled with Quinn about the wig his character was supposed to wear. The director wanted a vivid red hair color; Yul refused to wear it. Finally they both agreed on a softer shade that Yul would cover with a wide straw hat between takes. To dissolve the glue with which the wig was attached, it would usually take several annoyingly long applications of nail polish remover by the makeup artists.

The main friction between Brynner and Quinn was caused by the former's insistence on doing his own stunts, even in the most dangerous action scenes. Quinn, who would yell at him reminding him who was the director, did not want Yul to take any chances. Eventually Yul did as he liked. Yul also argued with Edith Head, the most important costume designer in Hollywood, about the way she dressed the actors in the film. Yul disliked Head's costumes because they were too "self conscious."[37]

Yul's professional relationship with some of his co-stars was more relaxed. Charlton Heston recalled that he had the same good screen chemistry with Yul that they had on *The Ten Commandments*.[38] Despite her past affair with Yul, Claire Bloom maintained that it was he who insisted that she appear opposite him; for this reason, Quinn resented having her in the picture and never addressed a single word to her during the entire shoot of the movie. Apparently Yul also all but ignored Bloom during the filming, something the British actress found deeply humiliating and painful.[39]

Some of the cast members were pro–Quinn, others pro–Yul, especially those who knew that it was originally his project. Lovely Swedish actress Inger Stevens, who was madly in love with Quinn, did not get along with Yul, who knew her from their *Studio One* days. Yul was very saddened when Stevens committed suicide years later, recalling how radiant she looked on the set even though she always hid an inner unhappiness.

In the film, Yul performed a French traditional song titled "*Allez l'eau*" on a seven-string guitar. He did his own arrangements of the songs, adding a touch of comedy to the presentation by having a couple of the actors playing pirates howl like dogs while he sang.

Between scenes, Yul took candid portraits of other members of the cast and crew. He enlarged and mounted the photographs and gave them as gifts to some of his colleagues, but first held a little gallery showing of 180 of his photos on a studio sound stage.[40]

DeMille rarely visited the set, but when he did he sat on one side observing all the scenes carefully. He would order an extra take for all the scenes he did not like. Then he would look at the dailies and he would scream with rage. Apparently each night he would return home and tell everyone that he was going to dismiss Quinn as director immediately.[41] Afterwards he personally checked all the film footage in the editing room.

The Buccaneer surpassed the $3 million budget, Paramount had allocated. When the film was released in December 1958, it was an instant flop, panned by all the reviewers. In a later interview, Quinn said, "It was the picture I should never have made." This was his first and last experience as a director in his entire career.[42]

8

A Bastard with
a Heart of Gold

"Yul is a really sweet man."
— Warren Beatty

The tension felt on the set of *The Buccaneer* prompted Yul to smoke three packs of cigarettes a day. He was constantly lighting a cigarette, a vice confirmed by all the photographs taken in those years. Even the characters he played on screen were often heavy smokers. Virginia urged him to give it up. After several vain attempts to quit, first switching to smoking a pipe (on Richard Brooks' suggestion), then cigars, Yul tried a new type of hypnosis. But he had no success and quickly went back to his old bad habit.

In spring of 1958, the Brynners went to Vienna, Austria, where Yul began to shoot *The Journey*. At first producer Anthony Havelock-Allan wanted Anna Magnani and Yul in the leading roles. Yul immediately liked the project and wanted Anatole Litvak as director, after the perfect professional relationship they had on the set of *Anastasia*. But Havelock-Allan was not convinced that Litvak was the right choice and backed off, leaving the project in the hands of Yul and Litvak (the actor and director financed the film after establishing their own production company, Alby — a mixed-up combination of their initials). Originally the story was set in China, but screenwriter George Tabori, a Hungarian immigrant in Hollywood, was inspired by real political events to change the setting to the Austro-Hungarian frontier.

The Journey tells of the peregrinations of 16 international travelers stranded in Hungary after the invasion of the Red Army. Their evacuation is interrupted by a Russian militia led by Major Sukov, played by Yul. Deborah Kerr plays Lady Diana Ahmore, an elegant British aristocrat who tries to help her Hungarian lover (Jason Robards) flee the country. Also in the international cast were French actress Anouk Aimée, as one of the leaders of the Hungarian resistance, British character actor Robert Morley, and Anne Jackson, the wife of Yul's old actor-friend Eli Wallach.

Shot on location around the hills outside Vienna and at the Hosenhegel studios, the picture got a great amount of press, largely because it was reuniting *The King and I*'s Yul and Deborah Kerr — and there was speculation about a romance. The truth was known several weeks later when Kerr left her husband Tony Bartley after 12 years of marriage for screenwriter Peter Viertel, who was in Vienna and often accompanied her off the set.[1]

Several newspapers accused the film of bringing anti-Soviet propaganda to neutral Austria, while others maintained that it was against the Hungarian resistance. The quarrels filled the pages of the 11 Viennese daily papers, forcing Litvak to release an official statement in which he declared his firm intention to continue his work in peace, and condemning those who criticized the film without even knowing what it was about.[2]

Many of the extras playing the Russian military were former soldiers, appearing before the cameras in their own uniforms and wearing Russian medals. They signed up for the picture under false names, since they were all refugees or defectors from the Red Army who had found sanctuary in Austria. During his stay in Vienna, Yul threw a party at the Palace Auersperg. Among the guests were a dozen of those former Russian soldiers. After a few drinks, they broke out with some militant Red Army songs that incensed the refugee Hungarians who *also* were extras in the films. Things got very tense when Hungarian dissidents in the crowd whispered that the Russians had been paid $1,000 each for three months' film work, while Hungarians got only $3.10 a day. Yul prevented a second Hungarian revolt by strongly denying the charge (and quickly ordering more wine).[3]

The making of the film dragged on for several extra weeks. Anne Jackson, who was pregnant, used to joke that she would have to give birth to the child on the location bus. In the film, one of the two kids playing the children of Jackson was Ron Howard, now the acclaimed director of features like *Splash* and *Beautiful Mind*, making his screen debut at age four. Howard still remembers his time on the set with great pleasure, and *vividly* recalls "Yul Brynner taking a shot glass, which I didn't know was made of edible sugar, and devouring it before my eyes."[4]

Kissing Deborah Kerr in *The Journey,* 1959.

The professional relationship between Yul and Litvak was not always idyllic. Yul wanted to enter his Mercedes Benz 300 in a sports car race in Vienna, but the director refused to allow him to risk his neck (and the film). The argument was so heated that at one point some bystanders were afraid it could turn physically violent. Yul stormed off and refused to work the rest of the day. He returned the following morning after he cooled down.

In Vienna, the Brynners' marriage went through hard times. In the past, Virginia had often threatened divorce, but for their son's sake she had always forgiven Yul's countless escapades. This time the situation was more serious and complicated. She had accompanied Yul to Austria, leaving Rocky in California with family friends. Before her departure, she worked full-time in a hospital, taking microscopic photographs in connection with cancer research. Thanks to Francis and Marianna Masin, a husband-and-wife research team, Virginia was able to take courses in microscopic photography at the University of Vienna. By the time Yul finished *The Journey*, she had earned a degree as a cytologist.[5]

While Virginia was busy with her studies, Yul found the time to have a secret affair with Frankie Tilden, a young singer and actress with whom he spent a long weekend in Fuschl, a little village near Salzburg. Soon news of the romance was in the European tabloids. When Yul returned to the States and was asked to comment about it, he replied, "After 14 years of marriage, Virginia isn't disturbed. These stories have happened too often. I have known Frankie's mother, who is Ina Claire of Vienna, for years and I did see both Frankie and her mother while I was making *The Journey*."[6]

This false statement was contradicted when 19-year-old Frankie revealed that she was expecting Yul's child. At first Yul denied any responsibility. Then, to the shock to Virginia, he admitted the truth and agreed to financially support Tilden. The young singer decided to raise the baby alone and named it Lark with Yul's approval.

In Vienna, Yul received a visit from Martin Ritt, an old friend and former CBS colleague, now an established film director. Ritt wanted Yul to star in his next feature. The two friends had in mind a picture on Spartacus, the Roman gladiator. Together they outlined a script and got permission from United Artists to produce a film called *The Gladiators*. At the same time, Kirk Douglas had optioned Arthur Koestler's novel *Spartacus*, confident that he would get funding from United Artists, who had produced Douglas' most recent film *The Vikings*. Arthur Krim, the head of United Artists, dismissed Douglas' proposition with a brief telegram saying that the actor's project covered the same story as the one proposed by Yul and Ritt, with whom he had already committed.[7] At first Douglas was disappointed, but then he considered joining forces with Yul and Ritt. After all, there were two interesting great parts, adversaries in the story who could be played by Yul and him. Douglas was also convinced that United Artists would be happier to have *two* major stars in the picture. Several days after Douglas called to make that proposal, Ritt dismissed it. As Douglas wrote in his autobiography, "Yul Brynner hated my guts. I thought that was odd —*he* had beaten *me* for the Academy Award."[8]

"I have no faith and no liking for Kirk Douglas's acting and at this point for his box office value," Yul wrote to Ritt in a letter, adding, "Frankly, it makes me quite sick to give an inch in this [to Douglas] and everything inside me rebels against it."[9] A few days later, Douglas saw a copy of *Variety* with a picture of Yul dressed as Spartacus and the words **The Gladiators. Next from United Artists.** The article said that the production would begin as soon as Yul and Ritt finished *The Sound and the Fury* at Fox.

Yul was brought aboard to play the role of Jason in *The Sound and the Fury*, based on William Faulkner's novel. To write the screenplay, Fox hired Irving Ravetch and Harriet Frank, Jr., a husband-and-wife team, supervised by producer Jerry Wald and Ritt. The Ravetch-Frank-Ritt trio had already worked together in *The Long Hot Summer*, based on Faulkner's novel *The Hamlet* and his short story *Barn Burner*, starring Paul Newman and his wife Joanne Woodward.

Faulkner's *The Sound and the Fury* was updated to the '50s; all but eliminated was the novel's use of flashbacks. Consequently the film script dealt almost exclusively with the events in the book that took place in the present. Producer Jerry Wald explained that the film could concentrate on the current plight of the Compson family and gradually reveal events of the past.

The Sound and the Fury was director Ritt's fifth film and the third one starring Joanne Woodward, an actress he highly respected. Originally Wald thought of Lana Turner for the role of Woodward's mother, but eventually Margaret Leighton played the part.[10] Yul was the first actor to be cast as Wald revealed in an article before the opening of the film. "Temperamentally, Yul fit the role perfectly. Yet he has an undisguisable accent and a touch of exoticism about him that at first glance seemed out of place in the local of our story. We made this acceptable by changing the nationality of Jason and his aging mother to French—from the Bayou country of Louisiana."[11]

The director traveled across different Southern states looking for the right location for the film, but he did not find any place suitable. For

Yul Brynner in *The Sound and the Fury*, 1959.

this reason, the town of Jefferson, Mississippi, was recreated on the 20th Century-Fox back lot. It was a wrong choice because it gave an artificial flavor to the film.

When *The Sound and the Fury* opened, many critics disapproved of the changes made to the novel. They also found Yul's character odd: He had a full head of hair (Yul again wore a wig) and spoke with a strange accent. Joanne Woodward was also criticized because she was not very believable in the role of a 16-year-old girl. She was in her seventh month of pregnancy and had to find many ways to camouflage it.

The Sound and the Fury and *The Journey* came out in the spring of 1959, one month apart from each other. They were both box office disappointments. The first disappeared from the theaters after few weeks and was Yul's first Hollywood flop. Many years later, Martin Ritt remarked, "I didn't like [*The Sound and the Fury*]. I made some mistakes on that. I shouldn't do Faulkner again. There's something in the language that's too rich ... it's almost untranslatable."[12]

On November 15, 1958, actor Tyrone Power was rushed to the United States Torrejon Air Base Hospital near Madrid after having a heart attack on the set of *Solomon and Sheba*. He died in the Mercedes

Yul and Joanne Woodward rehearsing a scene of *The Sound and the Fury.*

of his co-star Gina Lollobrigida on the way to the hospital. After Power's death, producers Edward Small and Ted Richmond raced to find a replacement to save the picture. Each day of inactivity cost the production thousands of dollars. First United Artists wanted Spanish actor Virgilio Texeira, who already had a small role in the film. The producers refused, demanding a major Hollywood star. Robert Taylor, Gary Cooper, William Holden and Charlton Heston were considered, but they were all engaged in other projects. Then Yul was chosen. Luckily he was available until the following February, when the shooting of his next picture was scheduled to begin.

At a press conference, Yul stated that, in honor of the memory of his friend and colleague Tyrone Power, he was accepting this part. Although his friendship for Power was a noble reason to play the role, the offer of a salary between $700,000 and $1,000,000 (paid by the Fireman's Fund, the film's insurer), plus 15 percent of the gross over $9 million, seemed a more realistic explanation for Yul's decision to immediately leave for Spain.

When Tyrone Power died, director King Vidor had already shot half of the picture. Since Yul walked differently and had a larger build than Power, even shots in which Power had his back to the camera had to be filmed again. All the costumes had to be quickly altered to fit Yul. Because Yul wore a wig whose color did not match the color of Power's, every scene with co-star Lollobrigida had to be retaken.[13] Yul was signed on in such haste that he did not have enough time to study his role as he usually would do, and rushed to learn his lines.

Solomon and Sheba's exteriors were filmed on location in Zaragoza, the interiors at the Sevilla Studios in Madrid. The cast also included Italo-American Marisa Pavan and British actor George Sanders.

Yul arrived in Madrid with an entourage of seven, including assistants, secretary, chauffeur and bodyguards. As Sanders wittily wrote in his autobiography, "The function of one member of this retinue appeared to consist of placing already lighted cigarettes in Brynner's outstretched fingers. Another was permanently occupied in shaving his skull with an electric razor whenever the suspicion of a shadow darkened that noble head. While these services were being rendered unto him, Brynner sat in sphinx-like silence and splendor wearing black leather suits or white leather suits, of which he had half a dozen each, confected for him by the firm of Dior. I never discovered the duties of the remaining five members of his staff, but they were no doubt doing work that was equally essential…. I came to the conclusion that Brynner is a very shrewd fellow; he has one very intense expression that he uses all the time on the screen, and one intense expression is more valuable to a film star then a dozen faces."[14]

Yul did not waste any time making himself known. If Lollobrigida was 20 minutes late, he managed to arrive 20 minutes after her; if she was escorted by five assistants, he had seven. King Vidor said in an interview, "With Power, [Lollobrigida] was all sweetness and honey, but when Brynner started to come on and throw his weight around, she tried to keep up with him and she started to swing her weight around."[15] But as soon as Yul was away from the set, and in the company of his friends, he would make fun of himself and his whims as a star, confessing how much he liked to shock the people around him. French actor Jean-Pierre Aumont, husband of *Solomon* star Marisa Pavan, described in his memoir a memorable dinner with Yul in a traditional Spanish restaurant:

> We were sitting in the same restaurant where eight days earlier we had dinner with Tyrone a few hours before his death. We had to struggle to cancel

his tender spirit ... Yul was exactly the opposite. He was as outgoing as Tyrone was reserved. From his entourage he has only brought with him a young brunette with gypsy's eyes to whom he does not pay too much attention. Without looking at the menu he orders "criadillas." "What's that?" "Bull's testicles." I should have imagined it. The macho inside Yul gets fed only with bull's testicles. He asked me: "Have you ever thought about how fragile testicles are, no difference if it's bull's or ours? I always think about it. Reflect on it. Our other less necessary organs are much more protected. The head is protected by a shell of bones. The thorax is shielded in a cage protecting liver, spleen ... [And] the organ which should be the most noble, the most respected, the most celebrated of all because it is the only one to generate life, is at the mercy of every little kick, fall or fight. Have you ever thought that we could still reproduce ourselves without legs, arms, bladder, tongue or nose, but it's impossible to reproduce mankind if something little happens to the least protected of our organs?" I ponder about those sad reflections. Marisa coughs. The gypsy pretends not to understand. Yul orders another portion of testicles. "Only five or six," he points out, "I'm not very hungry." When they are finally served they look clearly smaller than the previous ones. Yul complains about it to the waiter. "Yes Mr. Brynner I agree with you, but those are the last ones we have. Those are just different but not bad at all. You must know that the day we bought them it was not the bull to be killed but the matador!"[16]

The retakes on *Solomon and Sheba* dragged on for months. Yul left the set for Switzerland to go under minor surgery for an ear problem. At first, Yul and Lollobrigida did not have good chemistry on the set. She got upset after Yul had furtively photographed her with a huge telephoto lens while she was in a huge tub doing a scene taking a bath (wearing skin-colored tights). Gradually, thanks to Yul's *savoir faire*, the relationship improved. Having an interest in photography, Lollobrigida was impressed by Yul's picture and by his kindness (he taught her how to use his camera, which she borrowed for a while).[17]

To the reporters who frequently asked Yul for his opinion of his Italian co-star, he discreetly replied, "Gina makes my coming to work in the morning a pleasure."[18] In a recent TV interview, the Italian actress confessed that of all the famous stars she had worked with, Yul was the only one with whom she had a brief romance. Lollobrigida was also Yul's date on the night of the Spanish premiere of *The King and I* in Madrid.

After *Solomon and Sheba* was completed, a record $1 million was spent on publicity. The film opened in December 1959 and was unani-

Yul and Gina Lollobrigida in *Solomon and Sheba.*

mously panned by reviewers, who considered it one of the worst movies ever made. King Vidor disliked Yul's performance: "When Brynner took over ... he fought the idea of a troubled monarch and wanted to dominate each situation without conflict. It was an attitude that affected ... the integrity of the film."[19]

Despite the terrible reviews, the picture grossed $5.5 million in the

United States and $10 million in Europe. It not only recovered the production cost but made Yul a rich man (he got 15 percent of the gross). Ironically, Yul's shaky financial situation (he had recently gone into debt to maintain his extravagant lifestyle) improved thanks to one of the worst pictures he ever made.

Yul had to make a difficult choice. At that time, the American tax system obliged him to pay in taxes almost three-quarters of his revenues and the only exception the government made was to citizens who had their permanent residence abroad for a minimum of five years. Virginia, as Rock Brynner revealed, was against moving her family abroad; she believed that would be dishonest, immoral and unpatriotic.[20] Nevertheless, for Yul the economical stability was more important than the patriotic sentimentalism that did not suit his nomadic personality. Hence at the beginning of 1959, he decided to move to Lausanne, Switzerland, where 20 years earlier he was treated for his opium addiction. Yul took his faithful assistant Don Lawson and a secretary. While Rocky was enrolled in an exclusive boarding school, Virginia opted to stay in the States planning a show business comeback. However, the end of the Brynners' marriage was in near sight. Yul's decision to change residence was the *coup de grace* to a stormy union that lasted 15 years, gone through many crises, and was now over with Yul opting to leave his wife (and her grave alcoholism problem) behind.

Before his departure to Switzerland, Yul had begun to collect stamps, a hobby initially shared with Rocky (about whom Yul felt guilty for not devoting enough time). But this soon became another expression of his narcissistic personality: He aspired to have one of the most important collection of rare stamps ever. Yul transformed a small hobby collection (inherited from a friend who lost interest in it) into an investment, collecting exclusively United Nations stamps. He ordered his secretary to write each United Nations head of state requesting a corner block of their stamps and asking them to personally sign them. In a few months, his 35-volume collection was one of the most complete in the world. Appraised at about $250,000 it was kept in a bank in Switzerland. Yul periodically met collectors from all over the world to buy, trade or sell the rarest stamps.[21]

Collecting stamps gave him the opportunity to get involved in a very important humanitarian mission. The United Nations asked him to provide some advice about the postage stamps that were to be issued during the World Refugee Year and to assist in the making of a documentary on that subject. Yul soon realized that August R. Lindt, the High Commissioner for Refugees, was interested in a more active participation. Therefore Yul signed a two-year contract as special consultant with the Office of the High Commissioner of the United Nations, to help make people everywhere aware of the problems of refugees, particularly refugee children.

While in Austria during the making of *The Journey*, Yul had come in contact with a group of Hungarian refugees who worked as extras. Still none of this made a lasting impression on him until he visited a refugee camp. The sight of all those children moved him so strongly that, months later, when the U.N. asked for his help, he could not refuse.[22]

Early in 1960, Yul, in collaboration with Magnum's photographer Inge Morarth, toured several refugee camps in Europe and the Middle and Far East to make a photographic report which was published as a book. Yul donated its earnings to the Office of the U.N. High Commissioner for Refugees.

He also narrated *Mission to No-Man's Land*, a 30-minute documentary on the conditions of the refugee camps made by Stanley Wright and BBC-TV, and supervised by Anatole Litvak. It was the first of a series of documentaries in which Yul emphasized the nature of the sad situation. In an interview concerning his philanthropic activism, Yul explained, "I'm doing this not as an actor but as a member of the human race. We are trying to get countries to speed up the process of immigration and repatriation.... My personal interest has been trying to find some way to make the world at large aware that there are millions of children who know no other life than that of a refugee camps"[23]

In December 1960, CBS aired a special program called *Rescue: Yul Brynner*, which showed all the refugee camps Yul photographed. Twenty years later, in an interview with *The New York Times*, Yul revealed that in the beginning, his choice to work for the U.N. was also dictated a little by selfish elements. "I wanted to do that work, but it also did reconcile this celebrity image that I had such a distaste for. I was able to take that overflow attention and use it to make people aware of something important. That did something good for me."[24]

Yul always wanted to star in a film directed by Stanley Donen, whom he greatly admired. As the director explained, "I signed a four-picture, non-exclusive deal with Columbia in the late '50s to produce and direct. I had gone to the Coast to see about casting a film I'd been working on all summer. I had just arrived, in fact, when I got a call from Yul Brynner, who insisted I come over immediately to read a play. Yul said, 'I'll play in it on the condition you direct.'"[25] Donen liked the idea and agreed to make *Once More, With Feeling.* The director, a former dancer and choreographer, had worked with Gene Kelly in several films (including *On the Town* and *Singin' in the Rain*) and had directed such hits as *Seven Brides for Seven Brothers, Funny Face* and *Indiscreet.*

After reading Harry Kurnitz's play and seeing it performed on Broadway by Arlene Francis and Joseph Cotten, Donen bought the rights to make into a film. Opposite Yul, the director cast Kay Kendall, who agreed right away to co-star after Columbia decided to shoot it in Paris instead of London (where the story took place) because of tax problems. Filming began in late April 1959 at Paris' Boulogne Studios. *Once More, with Feeling* had a $3,000,000 budget and Kendall was in the latter stages of leukemia (diagnosed in the fall of 1956); if this had been detected by the insurance examiners, she would not have been allowed to work.[26] Nobody knew about it but her husband Rex Harrison. Despite looking slightly underweight, Kendall seemed in good shape.

In *Once More, with Feeling,* Yul played Victor Fabian, a tyrannical orchestra conductor, and Kendall his harpist mistress, who decides that in order to leave him and marry another man, she must wed and then divorce the despot. The character of Fabian intrigued Yul, not only because he had never played in a comedy but also because it gave him the opportunity to comically transpose the arrogant egotistic tyrant, played in his previous films. Unfortunately the script was unfunny and the final result was extremely disappointing.

Two weeks into shooting, Kendall suddenly collapsed on the set and was rushed to the American Hospital in Paris; her personal physician was quickly flown in from London. Columbia immediately threatened to replace the British actress in order to avoid costly delays. Yul stated clearly that if Kendall was fired, he would quit the production.

At first the press published the news that Kendall was ill with pneumonia or bronchitis, but a few days later some newspapers reported a "serious blood disorder."[27] In the meantime, Donen filmed all the scenes in which Kendall did not appear. On June 8, 1959, eight days after her crisis, Kendall miraculously returned to the set to finish up her work.

Makeup artists' and hairdressers' great ability, along with Givanchy's extraordinary gowns and Cartier's magnificent jewels, were able to create a glamorous illusion to hide the terrible truth.

Argentinean novelist Manuel Puig, then an assistant on the set, remembered how gladly he ran to the deli for hamburgers and sandwiches for Kendall. She was in fact ravenous all the time — apparently one of the symptoms of the leukemia.[28] Puig's biographer also maintained that Puig had a brief homosexual encounter with Yul during that time, and that Puig graphically commented on the actor's genitals.[29]

Kay Kendall died three months after *Once More, with Feeling* was completed. Yul talked about the tragic loss of his co-star with columnist Louella Parsons: "Kay worked with great and wonderful spirit and finished the picture with flying colors…. None of us realized that the poor girl was actually suffering from leukemia. She was so gay and bright."[30]

When the film opened in March 1960, Columbia Pictures promoted Yul as a main star and stressed the funny qualities of the movie, carefully avoiding mention of Kendall's tragedy. *Once More, with Feeling* received mixed reviews and was generally considered "forced and funless." Even Donen admitted in an interview, "It was not very good. It should have been romantic. I thought Yul was good in it, though."[31]

In September 1959, poet-artist-filmmaker Jean Cocteau was ready to film *Le Testament d'Orphée*. The picture was the last installment of a trilogy (which included *Le Sang d'un poet* and *Orphée*) about life and death in which Cocteau was an intermediary between reality and fantasy.

Yul had met Cocteau during his first years in Paris, when he was playing the guitar in the Russian night clubs. The poet approached him knowing Yul could show him where to buy opium. Since then they became very close and Cocteau introduced him to many famous friends like Picasso, Colette, Marcel Marceau and Jean Marais. Knowing that Yul was now living in Switzerland, Cocteau asked him to play a cameo in his film. For the sake of their old friendship, Yul could not refuse. He went to Les Baux de Provence, a small village near Arles in the south of France, where the picture was scheduled to be filmed.

Yul was in the first scene shot, playing the usher into Hell. He wore an elegant tuxedo and, with his cavernous voice, his final words were, "Abandon here all hope" an appropriate reference to Dante's *Inferno*.

Kay Kendall and Yul in *Once More, with Feeling*.

Besides Yul, Pablo and Jacqueline Picasso, Spanish matador Luis Domin-guín and his wife (Italian actress Lucia Bose) played small parts as well. *Le Testament d'Orphée* was released in the United States two years later, but Cocteau's obscure dialogue and surrealistic images were not understood. During a special screening for potential distributors, many in the audience left the room before the end. Yul, who also attended was outraged by it and ordered the projectionist to stop the film. He yelled, "Cocteau was right when he told me that this movie should be forbidden to imbeciles!"[32]

On October 17, 1959, Yul boarded a flight bound for the Greek island of Rhodes. Stanley Donen, who was having some financial difficulties after a stormy divorce, asked Yul to star in his new film *Surprise Package*. The director had purchased the rights of Art Buchwald's play *A Gift from the Boys* and asked screenwriter Harry Kurnitz to write a script based on it. Five weeks later, a crew was ready to shoot in Greece. (The setting of the play was Sicily, but Donen opted for Rhodes since the autumn weather was milder there and the landscape more colorful "uncontaminated" — it had never been used as a film background before.)

Mitzi Gaynor, Noël Coward and Yul played the leads. They all arrived from England together with a group of 45 British technicians. At the time, living conditions on Rhodes were very simple. Electricity was only available a few hours a day; drinking water had to be carried directly from one spring in the area in clay-brown jugs; donkeys were the most common means of transportation.

The moviemakers lodged at the Hotel Miramare in Lindos, the main town on the island. Donen set up a screen on a patio and each day guests were allowed to view the daily rushes. Yul was surprised that no one in the street recognized him, but the mystery was soon solved when he discovered that two-thirds of the population had never been inside a movie theater. During the shooting of a scene in which Yul had to scream at Gaynor and threw her to the ground, the local children became so upset that they protectively gathered around the actress. Yul tried to explain that he and Gaynor were only acting. Yul and Mitzi even held hands between takes to show that there were no hard feelings, but the children's reactions remained the same. The children cheered when the strange American "game" was over.

The Archbishop of Rhodes, knowing of Yul's humanitarian mission, asked him to visit a home he had established for aged refugees. Yul gladly went with him and distributed to the guests care packages.

Surprise Package was shot in black-and-white for budget reasons. It was the story of Nico March (Yul), an American gangster deported by the police to a tiny island in the Mediterranean Sea. There he tries to steal a jewel from an exiled monarch (Coward). The con's plan does not succeed. He chooses to live peacefully with his girlfriend (Gaynor), "the surprise package" his friends sent him from America.

Discussing his casting choices, Donen explained, "Yul was certainly the ideal. Mitzi and Noël were first choices, too."[33] Once again Yul played a bossy, authoritarian character — and once again the lack of wit in the script and the absurdity of the plot made the picture into a flop.

After several weeks in Greece, the crew returned to England to complete interiors at the Metro-British studios in Elstree. *Surprise Package* premiered in England on September 1960 and received lukewarm reviews which mostly praised Coward's performance. American critics later panned the film, which disappeared from screens after a few days.

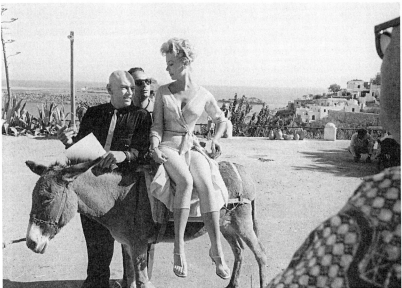

Top: Mitzi Gaynor and Yul in *Surprise Package. Bottom:* Yul Brynner with director Stanley Donen and Mitzi Gaynor on the Greek set of *Surprise Package* (1960).

Just before replacing Tyrone Power in *Solomon and Sheba*, at a party in Versailles, Yul met Doris Kleiner, a beautiful, classy and sophisticated girl who was working for *haute couture* designer Pierre Cardin. Kleiner was born in Yugoslavia but spent most of her childhood in Chile. In the 1950s she moved to Paris, mingling with international high society, and became one of the most elegant women in Europe.

Yul and Doris immediately fell in love. Her charm was a great comfort for him, especially during the difficult separation from Virginia. Gilmore had refused Yul's offer, as part of the alimony agreement, of a percentage of the gross of his next film, *The Magnificent Seven*, lacking confidence in that project and in her former husband's career.

"He had a fantastic personality," Doris remembered when asked about Yul. "He was strong, he was gregarious, he was sexy, he was good-looking, he was talented. He was marvelous! He was at the prime of everything everybody can have. And he had a wonderful 13-year-old son and there he was, this hunk of a fellow with no hair!"[34]

Each time Yul went to Europe he met with Doris; then when he moved to Switzerland, he asked her to live with him in a beautiful villa he had rented by a lake.

Doris also met Rock, whose custody after the divorce was given to Virginia. But Virginia agreed to let him study at an exclusive Swiss school so he could be closer to his beloved father.

Doris introduced Yul to her circle of friends and, as Victoria Brynner pointed out, "She brought to him a whole sophistication and taste which he knew about instinctively but he really did not know materially speaking."[35]

In March 1960, when Yul went on location for *The Magnificent Seven*, the couple decided to get married in Mexico during the shooting of the film.

9

The Magnificent Seven

"Yul is a good actor for sure, but when it comes to riding horses or handling guns he's laughable."
— Steve McQueen

The same night Yul won the Academy Award for Best Actor for his performance in *The King and I*, *The Seven Samurai*, a Japanese film by Akira Kurosawa, did *not* win in the category of Best Foreign Picture.

Hollywood producer Lou Morheim owned the American remake rights, which he bought from the Toho production company for the ludicrous sum of $250. Yul and Anthony Quinn were impressed by Kurosawa's masterpiece and both showed an interest in directing a Western based on the Japanese film. Quinn explained in his autobiography that, despite their mutual disrespect, he and Yul jointly purchased the American rights from Morheim. "We both wanted to make Kurosawa's picture into a Western," Quinn wrote, "and could not see the point in bidding each other up and inflating the price, so we became partners. As it turned out, I did not have the same scheming head for business as my new associate. In the months ahead, Brynner would dupe me from my share of the picture.... I never forgave him his trickery."[1]

In February 1960, Quinn filed a $500,000 breach of contract against Yul and Alciona Productions, Yul's production company. In his complaint, Quinn alleged that in the final screenplay of *The Magnificent Seven*, his business partner used script suggestions that he (Quinn) offered without his permission. In addition, he sued United Artists for $150,000 citing exclusion from the production, scheduled to be filmed in Mexico. Yul's attorney Leon Kaplan denied Quinn's charges, maintaining that the entire project was sold to the Mirisch Co. with Yul and Quinn's authorization and that Mirisch would co-produce the film with director John Sturges, who was considered one of *the* best action films

93

directors. According to Kaplan, there was never any discussion of Quinn's participation in the picture.[2]

Quinn lost the battle and had to pay the legal expenses. The truth was that, without notifying his business partner, Yul sold the rights to the Mirisch Co. with the promise that Sturges would cast him in the leading role.

Major problems arose during the process of writing a screenplay. Walter Bernstein (a screenwriter blacklisted during the McCarthy era) wrote the first draft of *The Magnificent Seven* as a faithful Western adaptation of the original Japanese film. Once Sturges became the producer, he also hired Walter Newman, author of the brilliant *Ace in the Hole*, to update Bernstein's script, whose characters were (as in *The Seven Samurai*) middle-aged men. For personal reasons, Newman could not be on the set in Mexico, where the film was scheduled to be shot; therefore the production hired William Roberts as a script doctor. When the Writers Guild of America demanded Roberts' name in the credits, Newman was so enraged that he requested *his* name be removed — leaving the false impression that Roberts was the main author.

United Artists agreed to finance *The Magnificent Seven* primarily because of Yul's participation and they did not much care about the rest of the cast. Sturges assembled a group of relatively unknown but talented actors: Steve McQueen, James Coburn, Horst Bucholtz, Robert Vaughn, Charles Bronson, Brad Dexter and Eli Wallach.

The plot was simple yet powerful. The inhabitants of a Mexican village, unable to defend themselves from continuous raids by bandits, seek the help of Chris, a mercenary gunslinger played by Yul. The gunfighter recruits a group of six other hired guns to fight the marauding Calvera (Eli Wallach) and his band.

Once the casting was completed, the crew moved to Cuernavaca, a then-small, unknown village 50 miles from Mexico City (now a popular holiday destination). Yul received movie star treatment including a fantastic villa with swimming pool and servants, a huge dressing room trailer, a limo and a full staff of assistants. The rest of the cast stayed at the modest Posada Jacaranda, the only hotel in the area.

Most of the filming was done in Tepoztlan, a tiny village outside Cuernavaca. The Mexican government authorized their shooting on location on the condition that a censor was always on the set, ready to make changes if any negative or offensive stereotypes were used in portraying the locals. Hence an official censor, a Mexican woman, often interrupted the takes, ordering immediate modifications. Among many alterations, she demanded that the Mexican peasants always wear clean clothes and that the story clearly show that the villagers, before hiring the gunslingers, had tried to buy guns themselves (this made it clear that they were not cowards).

Yul was excited to play Chris, leader of the Magnificent Seven. He described his character as "a dirty bum" with "only two clean things about him, his gun and his soul."[3]

Apart from the problem with the censor, the atmosphere on the set was very relaxed. Much has been written about an alleged feud between Yul and Steve McQueen, but most of the episodes reported by the press (and by McQueen's biographers) were fabrications made up by reporters who were on the set. There was indeed a sort-of competition between the two actors; McQueen in particular used tricks to upstage not only Yul but *all* his colleagues. But the "conflict" was not the sensational, violent one described by the media.

McQueen, who had previously worked with Sturges in *Never So Few* opposite Frank Sinatra and Gina Lollobrigida, was then on the rise thanks to his popular TV series *Wanted: Dead or Alive*. To play the role of Vin in *The Magnificent Seven*, McQueen simulated a car accident that would free him from his TV contract. After he read the script and noticed that his character had only seven lines of dialogue, he called Sturges complaining that his part was "a kind of ass-wipe to Yul" and demanded that it be expanded.[4] With infinite patience, Sturges tried to keep the situation under control and found time for each actor to discuss the character they were playing. But apparently it was not enough for McQueen.

In a scene in which Yul gave a speech to the group with his back to McQueen, Steve began flipping a coin, trying once again to upstage Yul. There were other, similar episodes (McQueen moving his white hat, rattling his bullet-casings, etc., to get attention). Once Yul heard about McQueen's antics, he took off his cowboy hat in their next scene together. Suddenly, no matter what amount of scene-stealing was going on, his bald, shiny head become a magnet for the audience's eyes.[5]

According to another legendary anecdote, Yul built himself a little mound of earth so that he would look as tall as McQueen. The latter responded by casually kicking at the pile each time he passed, thus reducing Yul's height.[6]

The Magnificent Seven

Sturges admitted that there was friction between the two stars but downplayed the suggestion that it ever amounted to a feud. He explained, "Yul was like a rock, while Steve was volatile."[7]

When a local newspaper printed an article about the Brynner-McQueen rivalry, the news quickly spread to the American press. When Yul read it, he walked up to McQueen, newspaper in hand, grabbed him by his shoulder and ordered him to tell the press they were *not* fighting on the set. Yul added that he was an established star and did not feud with supporting actors. McQueen, irritated by Yul's behavior, yelled at him to keep his hands off him and to go to hell.[8] The following day, in a brief statement for the press, Yul denied that there was bad blood between him and McQueen, stating, "I never feud with actors, I feud with studios."[9]

Off the set, the cast members spent most of their time playing poker or gin rummy, drinking and enjoying the local food. Solitary and taciturn Charles Bronson often stood apart.

Yul, Robert Vaughn, Charles Bronson, Horst Buchholz, Brad Dexter, and James Coburn in Mexico on the set of *The Magnificent Seven.*

During the stay in Mexico, Yul was officially divorced from Virginia. Only five days later, Yul married Doris Kleiner. The informal ceremony was held in the office of Yul's attorney Edgardo de Villfranco. Judge Manuel Soto performed the rite in the presence of a few close friends. Don Lawson, Yul's assistant, was the best man. The wedding reception was held on the set of the film, using the set from the scene of the party thrown by the villagers to welcome the Magnificent Seven.

It was a fantastic fiesta with almost 300 people, champagne, tequila, fireworks and the dance music of a Mexican band until dawn.

When *The Magnificent Seven* was completed, United Artists was dissatisfied with the final cut and decided to release the picture with limited advertising. The American critics had contrasting reactions to the film, which ran in many cities for only for a week. Several months later, when the movie opened in Europe, its success was so big (thanks in part to the sensational score by Elmer Bernstein, one of the most popular film themes in history) that United Artist re-released the picture in the U.S. It became an immediate hit.

The Magnificent Seven started a trend that culminated in the '60s with the "spaghetti Westerns" by Sergio Leone. The film was so successful that it spawned three (awful) sequels, only one of which had Yul in it. The picture launched the careers of all the young actors of the cast and marked the peak of Yul's popularity. Ironically, Yul's next successful film was *Westworld* 13 years later — in which he played a robot version of his *Magnificent Seven* character.

When Yul returned to Paris (where he bought a pied-à-terre), he was invited by Anatole Litvak to be the official photographer on the set of *Aimez -vous Brames?*, starring Anthony Perkins, Ingrid Bergman and Yves Montand. Yul enjoyed taking scado of pictures, many of them candids, and also appeared as an extra along with Françoise Sagan, author of the novel on which the film was based. The scene was shot on a set that was a faithful reconstruction of the trendy Parisian nightclub, Epic Club. Yul drank the movie company's liquor like a fish to compensate for the fact that he was not paid for his services.

That same year, 1960, screenwriter Norman Krasna wrote a script for Yul called *The Billionaire*. The story concerned a tycoon (resembling producer Howard Hughes) in love with a showgirl. Yul was not interested in playing in another comedy after two flops with Stanley Donen and passed on the part. Gregory Peck also refused it. After many other stars turned down the role, Yves Montand and Marilyn Monroe finally played the leads and the film was re-titled *Let's Make Love*.

For more than a year, Yul stopped working and instead traveled around the world on behalf of the United Nations refugee organization. At the same time, selecting the right script became more difficult since

Doris Brynner, Yul and an unidentified woman on the Mexican set of *The Magnificent Seven.*

he had to reject all Hollywood screenplays because he could not work in America due to his tax problem. But the European scripts did not seem good enough for his standards. Finally, in the spring of 1961, a team of accountants found a way for Yul to return to work in the States. Yul talked about his sabbatical with the press, claiming that it was long-planned: "I had gotten married and wanted to live like a civilian," he said. "It was like getting out of the army. And the first three or four

The Magnificent Seven (1960) publicity shot. Left to right are Yul Brynner, Steve McQueen, Horst Buchholz, Charles Bronson, Robert Vaughn, Brad Dexter and James Coburn.

months were difficult. I forgot the discipline we live under in this business."[10]

Escape from Zahrain was the picture Yul agreed to make with director Ronald Neame. At first Paramount set the film to be shot on location in Middle East, but at the last moment, after Yul and Neame had signed their contracts, the studio executives changed their minds, realizing that filming in California's Mojave Desert and using local extras would dramatically decrease the film budget. Hence in the summer of 1961, with a mediocre script and a limited budget, cameras started rolling in Hollywood. Yul and Doris stayed in a bungalow at the Beverly Hills Hotel, not far from Elizabeth Taylor and then-husband Eddie Fisher. The Brynners became very close friends of the Fishers, seeing each other during the entire time they stayed in California.

The cast of *Escape from Zahrain* included Sal Mineo and James Mason in a cameo. Mineo was cast at Yul's suggestion; Mason was an old friend of Neame and accepted the role as a personal favor (he was promised that his name would not appear in the credits. The picture told the story of five men who escape from a Middle Eastern prison and set out across a desert. When the film was released on July 1962, it got terrible reviews. *The New York Times* defined the plot as "nonsensical ... [it] never rises above the level of a comic strip" and Yul's character, the silent Arab leader Sharif, was "patently absurd."[11] Neame told a reporter that the only positive thing that came out of the experience was the opportunity to work with Yul, whose professionalism he had always respected; they quickly became close friends.[12] Yul's memories of that film included frequent sandstorms and also the pleasure of working again with his friend Mineo, of whom he said, "Sal treated me like a father. To me he was like family, like one of my own kids."[13]

After appearing in a printed advertisement for Air France, Yul left with Doris for Argentina to star in *Taras Bulba*. Directed by J. Lee Thompson, who was fresh from the success of *The Guns of Navarone*, *Taras Bulba* was co-written by Waldo Salt and Karl Tunberg and based on Nikolai Gogol's popular novel. Originally Burt Lancaster was to play opposite Yul, but at the last moment he was replaced by Tony Curtis.

Producer Harold Hecht traveled around the world to find a location which resembled the Ukrainian mountains, where the story was set. He finally chose Salta, a Spanish colonial town in the Andes foothills.

Gogol's novel had already been adapted three times by moviemakers. A 1936 version was filmed in France starring Harry Baur and Danielle Darrieux. Yul had worked on the set, helping the makeup artists make fake mustaches for 300 extras.

The film tells the story of the sixteenth century Cossack leader Taras Bulba, who fights against the Poles and whose son Andrei deserted after falling for a Polish girl. The relationship between father and son stimulated Yul's interest in the script. Although he was again playing a tough, authoritarian character, he did not have any problem showing his deep feelings of love for his son, whom he is forced to kill out of loyalty to his people. Yul spent 15 weeks in preparation for the film, giving screenplay with meticulous attention and developing an enthusiasm for his character. He explained, "Bulba is a great leader. He is a great patriot. He is a mythical figure. In my mind he is 15 feet tall in order to make things he does convincing."[14]

Yul suggested that the director shoot the film chronologically so he

Yul and Tony Curtis in Taras Bulba.

(Yul) could better plunge into Taras' character, who ages throughout the story. Due to practical reasons which involved the presence of over 6000 extras — some gauchos, some hired from the Argentinean army — the idea was overruled.

In early October 1961, the Brynners arrived in Argentina, where the production company had rented a cottage for them, with a butler, maid, driver and guards. Tony Curtis and his wife actress Janet Leigh were next door. Curtis remembers Yul as "a charming and funny man" and "the most fascinating of those players. He had a fabulous pomposity about him, an aloofness. A sense of grandeur about himself and everything he did. That was the nature of the man, and that was the way he behaved, both on and off the set.... I like working with him very much. I'll never forget that moment when, as my father, he shoots me."[15]

On the set, the most difficult task was to organize the extras in the battle scenes, many of them performed on horses. J. Lee Thompson recalls that the gauchos were told that if they fell off their horses, they

Yul as Taras Bulba.

would get a considerable amount of extra pay. The people who were to fall were selected, but when the shot was taken the obvious happened and 400 of the 500 gauchos fell to the ground. That evening, only those who had been instructed to fall were paid extra. This upset the other gauchos, who decided to strike and not come back to the set the following day. That night, Yul ordered hundreds of steaks and had them sent out to the fields where the gauchos lived with their horses. Later he showed up at their camp and for three hours gave a concert, playing and singing Russian, French and English songs—a sort of "Argentinean Woodstock."[16] Yul's behavior impressed the gauchos so much that they all came back the next day.

As Taras Bulba, Yul wore a fake ponytail glued to his scalp and once again did all of his scenes without a double. He did have a minor accident while riding his horse; when he was rushed to the hospital, no fractures were found.

Despite the presence of his wife and three daughters, Tony Curtis did nothing to hide the huge crush he developed on co-star Christine

Yul meets the Queen of England in 1962.

Kaufmann, who played the Polish woman for whom Bulba's son betrays his father. (A couple months later, Curtis divorced Leigh to marry Kaufmann.) Yul, still a newlywed, spent his free time playing cards with Doris in his mega-trailer, which was specially equipped with all sorts of comforts he had expressly requested.

Filming in Argentina lasted over eight weeks; the crew then moved to Hollywood to complete some interiors. The film budget went from $3 million to $9 million and it grossed less than $10 million. But Yul had established such a good relationship with producer Harold Hecht that he signed up for Hecht's next film *Flight from Ashiya*.

In March, a few months before going to Japan to make *Flight from Ashiya*, Yul was formally introduced to the Queen of England, Princess Margaret and other foreign celebrities like Claudia Cardinale, Leslie Caron and Melina Mercouri. When Doris informed him that he was soon to become a father again, Yul rented a magnificent nineteenth-century villa. In the summer of 1962, Yul took Rocky with him to Japan while Doris, under doctor's strict orders, was confined to bed due to pregnancy complications.

Michael Anderson, the director of *Flight from Ashiya*, chose Japanese master cinematographer Kazuo Miyagawa, whose previous films included *Rashomon* and *Ugetsu Monogatari*. After only one day of shooting, Miyagawa was replaced by Joseph McDonald. The official explanation given by the producers was Miyagawa's lack of familiarity with the Panavision lenses and the different screen ratios used in American pictures. The truth was that the master's technique included showing the stars' wrinkles, their scars and their physical defects—a method too far removed from the Hollywood norm of always making the stars look perfect.

Flight from Ashiya, adapted by Waldo Salt from a novel by Elliott Arnold, concerned the air-sea rescue of a group of Japanese survivors from a typhoon. Throughout there was a series of flashbacks depicting the lives of the three aviators (played by Richard Widmark, George Chakiris and Yul) and their wives (Shirley Knight, Eiko Taki and Suzy Parker).

The picture was shot in different locations in Japan, where Yul was considered a major star and was always received with enthusiasm. A group of distant relatives visited him on the set in his special air-conditioned trailer, shipped by boat from the States. During his stay, Yul's special demands often upset Japan's best hotel chefs: He would order *oyako donburi*, a working man's rice dish with eggs and chicken, which he also forced on his personal entourage.[17] *Flight from Ashiya* was released in the spring of 1962. In his review, *The New York Times*' Howard Thompson wrote, "Occasionally it's diverting to see just how consistently bad a picture can be.... [This one] is synthetic and hollow from the fade-in. The dialogue, especially the romantic pearls, is atrocious."[18] Other reviews were also very poor and Yul added another flop to his filmography.

Before leaving for Japan, Yul had viewed and approved a rough cut of *Taras Bulba*. He loved the film and felt proud of the final result. On his return, he attended a public screening of the final cut and was shocked. His rage was so intense that he reportedly cried and did not sleep for several nights. The picture he watched was unrecognizable. The film, which he thought was the best of his career (better than his favorite, *The Brothers Karamazov*), had been ruined by Hecht. The producer, nervous about the excessive length of the film, decided to cut all the most interesting dialogues and to leave all the fighting scenes, trans-

Yul in a scene from Michael Anderson's *Flight from Ashiya.*

forming *Taras Bulba* into an "equestrian melodrama." Yul suddenly lost all his faith in Hecht. The situation increased the contempt and the disdain he already had for incompetent studios executives. That heartbreaking experience stayed so vivid in Yul's memory that in a 1970s interview he declared, "I really was very close to leaving the business altogether that time. I just wanted to go and start into something entirely different. To become a kind of roaming reporter … with the camera … Then came along a role and the pain healed."[19]

In November of 1962, Yul celebrated the birth of a beautiful daughter, Victoria. The joy was so immense that it brought him a sort of anxiety, fearing the loss of the privileges he had as a star and of the financial stability he had finally achieved. But those concerns did not stop him from continuing to be involved in charitable events. He in fact donated $2,300 to start an international school for children from underdeveloped countries in collaboration with the Lausanne city council.[20]

10

Surprise Flops

[Kirk] Douglas has to fight the same thing Yul Brynner has to fight. They both have these images as strong, macho men. Sometimes they have to change this. They want to be strong all the time, but now and then they have to be weak.
— King Vidor

Movie stars often agree to make bad pictures with the presumption that their extraordinary acting skills will elevate it. In the 1960s and 1970s, Yul made this common mistake. He accepted work in mediocre productions, perhaps thinking subconsciously that his star presence would guarantee their success. This quickly became a trap; his fans got accustomed to seeing him play the same type of character and dismissed him when he did anything slightly different. Nevertheless, Yul never stopped taking acting classes or hoping to play different types of parts, but in reality he was rarely able to escape his restrictive stereotype. Exhibits A and B: *Kings of the Sun* and *Invitation to a Gunfighter*, pictures he agreed to make in 1963 and 1964.

The first film was a multi-million production filmed in Mexico. Yul played the leader of an Indian tribe who fights against the descendants of the legendary Mayans and is eventually condemned to death. In a *Los Angeles Times* interview, Yul said that *Kings of the Sun* "has something to say about capital punishment and peaceful co-existence. I think it is one of the best jobs Lee [Thompson] ever directed ... [He] has an extraordinary talent for sweeping from the spectacular to the personal story."[1] Yul's valid performance was not enough to save the film from sinking at the box office. The improbable plot and the silly dialogue were unanimously condemned by critics.

Invitation to a Gunfighter was made at the Revue Studios in Hollywood. It was supposed to be a Western with the same successful ingredients that made *High Noon* an international hit. Yul agreed to make it mostly for the opportunity to work with Stanley Kramer, the film pro-

Yul, George Chakiris and Brad Dexter in *Kings of the Sun.*

ducer and one of *the* most talented Hollywood directors. George Segal and Janice Rule were also in the cast. Kramer wrote in his autobiography that "Brynner just didn't create the electricity we thought he would, in part because the script was never more than workmanlike."[2] *Invitation to a Gunfighter* had a complicated plot and pretentious affected dialogue which made it a bore. Allen Eyles, editor of the prestigious British magazine *Films and Filming*, wrote, "Yul Brynner is a serviceable performer who has been too long without a good part. This at least is a good part—but a bad film."[3]

A perfect role for Yul would have been Capt. Von Trapp in *The Sound of Music*, the upcoming movie based on the stage musical hit. Yul fought very hard for the part, but director Robert Wise was not convinced that he was the actor for that character, whose personality was too similar to the king of Siam from *The King and I.* Moreover, Yul had an accent; all the characters in the movie were Austrian, so naturally they had to sound the same. "One of the strikes against Yul Brynner and some other foreign actors," explained Wise, "is that they would have a different accent than everyone else."[4] Eventually the director cast only English or American actors. A special dialogue coach stayed with the American cast members during the entire shoot helping them speak with the same English inflection.

Between films, Yul found time to be part of *The World's Greatest Showman*, a NBC-TV tribute to the late Cecil. B. DeMille, and to work as the official photographer on the Parisian set of Anatole Litvak's thriller *Five Miles to Midnight* starring Anthony Perkins and Sophia Loren.

In September 1964, Yul agreed to appear in *The Sabouter: Code Name— Morituri* simply for financial reasons. The huge expenses of running a villa in Switzerland and maintaining his jet-set lifestyle forced him to be less selective about the very few scripts he was given. For the same reasons (monetary), Marlon Brando agreed to co-star in the picture. Strangely, Yul did not complain about being part of a production in which he was not the major star. (He had briefly met Brando in the 1940s when Virginia appeared with him on Broadway in *Truckline Café*.) The studio got enormous publicity out of the fact that the two stars were working together for the first time. False rumors were spread about friction between these two strong egos. At a studio press conference, Yul and Brando entered from doors at opposite ends of the room and then, 50 feet apart, stopped and angrily looked at each other. After a long silence, they then both burst into laughter and embraced each other.[5]

In his autobiography, Brando wrote that making *Morituri* was a pleasant experience, especially since he was working with old friends Wally Cox and William Redfield. He added, "Yul Brynner ... wasn't a great actor but ... taught me a lesson about making movies. Yul was a nice man, but like David Niven, he liked to hang out at chic places and be seen with fashionable people, which didn't appeal to Wally, Billy or me. Someone, probably Wally, joked, 'I wonder what Yul would look like if he ever put his legs together.' This was because he was constantly striking the magisterial pose he used in *The King and I*, with his legs separated, planted firmly on the ground, and his hands on his hips. But Yul did something in that picture that impressed me. In one scene I thought his acting was very stagy and artificial, but when I saw the scene on film it succeeded because the lighting was effective, and I learned he had suggested to the lighting man how to light that scene. I had never paid much attention to lighting, and it made me realize that the man who sets it up can do a lot for your performance or break your neck if he wants to...

Yul as Chief Black Eagle in *Kings of the Sun.*

From then on, I began checking with the lighting man before doing a scene, using a mirror to see what effect different light gave my appearance and performance."[6]

Yul had always a profound admiration for Brando. Asked years later who his favorite actor was, Yul replied, "Marlon Brando. He touches me the most and he makes some of the most obvious mistakes. I have a kind of sacred spot in me that is important to me, entailing purity of intention. I think Marlon has that too."[7]

Morituri's screenplay, written by Daniel Taradash, focused on the character of an anti-Nazi saboteur, played by Brando. Brando was sent on a secret mission aboard a ship commanded by Yul. Most of the film was shot aboard a ship rented in Japan by the production and sailed to Catalina Island. Yul demanded in his contract that a landing pad be built on the ship so he could get a private helicopter to take him ashore after each day's shoot. Brando requested the same service. Every day at 6 P.M., even if in the middle of a scene, Yul and Brando left the set to get in

Yul plays poker in a scene from *Invitation to a Gunfighter*.

their helicopter. The crew was very annoyed because suddenly they were forced to stop filming even if the light was right.[8] Shooting lasted six weeks, one week more than scheduled due to bad weather. Often Brando would retreat to his cabin to re-write some of his character's dialogue, sometimes just a few hours before shooting a scene. Director Bernhard Wicki had several arguments with the star.

The Sabouter: Code Name — Morituri was released in August 1965. It stayed in the theaters for only two weeks after being panned by reviewers and ignored by filmgoers. Yul commented on this fiasco with an air of superiority: "The reviewers should realize they are looking at a classic. Just having Brynner and Brando together is reason enough for raves!"[9]

Yul often played golf, a sport he had been avidly enjoying for a couple of years. At the exclusive Hillcrest Country Club in Beverly Hills, Yul played host to director Melville Shavelson, who was interested in having him in his next film, *Cast a Giant Shadow.* Yul had received the script the day before and read it until three in the morning. It was so impressive that he told Shavelson he would play any part the director wanted him to.[10]

Cast a Giant Shadow was based on the true story of Col. David "Mickey" Marcus, a West Point graduate and Jewish New York lawyer. In 1947, Marcus was persuaded by the Israeli government to organize and lead an army to defend the country from the Arabs after the British withdrawal from Palestine. Marcus was mistakenly killed by one of his own sentries on the night before the independence of Israel was declared.

Opposite Kirk Douglas, who played Marcus, were John Wayne, Frank Sinatra, Angie Dickinson and Senta Berger, all in small roles. Yul played Asher Goren, one of the leaders of the resistance and an advocate of the creation of the state of Israel.

Principal photography began in Israel in the summer of 1965. All the equipment was shipped from Hollywood and dozens of technicians were hired in Los Angeles, Rome and Tel Aviv.

Before his arrival on location, Yul sent his assistant ahead to find him a place to live. He finally rented two adjoining apartments and had a wall knocked down to make it one *big* apartment.

Shavelson, a very bright man, was not only the director but also the producer and the screenwriter. From the very beginning the set seemed cursed (there were several accidents and mishaps), making the shooting so difficult that years later the director wrote a book about it.

On the set, Yul was often by himself, trying to concentrate on his character. On one occasion a fan approached him and asked for an autograph. Yul pushed him away rudely because the admirer apparently broke his concentration. The episode was immediately reported in the local news. Shavelson described Yul as "something of an enigma … He can be a warm friend, a good father, a happy companion; or he can be shouting in anger. I still don't know which part is acting, which part is real."[11]

Photographer Zinn Arthur, who had worked with Yul on the set of *The King and I* and *Anastasia*, was also in Israel and was invited to a party Yul threw to celebrate Rocky's visit. Arthur recalled, "My wife had always been a great admirer of Yul's, and said he was 'the sexiest man.' That night she changed her mind when she saw him go through a full bottle of Scotch and allowed his son to consume a bottle as well. The biggest pleasure for all at the party was hearing Yul play guitar and sing."[12] Rocky was only 18 and already had a drinking problem. A couple of years later, he entered a rehabilitation program in the same Swiss clinic that Yul visited in the 1940s to fight *his* opium addiction. Rocky's psychological problems and his difficult relationship with Yul were touchingly described in the memoir that Rocky wrote after his father's death. In the book he makes it clear that, during his adolescence, he desperately wanted to get some attention from Yul, whom he adored. Unfortunately Rocky emulated all his father's vices: drinking, smoking and spending excessively. At one of the many parties organized during the shooting of *Cast a Giant Shadow*, Yul, Kirk Douglas and the rest of the cast were introduced to David Ben-Gurion, the first Prime Minister of Israel, who did not know who the bald actor was. Yul, very surprised, tried to explain to the politician that he was a movie star. The information did not impress Ben-Gurion at all. Yul told the Prime Minister that he had probably seen him in *The King and I*. "*The King and I*," Ben-Gurion repeated. "Which one were you?"[13]

Frank Sinatra's presence made Yul very happy, as the two had known each other for several years. When in California, Yul often visited Sinatra's villa in Palm Springs. The singer called Yul "the Chinaman" while Yul called Sinatra "Charlie." Yul was also a very close friend of Mia Farrow, Sinatra's very young girlfriend at the time (and later his bride).

In her autobiography, Farrow called Yul "a surrogate father."[14] In the 1970s, when Yul adopted two Vietnamese girls, he named one Mia in honor of Farrow.

Yul admired Sinatra's talent and dedication to his profession and of course the lifestyle: "Ol' Blue Eyes" was a womanizer, a heavy drinker and a chain smoker just like Yul. In a recent Sinatra tell-all biography written by his personal valet George Jacobs, Yul was described as one the most "penny pinching" friends the singer had, always "sponging off" Sinatra for food, drink and girls. This description was very atypical, as Yul is often remembered by friends and colleagues for his extreme generosity. Jacobs also maintained that Yul was secretly bisexual, "having had a secret affair with Sal Mineo."[15] This statement was another groundless and unbelievable one, especially when many biographers have described Sinatra as homophobic. The singer would have never included in his circle of intimate friends someone who was even suspected of having a non-heterosexual orientation.

One month before filming *Cast a Giant Shadow*, Yul, who had Swiss and American citizenship, officially dropped the latter, returning his passport at the American Embassy in Berne, Switzerland. The State Department made the news public while he was working in Israel. In a

Yul relaxing on his terrace in this undated photograph.

press release, Yul explained that he took this step "in order to normalize his family life." He maintained that his wife and daughter held Swiss passports and were not eligible for American citizenship because they lived abroad. Travel to film locations or private travel required different passports from different countries and visa applications from different places. This situation complicated their lives enough in normal times, but in times of international tension or war his family could become separated. Therefore he thought it was advisable to keep only the Swiss citizenship like the rest of his family — and he pointed out that his devotion, affection and loyalty to the United States were deeply ingrained in his heart and would never change.[16]

The truth, however, was completely different. Yul had reluctantly given up the American passport because he had broken the law, which granted him tax-exemption as an American resident in a foreign country, by spending too much time working in the United States. Therefore, almost $2 million of U.S. taxes and penalties were assessed to him. If paid, this sum would make him bankrupt. In order not to pay, his accountants advised him he must drop his American citizenship. Yul, full of anger and completely powerless, decided to follow the advice.

Cast a Giant Shadow was not very successful. At 141 minutes it was considered too long, especially and too many fictional elements were introduced into the fact-based plot, making it melodramatically unbelievable and heavy.

Yul next agreed to play a small part in *The Poppy Is Also a Flower*, a spy story involving the manufacture and distribution of opium and heroin. The picture was financed by Xerox Company and produced by Eulan Lloyd, who assembled a spectacular all-star cast: Grace Kelly, Omar Sharif, Jack Hawkins, Rita Hayworth, Marcello Mastroianni, Angie Dickinson and Trevor Howard, among others. They all played cameos and they all agreed to work for a $1 salary. All the profits were given to UNICEF for the battle against drug abuse. Based on a story by Ian Fleming, the creator of James Bond, it is set (and was shot) in different cities around the world, from Teheran to Naples, Rome to Monte Carlo. Yul agreed to play the role of Col. Salem as long he was allowed to wear black, his lucky color since *The Magnificent Seven*. He left for Iran, where he finished his job in only two days. In the States, *The Poppy Is Also a Flower* went straight to television, while in Europe it was successfully released to theaters after a benefit premiere in Vienna. Several months later, Lloyd decided to show the picture in American theaters, to give people who missed the TV broadcast the chance to see it (and raise more money for his cause).

That same year, United Artists proposed that Larry Cohen write a sequel to *The Magnificent Seven* after Yul agreed to participate. Steve McQueen also planned to be in the film, but the actor did not find the script convincing and backed off. Cohen remembered meeting Yul at the Beverly Hills Hotel and going over the script with him. Yul tried to get the screenwriter drunk so he'd agree to some changes that he wanted in the script.[17]

Yul in *The Return of the Magnificent Seven.*

The Return of the Magnificent Seven was an American-Spanish co-production, which required casting an equal number of Spanish actors in major parts. So instead of seven great actors (Cohen proposed Peter Falk and Telly Savalas), they cast some unknown Spanish actors who didn't have much charisma.[18] The picture was shot in Alicante, Spain where Yul arrived together with Doris and little Victoria. Victoria often visited her father on the set and enjoyed watching and playing with the extras dressed as cowboys.

117

Director Burt Kennedy used only half of Cohen's original script; he removed any examination of the psychological aspects of the characters and stressed hot-and-heavy action. Despite the mediocre box office results, United Artists released *Guns of the Magnificent Seven* in 1969 and *The Magnificent Seven Ride!* in 1972, both without Yul's participation. The only positive thing to come out of *The Return of the Magnificent Seven* was Elmer Bernstein's Oscar nomination for Best Original Score, although he did not win. (Bernstein was the first composer to be nominated for music when it was used for the second time.)

The James Bond films gradually came to dominate the 1960s' international film market; their influence was so strong that they contaminated *other* film genres, like war movies. When producer Paul Bertrand decided in 1966 to make *Triple Cross*, the true story of Eddie Chapman, a spy who collaborated with both British Intelligence and the German Nazis, it was not an accident that he hired Terence Young, the British director who had made three Bond pictures.

Young offered a major role to Yul. The actor could not refuse the $250,000 offer, especially after his last films were all box office disasters.

The filming of *Triple Cross* began in June 1966 and ran through the entire summer. Yul worked with Christopher Plummer, who played Chapman, and beautiful Austrian actress Romy Schneider. Despite Plummer "stealing" the lead in *The Sound of Music* from Yul, they had great respect for each other and became close friends on the set.

Triple Cross was a fiasco, as was Yul's next film *The Long Duel*, made at the end of 1966 in Granada, Spain. The picture was produced and directed by Ken Annakin, whose *The Longest Day* and *Those Magnificent Men in Their Flying Machines* were big hits. It was set in the 1920s, during the British colonization of India. Yul playing a rebel Indian sultan fighting against the English, who were represented by a loyal police officer (Trevor Howard).

Howard had previously worked with Yul in other three films (*The Saboteur: Code Name — Morituri, The Poppy Is Also a Flower* and *Triple Cross*) but he (Howard) could not stand him. The relationship was very tense from the very first day on location and by the time the production moved to England to shoot interiors, Howard and Yul were hardly on speaking terms. Actor Patrick Newell never forgot Yul's arrogance: [W]e used to play games with him and we were going to invent a game that didn't exist because whatever you said, Mr. Brynner always said, 'Well,

Yul and Christopher Plummer in *Triple Cross.*

as a matter of fact I was world champion pistol shot,' or 'I'm the world champion' of whatever it was you mentioned. So we were going to make up a sport to see what he said, and in Spain they play a game called callot. So someone suddenly said, 'There's this terrific game going on in the square of Granada,' and we were just waiting and then Brynner said, 'Of course I'm the South American callot champion.' I remember Trevor just standing up and looking at him, mounting a bad word and walking out of the room."[19]

In January 1967 the production moved to Pinewood Studios in England; the relationship between Trevor and Yul did not improve Newell recalls,

> At Pinewood one day there was a knock at my dressing room door, and Trevor came in and said, "Come to my room." I said, "Why?" and he said, "Just come into my room." ... I went into his room and it was pitch dark. He said, "Have you seen outside?" And I looked and there was this enormous caravan parked outside, closing off the light through his window. And he said, "Give you one guess whose that is." And I said, "It's Mr. Brynner's," and he said "Yes, it is."
>
> There was this veranda on the back of this caravan which Yul Brynner

had got from somewhere, and he was sitting on this veranda in his black shirt, black boots and black trousers—he always wore black—and smoking a big cigar and Trevor said, "That bastard! We'll see about this."

So we went out and Trevor said, "Morning, amigo. Lovely caravan. Quite big."

Brynner said, "It's the biggest in the whole world." And Trevor just turned round and gave it this tremendous kick. There was a loud "Boing!" and Trevor didn't say any more to him but just went back and called the first assistant director and said, "I want that monstrosity out of my window."[20]

There was a serious incident involving the two stars and an inexperienced female journalist who came on the set to interview Yul. Usually Yul was very charming with the press (especially if they were young and pretty women) but it was also his theory that reporters who asked stupid or personal questions deserved stupid answers, which is what happened on this occasion. He quickly became impatient and rude and did everything possible to embarrass the journalist in front of everybody on the set. Trevor saw the scene, turned red with fury and was close to hitting him, but the first assistant came over and bravely tore a strip of clothing off Yul, probably trying to separate the two. In an interview released shortly after the end of the filming, director Ken Annakin denied having any problems with Yul or with Howard, stressing that "they were both thoroughly professional and pleasant."[21]

A few months later, Yul came back to London to star in *The Double Man*, another spy thriller, opposite gorgeous Britt Ekland. The Swedish actress was extremely annoyed at the British tabloids for insinuating, when the film was still in pre-production, that her intention was to have

Yul in *The Double Man.*

Britt Ekland and Yul in *The Double Man.*

an affair with magnetic Yul. The stories caused some problems between Ekland and her jealous husband Peter Sellers.[22]

The Double Man was the brainchild of Hal Chester, a producer who heard about an unfinished picture with all second-unit work already done, including a lot of footage of skiing and mountains. After watching the unfinished picture with screenwriter Frank Tarloff, Chester asked Tarloff to write a script using the footage already shot. Tarloff wrote a first draft in collaboration with Alfred Haynes, but Chester did not like it. After a violent argument, Tarloff quit and sued the producer. (Tarloff's name did make it to the film credits.[23]

On the set, Yul had a special folding chair with very long legs. Graham Stark, who was working at the same studio on a different film, recalled, "Seated on top of this chair, Yul was able to view the world from high.... Britt Ekland was only too happy to introduce us. Co-starring in the film with Brynner, she gazed up at him ... and spoke in her delightful Swedish accent: 'Graham has shot some *beautiful* pictures of me, Yul.

121

You really must let him expose himself!' He made the descent, gave me a smile and assured me that now was the time. 'They don't need me for half an hour,' he said. 'We'll go out on the back lot and give you a chance to expose yourself!' When it came to my shooting him, it was really very easy, mainly due to our shared passion for photography."[24] Stark remembers Yul was in ecstasy after examining the sophisticated camera he (Stark) used to photograph him. It was a present from Peter Sellers to repay Stark for a favor. The sight of the camera alone was enough to satisfy Yul that the guy knew what he was doing, and he gave Stark the exact look he wanted. Years later, when someone asked Stark to comment on Yul's fearsome reputation, he only said that he behaved as a "little pussy cat," explaining that the pictures he took were a nice memory of a very patient sitter.[25]

In *The Double Man*, Yul played an American secret agent whose son was pushed off a mountain. He discovers that his son's murder is part of a scheme organized by a group of German spies to kill *him*, replace him with a double and infiltrate the American Secret Service.

Yul played an interesting double role in a film that today seems a bit dated, but at the time was mildly successful despite the low budget. Although the picture was almost entirely set on the Austrian Alps, it was mostly shot on fake snow in England during the summer.

That same year, a record titled *Yul Brynner Sings: The Gypsy and I* was released in English and French. It was a musical collaboration between Yul and his old friend Aliosha Dimitrievitch, who recorded 11 Tzigan songs—a dream Yul had for years.

Altogether, 1967 was not a memorable year for Yul. Besides the series of professional flops, his marriage with Doris was on the rocks. His extensive work travels and the regular escapades (including a fling with blond Swedish star Anita Ekberg, who described him as "very masculine and wild") were the problem. Yul and Doris decided to temporarily separate.

Yul was very saddened to learn that his estranged sister Vera was ill with terminal breast cancer. A few weeks later, while he was in New York, he decided to visit her with Rocky. Yul felt guilty about his cold behavior and searched for forgiveness. Brother and sister remembered all the happiest moments they shared during their childhood and it seemed that they resolved all their issues. Vera Bryner died in December 1967 at age 51 after a brilliant career as a soprano, survived by her husband and a daughter. It was a painful and difficult moment for Yul, losing his last and only bond to his "mysterious past."

11

Terrible Choices

"I have never played anyone I thought was like me."
— Yul Brynner

In the mid–60s, Italian director Sergio Leone achieved great international success with his "spaghetti Westerns," European adaptations of Hollywood's great Westerns from the '40s and '50s.

Hollywood immediately seized the opportunity to begin imitating the Europeans. Most of Leone's films were shot in Spain, where everything was cheaper than in Italy or other places, and where the landscape and architecture was similar to Mexico's.

In the spring of 1967, Sam Peckinpah completed a script about Pancho Villa and the Mexican revolution. Hollywood producer Ted Richmond bought the rights with the idea that Peckinpah would direct the film and Yul would star in it.

Yul was very surprised to find Peckinpah's script, *Villa Rides*, depicting Villa as violent and evil, something that did not fit a national hero who fought for the human rights of his people. The actor thought that his fans would never accept such on-screen behavior. Peckinpah had sent Yul a note along with the script humbly soliciting Yul's suggestions. But the star had only one suggestion, and that was to have Richmond replace Peckinpah. The screenwriter later recalled, "Brynner asked for me to be taken off the film because I didn't know anything about Mexico. That surprised me because I was then married to a Mexican and I'd been in and out of Mexico for years."[1]

Richmond hired Robert Towne, author of *Bonnie and Clyde*, to revise *Villa Rides*, leaving almost nothing of Peckinpah's original screenplay; Towne received the writing credit. "That was all right," Peckinpah commented. "I took the stuff they threw out of that picture and used it in *The Wild Bunch*."[2]

In the original script, Peckinpah was told by Paramount to include

Robert Mitchum and Yul in *Villa Rides*.

a "white face" amidst all the dark revolutionaries. He invented the character of an American gun smuggler. For this role, the producers thought immediately of Robert Mitchum.

Towne claimed that *Villa Rides* was made because Yul and Mitchum were signed to contracts that guaranteed them money whether the picture was made or not.[3]

Principal photography began in fall 1967 in El Casar de Talamanca, a tiny village outside Madrid. For the fifth time, Yul played a character wearing a wig, and this time with a fake mustache too. Besides Robert Mitchum, the cast included Charles Bronson, Fernando Rey, Maria Grazia Buccella and, in a small role, Jill Ireland, Bronson's future wife.

Yul was again suffering from terrible backaches that required him to rest regularly; he often had to be helped to mount his horse.[4] He thought director Buzz Kulik was too inexperienced (he was indeed a TV director at his first film experience) and showed scarce enthusiasm for a project which spared no expense faithfully replicating Mexico during the years of the revolution.

As usual, Yul had on the set his deluxe air-conditioned trailer in which he allowed Mitchum to rest between takes (and to enjoy the company of British identical twins he had met in Madrid). A couple weeks after shooting began, Doris and later Rocky visited Yul on the set. Rocky remembered the great respect Yul had for Mitchum, considering him an extraordinary, professionally humble man, proud of his own work and trying always to give his best.[5]

Villa Rides was released in the early summer of 1968. Paramount feared that the violence would be considered excessive in the wake of the recent assassinations of Martin Luther King and Robert Kennedy. Many critics did not appreciate the gratuitously violent scenes, but the picture did respectable business at the American box office and also in Europe when it opened there in 1969.

During his stay in Spain, Yul often visited his matador friend Luis Dominguín, who like Yul had been an extra in Cocteau's *Le Testament de Orphée*. Soon Charles Bronson, Robert Mitchum and Yul became regular guests at Dominguín's ranch, where the matador and his Italian wife, actress Lucia Bosé, had parties, lunches and dinners. Dominguín was helping some friends make a picture called *The Picasso Summer*, starring British actor Albert Finney, and Yul offered to appear in one scene for free. In the short sequence, shot on Dominguín's patio, Finney explains to some guests (extras included Doris Brynner and Lucia Bose) why he wants to meet Picasso. Yul, Bronson and Mitchum were extras in another scene, appearing amidst a crowd of local people watching Dominguín bullfighting in his own private bullring.

The harmony of this group did not last long after Picasso, who was a close friend of the Dominguíns, did not show up on the set after promising to appear in a scene. The explanation for Picasso's behavior: Lucia Bose had apparently fled to him for consolation from the grief and humiliation of discovering that her husband was having an affair with Doris Brynner. Picasso, in solidarity with Bose, whom he loved as his own daughter, now refused to participate in the movie. No one was able to change the painter's mind.[6] When the news of this incident reached the tabloids, *Confidential* published a photograph of Yul on the cover of the October 1968 issue with a large caption that read: "Yul's wife Bulled by Bullfighter." Inside, a four-page spread told Picasso's story in detail, with few inaccuracies.

Yul, no longer in great demand, became concerned by the drop in

Yul on the Spanish set of *Villa Rides.*

the number of scripts submitted to him. The situation forced him to accept every part he was offered, even in low-budget productions. This was not the case with *The Madwoman of Chaillot*, a picture that featured an exceptional cast: Katharine Hepburn, Giulietta Masina, Danny Kaye, Charles Boyer, John Gavin and Richard Chamberlain.

Yul and his colleagues were very disappointed to learn that director John Huston had walked off the film 18 days before production was to begin. Huston quit after disagreeing with producer Ely Landau, who insisted on making radical changes to the original script (he wanted to update the nineteenth-century story). Bryan Forbes was signed as the new director.

Except for Hepburn, the cast stayed at the fabulous Hotel La Voile d'Or in Cap Ferrat, not far from Nice, where the film's exteriors were shot. Yul, playing the small role of an arrogant, brutal man with a subtle sense of humor, was the leader of a group conspiring against a bizarre old woman.

A visit from Italian director Federico Fellini (husband of Giulietta

Masina) caused great commotion on the set; Forbes felt intimidated as *il grande maestro* observed him directing.

Yul had met Fellini several years earlier when the Italian director, together with Vittorio de Sica, attended a New York performance of *The King and I*. After the show Yul had dinner with the two directors, who congratulated him on his brilliant performance and suggested that he try to play Shakespeare's *Julius Caesar*, a role they considered perfect for him.[7] Yul was so impressed by that idea that for years he had the unfulfilled desire to play that role or *Macbeth* on stage.

In *The Madwoman of Chaillot*, Yul had only two scenes with Hepburn. Off the set Yul made her a gift of a bicycle, which the actress appreciated and used while in Nice. When Yul took out his camera to snap a candid shot of her, she became so upset that she ordered him off the set when his presence was not required.[8]

The extraordinary performances given by the stellar cast (one critic called Yul's performance "gilt-edged," adding "too bad it's so brief") were not enough to save the uneven, boring film from sinking at the box office. Reviewers considered it a complete mess.

The most bizarre role in Yul's whole career was a 53-second, uncredited cameo in *The Magic Christian*, which Peter Sellers directed. Yul lip-synced "Mad About the Boy" (actress Miriam Karlin provided the voice) by Noël Coward while dressed as a woman in a gay nightclub in London. At the end of the performance, he took off his blonde wig and showed his shiny pate. It was a funny, unusual way to debunk the image of macho which still was haunting him. Peter Sellers cast each part with a famous face (Ringo Starr as the lead, Raquel Welch, Christopher Lee, Richard Attenborough, Roman Polanski, Laurence Harvey, John Cleese and Princess Margaret in smaller roles), but *The Magic Christian* was a box office failure and quickly forgotten.

Yul's next picture, *The Battle of Neretva* had the same fate. The film, an international co-production, featured Orson Welles, Sylva Koscina, Franco Nero and Hardy Kruger. Shooting began in early 1969 in Jablanica, the former Yugoslavia. Based on true war episodes, the film told the story of a group of Yugoslavian partisans led by Vlado (the future Gen. Tito) who ward off German incursions during the winter of 1943. On the set, Yul had his $70,000 mega-trailer that he brought from California; in it he had installed a king-size bathtub and thermostat to adjust the temperature, luxuries envied by the rest of the cast.

On location, Yul was supposed to run across a bridge 200 feet above a flooded river while explosive charges were going off all around him. One went off prematurely, blowing Yul halfway off the bridge. He managed to grab a steel bar and hang in mid-air until he was rescued.[9]

In an on-set interview, Yul said, "I sometimes think over a screenplay for a few weeks—even a month. I decided on this one before I had finished reading it. It's the great, little-known super-drama of World War II. I only wish I had brought my cameras along. This time I didn't. I guess the cold worried me, I've never seen backgrounds like the mountains, forests and rivers of this rugged land."[10]

Director Veljko Bulajic had a $12 million budget and shot almost six hours of film. The picture was significantly reduced to a three-hour length, but the American distributors edited out an extra hour, making it unwatchable. The plot became trivial and incoherent when reduced just to action scenes. Surprisingly, *The Battle on the Neretva* got a Best Foreign Language Film nomination, but the Oscar went to Costa-Gravas' *Z*.

A few months after his return from Yugoslavia, Yul flew to London to work in *The File of the Golden Goose*, a dreadful, action-packed B movie. Directed by Sam Wanamaker, who had played a small role in *Taras Bulba*, the film was another of Yul's bad choices, necessitated by personal economic conditions. *Golden Goose*, a low-budget production with a confusing script, did not have a long life in the theaters.

In the summer of 1969, the brutal murder of actress Sharon Tate, the eight-month pregnant wife of director Roman Polanski, shocked the Hollywood community. Yul, together with Peter Sellers, Warren Beatty and other celebrities, announced a reward of $25,000 for the arrest and the conviction of the murderers. "We handed the money over to Roman Polanski and his lawyers in the hope that that would bring the killers to justice," Sellers said in an interview.[11] Sellers and Yul's friendship for Polanski seemed the sole reason behind this generous gesture. But in 1993, journalist Paul Krassner gave another explanation for Yul's personal involvement. In his non-fiction book, Krassner claims that while he conducted research for an article on Tate's murder, he met a private investigator who informed him that the Los Angeles Police Department removed some pornographic films from Tate's apartment after her murder. The material showed some celebrities in compromising sexual situations. Krassner was told of the existence of a videotape of singer Cass

Elliot from the Mamas and Papas in an orgy with Peters Sellers, Yul and an actor who was still alive.[12]

In the fall of 1969, Yul and a group of friends chartered a plane from Paris to Dublin where Rocky, a student at Trinity College, debuted on stage at the Dublin Theater Festival. The one-man play was *Opium*, based on a book by Jean Cocteau; Rocky directed and performed.

That evening, Yul looked very tense. He later admitted to his son that he almost threw up as soon as the curtain rose. He wore a bright pink scarf to be easily recognizable in the crowded theater from the stage. At the end, during a standing ovation, Yul was visibly moved, whispering with pride to his friends, "It was fantastic."[13] *Opium*'s great success gave Rocky the opportunity to perform the show first in London and then in October 1970 on Broadway. The American reviews were not as favorable as the European ones, and the show ran for only eight performances. Yul missed his son's Broadway debut because he was making a film in Europe.

During the last years of Yul's marriage with Doris, they mutually agreed to be an open couple. Doris maintains that she always loved Yul and she felt he probably shared the same feeling for her, but as a couple they had reached a point where it was impossible and pointless to keep living together.[14] Yul's constant interest in other women was probably the principal reason for the end of the 11-year marriage. Yul had been seeing Jacqueline Thion de la Chaume, a sophisticated, elegant French noblewoman who was the widow of Philippe de Croisset (son of French playwright Francis de Croisset), the victim of a car accident. For a while, Yul kept running into de la Chaume at many Paris social events they attended. Jacqueline belonged to Parisian high society and had worked in public relations for fashion designers like Guy Laroche and Courrages. At the time she met Yul, she was fashion editor of the French edition of *Vogue*.

His divorce from Doris had dried up Yul's finances, but his dire economic situation did not keep him from borrowing money to buy (with Jacqueline) the Manoir de Criqueboeuf, a sixteenth-century manor house with 50 acres of land in the North of France. It was the first time that Yul owned a house; his nomadic lifestyle had previously prevented him settling anywhere. Even the villa in which he and Doris had lived for many years was rented.

Despite her busy social schedule, Jacqueline had always wanted to live in a calmer environment more suitable to her docile and sweet personality. Yul was now 48 years old and he also now seemed more interested in a serene lifestyle.

After buying Criqueboeuf, Yul developed an interest in gardening. He personally chose the trees and flowers to plant (with a predilection for Oriental flora as an echo of his childhood). The previous owner had added a pool with two penguins inhabiting it. But the animals created two major problems: They rapidly ate all the plants around the pool; and the enormous quantity of fish they required filled the house and garden with their aroma. Yul offered the penguins to a local zoo and transformed the pool into a tropical water garden.[15]

In the winter of 1971, after renovations were completed, Yul and Jacqueline, now married, moved to Criqueboeuf. Yul received a shipment from Switzerland of his precious collection of paintings, antiques and fine wines and spent most of his spare time fixing and furnishing the new home. Rock never remembered seeing his father happier than at that time. Yul declared to a British newspaper that he had suddenly found peace in his life and he did not need to go looking for anything any longer.[16]

A couple of months later, a terrible fight between Rock and his father spoiled the harmony. Rock was going through a difficult time due to his serious alcohol problem and was in desperate need of Yul's help. Father and son did not speak for almost two years.

Between 1970 and 1973, Yul made six films, none of them memorable or successful. He had reached a stage in his professional life in which the economic element was more important than quality. He could not be choosy, especially now that the monthly cost of the Normandy manor was in the thousands of dollars.

After the success of *20000 Leagues Under the Sea*, Kirk Douglas read *The Light at the Edge of the World*, another adventurous novel by Jules Verne, at the suggestion of a Hollywood producer. Douglas was so impressed by the story that he decided to personally produce and star in a film adaptation.

Douglas recalls in his autobiography, "Yul Brynner played the brutal pirate captain. I got him the job, in spite of *Spartacus*. Yul always had to have the biggest everything just as when we were shooting *Cast a Giant Shadow* in Israel. Yul found the largest house in town, on top of a hill, and rented it. He had the largest trailer — oversized. It created tremendous problems when it had to be moved around on the rough locations. It had every modern convenience, including a butler who cooked meals. Yul would invite you over, in the middle of the wilds, to have a drink, oysters, fried shrimp, all kinds of hors d'oeuvres, at his trailer. It was quite a treat. I wondered how Yul Brynner had learned to live so well."[17]

The Light at the Edge of the World was shot in Cadaques, a Spanish fishing village not far from the French border, where Salvador Dalí owned a magnificent villa. That summer, before going on holiday, the painter organized a dinner at Le Train Blue, a restaurant inside La Gare de Lyon in Paris; among the 20 guests were Douglas, Yul and his wife. That evening, Dalí enjoyed playing a word-game in which the contestants had to identify their parents through a series of charades, clues and expressions. It was just what Yul wanted. He in fact went wild, lying about his family's origins.

Once on location, Yul and Douglas were often invited to the villa where Dalí lived with his wife Gala. Permanent guests there were Amanda Lear, the painter's muse, and Carlos Lozano, an intimate friend who, years later, wrote a scandalous book about his friendship with Dalí, claiming that one night he was the object of sexual advances from Yul.[18]

Despite the presence of two stars like Douglas and Yul, *The Light at the Edge of the World* was a fiasco. Yul's performance as the sadistic pirate was generally considered "overly flamboyant." The producers blamed the American censors for the film's failure: 20 minutes of footage was cut because it was considered too violent or too sexually explicit, spoiling the flow of the plot.

Yul's next picture did not have a better reception. *Romance of a Horsethief* was shot in Vukovar in the former Yugoslavia during the summer of 1970. Abraham Polonsky, the director, had made his directorial debut in the late '40s but his career was interrupted when he was accused of being a Communist during Senator McCarthy's era. Polonsky had to wait almost 20 years before he could make another film.

Romance of a Horsethief follows the story of a Jewish community in a Polish village in 1904. The village defeats a company of Russian Cossacks, led by Yul as Capt. Stoloff, who tried to confiscate their horses. Eli Wallach, Jane Birkin and her husband, French singer Serge Gainsbourg, were also in the cast. Birkin recalls that shooting the film ended up being a very pleasant experience; the actress had met Yul in London several years earlier and was a big fan.

One day Gainsbourg broke up the monotony of the long, boring nights by organizing a masked ball for the crew. Polonsky dressed as *The Wizard of Oz*'s Tin Man, Yul as a clown and Wallach as a gangster while the French singer showed up as a female clown. Off the set the only lively moments were the scenes of jealousy between Birkin and Gainsbourg, who repeatedly flirted with Italian supporting actress Marilù Tolo (for whom he had composed the song called *Marilù* in 1968).

The friendship between Birkin and Yul became so close that the following year, when the actress had Charlotte, her first baby (now an acclaimed international actress), Yul was the godfather. A few hours after Charlotte's birth, Yul raced to London to visit Birkin in the clinic where she gave birth.[19]

On location, Yul drove a black Mercedes, an exact replica of the one used by Yugoslavian president Tito, whom Yul personally met at an official reception. Yul told the Communist leader how often the local police would mistake his car for the presidential one. Tito, amused by the story, told Yul how funny it would be to trade places. The actor declined the offer, explaining that accepting it would have meant a step back for him — since in the past he was a king![20]

In *Adios Sabata* and *Catlow* Yul played without variation his *Magnificent Seven* character, Chris, the invincible cowboy all dressed in black and always ready to gunfight. *Adios Sabata* was an Italian production filmed in Spain. Producer Antonio Grimaldi invited Yul to Rome to promote the film and to help revive interest in Western pictures, which now was in decline. The imaginative story of *Adios Sabata* was set in 1867 Mexico, at the time of the conflicts between Benito Juarez and Emperor Maximilian of Austria. Yul played master gunslinger Sabata, this time helping some Mexican revolutionaries steal a wagonload of gold.

In *Catlow*, based on a novel by Louis L'Amour, Yul was an outlaw who tries to avoid interference as he plots to pull off a $2,000,000 gold robbery. Both films were full of stereotypes and situations that belonged to the classical repertoire of the Western genre. Both pictures quickly disappeared from screens, except in Japan where *Adios Sabata* inexplicably became a cult movie.

In 1971, Yul was one of the great performers invited to New York for the twenty-fifth anniversary of the Tony awards. Yul, who at that time had not done *The King and I* for years, performed with Patricia Morison "Shall We Dance." The performance was a triumph; it seemed like every person in the house had burst into tears. Many top stars were there, but it was Yul who received the longest standing ovation of the evening.

The success Yul had once again had as the king brought him an offer from producer Larry Gelbert, who proposed that he star in a TV series based on *The King and I*. The idea was accepted with great enthusiasm by CBS, and they agreed to produce the project. Yul quickly signed the contract, eager not only to again play the character that gave him the highest popularity but also to receive a fat TV salary. (CBS included in the contract a five-year option if the series would become a hit.)

Yul convinced the producer to cast as Anna his dear friend Samantha Eggar, with whom he had worked in *The Light at the End of the World*. Yul explained that choice in an interview: "A lot of people do not like Samantha because she is too intelligent for them. I met her when she was making *Lady in the Car* in Paris a couple of years ago. She glared at me when we were introduced, but half an hour later she was eating out of my hand. I fought for her for the series."[21] In the series, the producers decided to change the nationality of Anna from British to American — even though the female lead *was* actually British, and now had to hide her accent! The first *King and I* episode was one of the most expensive pilots in television history, but when it aired in October 1972 it had a rating so low that after only six episodes the show was cancelled.

Yul took advantage of the fact that he was in Hollywood for *The King and I* to make *Fuzz*, a film starring Burt Reynolds and Raquel Welch. It was a grotesque police movie filmed in Hollywood and Boston in which Yul played a deaf blackmailer who threatens to kill the wife and the daughter of the Boston mayor. It was again another flop. Burt Reynolds later (arguably) contended, "The movie may not have set box-office records, but it was well worth the price of the admission ticket just to watch Yul perform. He was a thoroughgoing pro. Every time he completed a scene I wanted to applaud."[22]

In September 1972, Yul and Jacqueline flew to the Seychelles islands to shoot *Mermaid with Oranges*, a TV film for ORTF French Television, directed by David Hemmings, the star of Michelangelo Antonioni's *Blow-Up*. Hemmings recalled that Yul arrived in a pirogue, "dressed

Top: Yul, Philippe Noiret and Henry Fonda in *The Serpent*. *Bottom:* Yul in *Adios Sabata.*

entirely in Magnificent Seven black as usual, and cool as ever, he walked the full length of the main street, followed by 200 kids and most of the population of the island to the house [where] he was to stay. He was an absolute star and people loved it. He loved it too. Making that film was, I'm sure, one of his better times ... Sad to say, in the perverted way of our industry, we'd just finished filming when we discovered that the production company had gone bust. Yul was never paid at all."[23] And the film was never released.

Yul was again unlucky with *The Serpent,* a French-

Italian-German production of an international spy-story starring Henry Fonda, Dirk Bogarde, Philippe Noiret and Farley Granger. The picture was entirely filmed in a Paris studio, where CIA offices were accurately reconstructed. Dirk Bogarde in his autobiography remembered, "Mr. Brynner was exuberantly polite and spent a great deal of his time amusing the crew with funny faces and varied tricks which delighted them."[24]

The Serpent got such bad reviews in Europe that it did not get much distribution in America. It was released in the U.S. on video in the '80s.

12

Westworld

"If anyone really built a place like Westworld, they probably would make the gunfighter robot in the image of Yul Brynner."
— Michael Crichton

For many years, bestselling author Michael Crichton intended to write and direct a science-fiction movie. The idea for one came to his mind in 1971 during a trip to Florida's Kennedy Space Center, where he observed the training of astronauts. He saw the trained astronauts as machine-like, working hard to make their responses, even their heartbeats, as predictable as possible. Next visiting Disneyworld, Crichton was impressed by the automated movements of wax statues of the presidents. These two experiences gave him an idea for a script which he completed in 1972.

Crichton's *Westworld* is a science-fiction thriller about Delos, a giant amusement park of the future, where visitors can live out their fantasies while interacting human-like robots in Imperial Rome, Medieval Europe or the American West. The robots suddenly rebel, not responding to the electronic impulses, and massacre the tourists.

Almost all the studios liked Crichton's original story, but they turned it down due to the anticipated high budget. Eventually MGM agreed to produce the film. The studio cut down on the expenses by cutting from the script the amusement park's "Futureworld."

Yul was impressed by the script; especially by its hidden message denouncing human infantilism toward new technologies. He perceived the story as an argument for technological terrorism, and enthusiastically accepted the role of the crazy cyborg gunslinger who chases one of the park visitors (Richard Benjamin). Once again Yul's performance was a tribute to the character of Chris from *The Magnificent Seven*.

Although Crichton was not involved in any casting decision, he was thrilled by the selecting of Yul, and them by his performance. "It's very hard to give the impression that you are a robot with no personality while at the same time having some sense of presence and personality"—this was the writer's answer to critics who claimed that Yul's role did not require any particular acting skills. He added, "If anyone really built a place like Westworld, they probably would make the gunfighter robot in the image of Yul Brynner."[1]

Westworld took 30 days to shoot and was filmed in different locations including the Mojave Desert, the gardens of the Harold Lloyd Estate (used the previous year in Coppola's *The Godfather*) and several sound stages at MGM. Crichton shot about 110,000 feet of film on a budget of $1.3 million. He finished the picture under budget and on time. Yul required a fitting for special contact lenses. The fitting was to take place in the San Fernmado Valley, about ten miles from Yul's Beverly Hills hotel. When he requested limousine service, producer Paul Lazarus III had to inform him that the film's low budget made such luxuries impossible. Yul's response was curt and direct. "Fine," he said, "I won't be wearing lenses in the picture." The producer asked his secretary if she would drive Yul, and she agreed; in her aging Mustang, she took him to the Valley for his fitting. Lazarus later wrote, "As long as he felt taken care of, he, like most actors, was happy."[2] Those special contact lenses, which gave his eyes a "metallic" look, protected him when a fake bullet exploded very close to his face, slightly injuring his eyes.

Westworld was full of amazing special effects. Yul refused to have a double, even in a dangerous scene in which he fell out a window. In a fight scene where the gunslinger has hydrochloric acid thrown on his face, Yul's face was sprinkled with bicarbonate that simply reacted to water, giving the impression that the flesh was burning.[3]

Once edited, the picture was shown to the producers who disliked it. Although it was re-edited with new scenes added, the new cut did not get a better response. Regardless, MGM decided to release it. Then, to comply with the censors, Crichton had to cut ten minutes of scenes considered too adult. Despite MGM's skepticism, *Westworld* was a hit, grossing over $10 million domestically. Yul's automaton was so realistically grim that his flawless performance was praised by many.

Westworld was Yul's first hit in 13 years. He later said that he should have taken that opportunity to retire from the film industry, leaving a better memory of his legacy, instead of making the mistake of working in additional mediocre pictures. The first was *Futureworld* (1976), a

Yul and Blythe Danner in *Futureworld*.

sequel to *Westworld* directed by Richard Heffro and starring Peter Fonda and Blythe Danner. This time the producers decided to use the previously rejected idea of an amusement park of the future.

Although Yul's name was on all the posters and in the film trailer, he appeared only in a cameo during an erotic dream scene with the female lead. Blythe Danner recalled how amusing it was to work with Yul, "a true gentleman."[4] Despite the film's huge budget, *Futureworld* was a box office disappointment. It *was* the first American film to be shown to general audiences throughout China, where in the past foreign films had been shown only to select audiences.

In 1975–76, Yul made his last two films. The first was *The Ultimate Warrior*, a science fiction B-movie with Max Von Sydow set in the post-atomic future. The second, *Death Rage,* was a police thriller filmed in Italy with Martin Balsam and Mas-simo Ranieri. Both movies were dis-

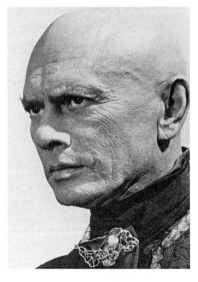

Yul in *The Ultimate Warrior.*

missed by reviewers and were poorly received at the box office. Antonio Margheriti (alias Anthony M. Dawson), the director of *Death Rage*, had such a great admiration for Yul that he planned to work again with him on an African-made movie in which Yul would have played a hunter. Yul's later unexpected success in the theater prevented him from returning on a film set.

Italian actor-singer Massimo Ranieri recalled what a gratifying experience it was to work with Yul in *Death Rage* after playing opposite him six years earlier in *The Light at the End of the World*. Ranieri explained that his first impressions of Yul were not positive as a result of Kirk Douglas' influence, and he considered Yul too pretentious and a rival. Now, under different circumstances in Naples, Italy, where *Death Rage* was shot, Yul appeared a completely different person. "I discovered an amazing human being with an extraordinary sensitivity," Ranieri told this author. "I was so moved by his stories of solidarity about the children refugees, and his collaboration with U.N. He also told me about the several travels he had done to Vietnam to help the war orphans. On the set he always showed great professionalism. One night he asked me in French, the only language we both spoke, [to recommend] a good place for a nice dinner. I went to pick him up at the Hotel Excelsior, where he was staying with his wife, and I took him to a typical Neapolitan restaurant. He loved that place so much that he went back several times and made friends with the owner. The last day of filming he ordered from the restaurant a huge case of mozzarella cheese to take with him to Normandy. A few months later, when I went to New York with Antonio Margheriti, [Yul] took me to a fancy Chinese restaurant, remembering that it was my favorite cuisine. Yul was truly an exceptional person, a true friend!"[5]

Yul and Jacqueline had been trying in vain to have a child. In the fall of 1974, at the suggestion of Mia Farrow who had just adopted a Vietnamese orphan (the first of many children), the Brynners went to Vietnam and adopted an 18-month-old baby girl they named Mia. In April 1975, they agreed to adopt a second child, Melody, a six-month-old.

Melody was on a plane bound for the U.S. when there was an accident in which 190 of the orphans aboard were killed. Yul and Jacqueline went through a terrible time when they heard about the crash because they did not know if Melody was alive or dead. When Melody was confirmed alive, Yul called Hugh Hefner, the billionaire owner of *Playboy* magazine, asking him if he would arrange to have his private jet bring 41 infant survivors of the crash to New York. Hefner immediately made his airplane available and Melody finally arrived at LaGuardia Airport.[6] Yul told the press, "[Melody] came out without a scratch or a bruise. That has to be some kind of a miracle!"[7] A few days later, in a different interview, Yul explained that he was "very much against" the "transplanting" of children into a different country or culture, but defended the airlifts of Vietnamese orphans as a humanitarian act. He added, "When you see the desperate conditions of those children who would perish without your help, then nationality does not exist at all. If a child, such as the children of Vietnam, has been totally abandoned, then it is not immoral to consider yourself his human brother or father."[8]

Yul often said that the epitaph on his gravestone should read "Here lies a man who adored children of all varieties." This undeniable truth was confirmed by his incessant humanitarian work for the U.N. His daughter Victoria remembers the great affection Yul always showed for her, especially when she was a child. In a 1975 interview, Yul admitted that becoming a father in middle age was an experience far more gratifying than when he was younger. The birth of his first son Rock had happened when he was too young and too busy with his artistic career to appropriately face fatherhood. With Victoria, who was born in 1962, and now with the two Vietnamese girls he was able to deeply appreciate the true meaning of being a father.[9]

At his house in Normandy, Yul cultivated a new hobby: breeding carrier pigeons. He had 75 birds with tags on their legs with Yul's name and phone number on them in case the birds strayed. He built their cages, opening them every day to let them out for exercise and training.

But he did complain to the press that not many parts were being offered to him. "People have a preconceived idea that I am very cruel and there are few characters I can play because of that. You cannot simply jump into a show. You are going to live with it a long time."[10]

For a long time Yul had been thinking of making a stage a comeback; the occasion arrived in the summer of 1974, when *Love Story* author Erich Segal visited him in Normandy. The bestseller writer offered him the part of Odysseus in *Odyssey*, a musical he had written based on Homer's epic masterpiece. A few days later, stage director Albert Marre (*The Man of La Mancha*) also visited Les Criqueboeuf along with producer Roger Stevens. The trio sat down with Yul and described the proposed show: *Odyssey* was set to begin a 43-week tour across North America in early December before opening on Broadway the following fall. Yul was enthusiastic and agreed without hesitation. He was convinced that an extensive pre–Broadway tour would enable him to perfect his performance.[11] "I always regretted that I didn't have that time with *The King and I*. Only in the fourth year of that play did I feel I was a competent actor," he later said.[12] Since *Odyssey* included five solo songs, Yul was soon hosting an American vocal coach for a month to work on his voice.

On November 3, 1974, before commencing the tour, Yul and Jacqueline had dinner with Marre and his wife at Trader Vic's, a Polynesian restaurant in the Plaza Hotel in New York. The party ordered, among many other dishes, some spare ribs. Five months later, Yul filed a multimillion dollar suit against the Hilton Hotel chain, owner of the restaurant, claiming that he with his wife and friends contracted trichinosis from the spare ribs, which were poorly cooked. The disease, which comes from parasitic worms, caused them to fall ill and weak, forcing Yul and Joan Diener (co-star in the musical and the wife of director Marre) to miss shows. Jacqueline averred that she sustained an "impaired and depreciated" marital association with her husband as a result of the tainted ribs. The lawsuit was ongoing until April 1979, when Yul testified before a jury in Manhattan Supreme Court. Three weeks into the trial, Yul settled for an undisclosed amount (some sources later revealed that it was $125,000[13]).

Odyssey premiered on December 9, 1974, in Cleveland with no reviews due to a newspaper strike. Yul played with a cast of 18, including Joan Diener as his wife Penelope. "I insisted on her," Yul told the press, hoping to quash the allegations of nepotism (director Marre had been accused in giving the female lead to his wife). The show was three hours long, touched briefly on the end of Odysseus' long journey but concentrating on his return home to Penelope.

Yul's list of special demands, which his secretary Carol Fisher sent to the managers of the different theaters and the hotels on the tour before Yul's arrival, soon became an industry joke. Every dressing room had to be painted a particular shade of brown and every hotel suite had to be stocked in advance with particular food products and beverages, including one dozen brown eggs ("under no circumstances white ones!") and a case of Chateau Gruaud Larose '66 ("the only wine I drink"). The list even specified the quality and the length of the telephone cords (at least two lines, both must be touchtone, and with 13-foot cords), beds (one king-size bed with one mattress and two cribs for the babies), closets (always extra wooden hangers) and, as the king of Siam used to say etc., etc., etc.

The show ran into trouble in each city where it was presented. In Boston, Dinier's name was left off the marquee of the Colonial Theatre. Since there was no time to alter the sign before the opening, the theater draped the entire marquee in black cloth, causing many observers to believe that Yul had died. When the show moved to the Kennedy Center in Washington, Erich Segal and composer Mitch Leigh did not speak to each other and the collaboration was on the verge of collapsing, since suddenly major changes had been brought to the text and to the music of the show without the author being notified. A few weeks later, during the Los Angeles run, Segal asked that his name be removed from the credits. Also in California, the director, after several fights with choreographer Billy Wilson, had him fired and took personal charge of the choreography.

When the show opened in Toronto, Yul went to see Marlene Dietrich, who was performing in concert. Many years had passed since the end of their stormy relationship, but Dietrich still had not forgiven him. That night, the German actress spotted him in the crowd. Yul, who was staying at the same hotel, called repeatedly, asking to see her, and she refused. She later changed her mind and went to tell him what she thought of him.[14] That was the last contact the two former lovers ever had.

Despite *Odyssey*'s problems and the generally bad reviews, it was always sold out, grossing (before opening on Broadway) over $4 million in a total of 348 performances. The show nevertheless arrived in New York in December 1975 with a burdensome deficit, which the production attributed to heavy operating costs on the road, extra rehearsal payments, unscheduled layoffs and a 25-day musicians strike that prevented an earlier debut.

Back in August, Yul foresaw coming problems and tried to terminate his contract, but was threatened with a $1,000,000 suit if he should leave the show. Then in November, when the producer considered closing the show early, Yul threatened to immediately walk out of the current engagement if he was not assured that the musical would continue on to Broadway.[15]

After a year of misadventures, on November 18, at a press conference at Sardi's, Yul announced the preview dates of an all-new Broadway version of the show (90 percent rewritten from its original), now renamed *Homer, Sweet Homer*. He also pointed out, "One of the major problems at first was the title, I think. *Odyssey* gave people the wrong idea. They didn't realize it was a comedy. Even some friends of mine who came to see it, came backstage afterward and told me they thought they would have to sacrifice themselves to go and watch Yul do this awful Greek tragedy. But when they saw it, they loved it.... I've gone through enormous disappointments in the theater. I had some disappointments in *The King and I*, the same as in this one, but I arrived finally at what I think is a happy harbor."[16]

Yul arrived to the press conference in a dark stretch limo, dressed all in black except for a light colored tie. "I always wear black," he said to the crowd. "I'm quite wide, I wear a 46 coat — and when I wear light clothes, I look like a wrestler who's escaped from a carnival or something so I always dress in black; it makes me look less bulky. Besides, it makes life a lot simpler."[17] He also pointed out that all his clothes were exclusively custom-made by French designer Balenciaga and the shoes by Gucci.

Homer, Sweet Homer opened at a Sunday matinee at the Palace Theatre on January 4, 1976. Actresses Lauren Bacall and Maureen O'Sullivan and members of the New York press were in the audience. The next day, the reviews were so awful that the producers shut down the show, which joined the list of nine other shows in the history of Broadway to close after only one performance. Yul did not worry too much because he had already received other interesting proposals. His only comment (to the *New York Times*) was: "*Homer, Sweet Homer* had an honorable career. Over 85 percent of our audiences gave us standing ovations; there must be something good about it; if there hadn't been we would not have continued ... I'd be delighted to do another on Broadway — I'm not discouraged."[18] After over a year of absence from home, Yul returned to Normandy for a well-deserved rest. He later posed for photos for two advertising campaigns: in the United States for Scotch Lauder's and in Italy for the Extra Brandy Rene Briand.

In France, George Shdanoff, the former assistant of Michael Chekhov and director of the Los Angeles Theater Company, invited Yul to play in Shakespeare's *Othello*. Yul was ecstatic about landing a role that had always fascinated him. However, just weeks before rehearsals were to begin, he withdrew from the production due to a viral throat infection. The truth was that he was suddenly concerned about performing Shakespeare with his accent. Shdanoff, who had personally invested in the idea based on Yul's participation, was forced to issue a statement announcing the postponement of the show.[19] Yul had lost interest in the project and avoided all the calls from Shdanoff, eventually breaking the friendship with his former coach. All his thoughts were concentrated on an unexpected offer received by telegram from Lee Gruber and Shelly Gross, two of the most important Broadway impresarios. The duo was urging him to return on Broadway in a revival of *The King and I*.

13

Long Live the King!

"He played the king, he lived the king and died a king."
— Deborah Kerr

Once the contract for *The King and I* was signed, Yul went into intense training to prepare his comeback in the role that made him a star 25 years earlier.

He ran three kilometers every morning backward, a trick he learned from his matador friend Luis Miguel Dominguín. Yul explained, "It's a marvelous exercise ... I built my body at the right age, during the teens. After you pass 20, it's already too late."[1] Soon, with the aid of a strict diet, Yul lost over 20 pounds and attained perfect physical shape. However, sudden severe backaches returned to afflict him.

July 26, 1976, marked the date of the beginning of the twenty-fifth anniversary tour of *The King and I* with Constance Towers, actor John Gavin's wife, as Mrs. Anna. The choreographer was Yuriko, a former pupil of Martha Graham, who had played the secondary role of Eliza in the original (1951) production.

During the rehearsals, Yul suffered from profound laryngitis and lost his voice completely. He had to mime his part for three weeks. Three days before the debut in Indianapolis, he was still completely silent. He decided to see a homeopathic healer in Houston whom he had met couple of years earlier. The healer treated him with full-body acupuncture, but the cure did not work. The night of the opening, Rock Brynner was in Indiana visiting his father, from whom he had been estranged for several years. Rock brilliantly suggested lip-syncing his father's voice. Yul and Rock had in fact incredibly similar voices. At first Yul was very perplexed by the idea; then he realized it was the only choice he had and agreed to it. That night on stage he only moved his lips, while from the orchestra pit Rock read the part. During the intermission, Yul whispered to his son to lower his voice because it sounded too young for a man his

145

age. The playback worked wonderfully, making the performance a triumph.

Before starting the stage revival of *The King and I*, Yul consulted Ernest Lehman, who was responsible for the original film adaptation of the show. The screenwriter recalled a surprising phone call from Yul, saying, "I'm gradually working into the play everything you did in the screenplay. But before I come into New York with it, I want your permission to do that." Lehman said, "My permission? Of course you have my permission. You do not have to ask me. First of all, it belongs to 20th Century-Fox, that screenplay, not to me." Yul said, "I do not want their permission. I want yours, as a writer." Lehman said, "You've got it."

"So I sent him a wire saying I was thrilled to be able to help, and I got a telegram back: 'You are a prince,' signed, 'King.'"[2]

Some critics charged that Constance Towers was the weakest of the actresses to play Mrs. Anna; it was even speculated that the actual reason Towers was cast was to make him look even stronger.[3] The actress denied all the gossip, explaining, "After working with him for a few months, I realized one reason he was so special and people reacted to him the way they did. I suddenly understood that he really liked women, and I don't mean that in a patronizing way. He really appreciated women and was sympathetic and sensitive to them. This communicated to the audience. He wanted you to come out on stage and be as beautiful and talented and brilliant as you could possibly be. That's what he encouraged you to be. He created an atmosphere where we weren't competing and I wasn't threatened by him and he wasn't threatened by me. I was just encouraged to go out and do the role and be the best I could possibly be, and it was a wonderful experience. He helped me, and if he saw something that could be improved upon, he was delicate and sensitive about presenting it to me. If he saw me doing something that he thought was wonderful, he complimented me on it.... I was so grateful for the help."[4]

There were a lot of stories circulating about Yul's difficult temperament and his constant striving for perfection. Some members of the cast, like Michael Kermoyan, did not remember any incidents, but recalled that once you became Yul's friend, he sometimes behaved like a child.[5]

During the long tour of *The King and I*, Yul gave many interviews, but every time he would meet with a journalist he would show up with his own tape recorder, explaining, "Too many times I have been quoted erroneously."

Yul Brynner on the stage of the Uris Theatre in New York during the revival of *The King and I*, 1977.

The show traveled across the States, then opened in New York on May, 2 1977. As soon as Yul entered the Uris Theater, he kissed the stage floor to show his gratitude about being back on Broadway, this time with all the honors.

The *King and I* revival sold out in every city and received wonderful reviews, which prompted the producers to extend the tour after New York to other cities, including London. After many long years on the down side, Yul's career finally reached its peak and gave him financial stability once again. The show grossed $17 million in New York before the tour was extended. Yul's share was said to be between $25,000 and $35,000 a week, and he expected to take in a million dollars by the end of the tour.

To welcome the public, an interesting photo gallery of 29 pictures, 18 of them taken by Yul, was displayed during the Broadway run in the upper promenade of the Uris Theater. The extra-large photos were candid images and portraits of the actors in the show; Yul took them during breaks and rehearsals using a telephoto lens so his subjects would be unaware. The Broadway success of *The King and I* was unbelievable: All the reviews praised the show and Yul's extraordinary performance. The night after the premiere, a party was held at Raga, an upscale Indian restaurant. It was a mob scene with dozens of photographers and over 300 guests trying to get to Yul.

All the theaters where the show was performed had to make major improvements. Yul demanded that his dressing room be repainted in his favorite shade of brown and refurbished with all the comforts he required. He knew that these requests could seem just the whims of a capricious star, but the reality was that he had to live and work for weeks in the same place, so it was absolutely necessary that his dressing room was as comfortable as possible. For years, many Broadway stars thanked him for cleaning up the dressing rooms of every major theater across America (Yul personally inspected the venues before the run would start).

In New York, he had several golden rococo decorations added to the white repainted walls of the orchestra pit. On the arch that ran over the stage, he insisted that some golden cherubs and peach-colored bulbs be installed. To a reporter who asked why he wanted all the soft lighting, Yul said, "Do you know what this place looked like? ... A public toilet.... The ladies look much prettier. It also adds a festive atmosphere." Some said that Yul insisted on those lights because they softened the glare that might show off his wrinkles. But Yul's mature look and voice were points of strength of the revival of *The King and I*. While 26 years earlier he looked too young in his role, now he was perfect being the same age of the king of Siam. "Now when I sit down in front of my mirror to start making up," Yul told *Newsweek*, "I find lines in my face that I used to draw. I don't have to put them in — they were etched there. My son looks at me and says, 'What a map!' ... My portrayal of the King is much more complete — I know much more in every way. I'm stronger physically than I was then — and I certainly have more energy."[6] Yul told another interviewer that, in the original production, "I was too young to understand the King's vulnerability, his innocence."[7]

When the show arrived at the London Palladium, Yul's dressing room was completely rebuilt at a cost of $65,000. A few days after the West End debut, Yul had a backstage pay phone disconnected once he had a private line installed in his dressing room. He said that the ringing of the public phone kept waking him during naps. Members of the cast retaliated by pouring glue on his dressing room doorknob. Every time the producers did not comply completely with Yul's demands, he refused to sing "A Puzzlement," his one solo number in the show. For this reason, Yul always got what he wanted.[8]

Suddenly Yul's health began to deteriorate: Frequent acute backaches with sharp pain at his legs often forced him to rest. Now when he was not in public, he moved around in a wheelchair wearing a large brown fedora down to his eyebrows in order to go unrecognized. During the tour, whenever possible, he departed from a small airport so that he could be driven to the stairs of the plane. One day Carol Channing, who was in London starring in a show at the same time Yul was playing in *The King and I*, watched him rehearsing a full hour, entering and going down six steps. Yul explained to her that because of the terrible fall at the *Cirque d'Hiver* when he was a teenager (and still about three four inches short of his full growth), he grew only on the side of him that was not banged up — and now had a four-inch lift under his right heel. He also claimed that he took his famous stance (with wide feet apart and fists on his hipbones) in order to maintain his balance.[9]

Despite his physical pain, Yul never forgot the troubles afflicting people less fortunate, especially children. While appearing in London in *The King and I*, he heard of Richard Chau, an 11-year-old refugee who had fled Vietnam by boat with his family and had just arrived in England. Chau could hardly speak English but he won a scholarship to a boarding school. However, the scholarship didn't cover his room fees and his family couldn't afford the extra money. Yul offered to pay the difference and the boy was so grateful that he wrote Yul about four times a year and told him about his grades until Yul's death.[10]

In a *New York Times* interview, Yul spoke of a moment of terror on opening night in New York at the revival of *The King and I*. "The princess is explaining something to Anna," he said. "Lady Chang [Thiang] tries to stop her from telling and I say, 'Oh, no, this is…' and I couldn't come up with the word, which is 'suitable.' So I went to my head and came up with 'convenient.' But I was shocked. It was inexplicable. Fortunately, something like that happens only once every 1,000 performances."[11]

A few days later, a armed man was able to get backstage at the Uris Theatre unnoticed; he was apprehended before anything happened. There had already been a series of unrelated petty crimes at the Uris: A dancer was mugged and some cast members had their money stolen. Suddenly Yul began worrying about his safety and that of his colleagues. He hired at his expense several security guards to patrol the theater and demanded a bullet-proof limo and six bodyguards. To some of those who accused him of being excessive, he explained that he learned that a jealous madman was trying to shoot him because the madman's girlfriend had a crush on him. Other times he would throw his hands in the air with colorful gestures, and with a grin exclaim, "What can I say? I'm just a maniac!"[12]

Rock Brynner recalls his father being very moody, often behaving bizarrely. Once, for instance, Rock walked into Yul's hotel suite and heard the sound of a power drill. He immediately thought his father was doing some carpentry, and was astonished to find him drilling his big toenail, splashing blood all over the place. Yul calmly explained that he had dropped a camera case on his foot, so to avoid losing his toenail, he was putting a hole in it, to relive the pressure.[13]

After each performance (which would last three hours), Yul would welcome his friends into his dressing room and then, if he was not suffering with a backache, he would dance until dawn at Studio 54, New York's most exclusive club.

Yul's *King and I* obligations did not keep Yul away from charitable social activities. He first worked for the Red Cross and the Salvation Army, then took the time to do a public service commercial for "I Love a Clean New York." On the streets of Greenwich Village, Yul (armed with a broom and close to a pile of trash) invited New Yorkers to keep the Big Apple tidy.

In April 1978, he flew to Geneva to attend, as honorary president, the Second World Romany Congress, meeting over 100 gypsy leaders from 26 countries to discuss issues and to appeal to the world to stop discrimination against gypsies and recognize them as a national minority. Yul, shamelessly lying, claimed that his mother was originally Romanian and that he had spoken the language as a child, but forgot it growing up.[14]

With eight performances a week and all the extra activities, Yul rarely had time for his wife and kids. Eventually he rented for his family an Upper West Side apartment that belonged to Henry Fonda. When the show moved to Chicago, Los Angeles and later to London, Jacqueline and the girls always traveled with Yul. However, the actual time he shared with them was less every day; the time he spent in the manor in Normandy amounted to just a few weeks per year. Now Yul's life went on exclusively in his dressing room where he had his meals, his business meetings and met his female "admirers."

Abandoned by her husband, Jacqueline sadly withdrew into herself.

In a rare interview released many years later, Thion de la Chaume said, "The one thing I've learned is that you never change anybody … take them [men] as they are. We're responsible for our choices in marriage…. Some people believe in giving up: I believe in going on."[15]

And she did go on with Yul for 14 years, devoting all of herself to him. Oddly, when his career was going nowhere, those were the happiest years of their marriage; then when he made his stage comeback, traveling all over the country, without a permanent home, Yul began to drift from his wife. Some tabloids reported the news of Jacqueline's attempt to commit suicide by taking pills and cutting her wrists. Yul was informed during a performance that she was in the hospital, but insisted on completing the show and then giving a dressing room audience to some fans before visiting her.[16] The straw that broke his marriage: His August 1980 announcement that he would take only a few months off at the end of the tour of *The King and I* and then resume playing in the show. Yul had signed an agreement of partnership with producer Mitch Leigh in which he committed to play *The King and I* in a coast-to-coast tour that would eventually conclude on Broadway, and share all the profits 50–50.

In spring 1981, Yul resumed his role in *The King and I*, exactly 30 years after he had made his debut opposite Gertrude Lawrence in the original production.

In many of the cities touched by the tour, local TV stations aired a commercial promoting the show. The response was incredible and the show sold out everywhere. Despite the amazing success, Yul was more demanding and whimsical every day. For instance, if he did not receive a standing ovation at the end of the performance, he would refuse to appear in any curtain call. At the age of 61, Yul traveled with a special hospital bed to help ease the occasional pain in his spine and legs.

In Philadelphia, one of the first cities on the tour, the show ran for several weeks. Yul asked his agent Robert Lantz to rent him "a lovely, big house in an area where I may have peace and quiet during the day." Lantz contacted a local real estate agent and found a place on Golf House Road in the exclusive Ardmore suburb. Yul signed a contract after he inspected the property and approved the choice. On the day after moving in the house, Yul was awakened by unusual noises. He climbed out of bed, looked out the window and cringed. Masses of people were swarming over the lawn. He had rented a house that sat across a narrow road from the Merion Golf Club, and the U.S. Open had just begun! Yul immediately packed his bags and moved to a hotel, refusing to pay the rent.[17]

In that period, Yul found the time to collaborate with Susan Reed on *The Yul Brynner Cookbook*, a volume of gourmet recipes divided into seven parts, each of them indicating Yul's favorite dishes from different cuisines corresponding to the countries of his multi-ethnic origins.[18]

Although he was still married to Jacqueline, Yul was having an affair with Kathy Lee (her real name: Kathy Yam Choo), a 25-year-old Malaysian dancer who had played Little Eva in the London production of *The King and I*. When the show returned to the States, Lee could not join the cast because she had no work permit, so she just traveled with Yul. In April 1983, while in San Francisco, Yul's divorce from Jacqueline became final and he immediately married Lee. During a break in the tour, the newlyweds went on holiday to France. On their return, the new Mrs. Brynner got the role of Eliza in the show.

"I'm very happy with her," Yul said in one of his first statements to the press after the wedding. "We're both passionate about the theater and we have fun together. Life is very good."

On September 13, 1983, in Los Angeles, Yul celebrated his four thousandth *King and I* performance. A party was organized in a tent in the parking lot behind the theater. The tribute was called *A Toast to the King* and many of the actresses who had played Mrs. Anna in different productions toasted Yul's achievement. Yul was offered a silver Buccellati champagne cooler engraved, "Every Day I Do My Best for One More Day" (from the lyrics of "A Puzzlement").[19]

Yul Brynner in an undated publicity shot.

Earlier that morning, Yul had learned that he had inoperable lung cancer.

A few days earlier, his wife caught a cold and made an appointment with her doctor. As she was preparing to leave to see him, Yul unexpectedly decided to go with her because for the past two weeks, while putting on his makeup, he had noticed a lump on his neck. Dr. Paul Rudnick examined him and asked him to return the next day to run a biopsy. When Dr. Rudnick learned that Yul was a heavy smoker, he prescribed a series of X-rays, which showed the presence of a malignant cancer in both lungs that had already traveled into his lymph system. Three other oncologists confirmed the first diagnosis. All the specialists stressed the need to quickly make a choice between a treatment of chemotherapy or radiotherapy. Yul chose the latter because the side effects could be less debilitating. Yul revealed the news of his illness only to his family and very close friends. Victoria Brynner received a moving phone call in which her father informed her of his condition, explaining that the doctors had given him three months to live.[20]

Despite Yul great efforts to keep his battle against cancer private, the news reached the media and was printed everywhere. The *King and I* box office registered a 40 percent drop in ticket sales.

Yul went to Los Angeles' Cedar Sinai Hospital for his treatment every day except those days when he had a matinee performance. He never missed a show for any reason even when the side effects made him terribly sick or extremely weak. It was another example of his exceptional physical strength, which he always proved to have during the most difficult times in his life — a confirmation of the show biz adage "the show must go on." It was the role of the king whose death he played every night that gave him the power to fight to live an extra day.

Yul's first reaction to his illness was one of anger. He had pain but refused to take painkillers. "With pain you at least know what you're fighting," he said in an interview with columnist Cindy Adams. "You have a concrete, palpable enemy which you must then come to grips [with]."[21] He would go into a deep meditation which he found extremely therapeutic. The seven weeks of radiation treatment burned the lining of his bronchial tubes and dried up his saliva. Without it lubricating his throat, he had to continuously use a liquid spray. He also kept one glass of water on each side of the stage so he could drink during the show when necessary. In December of that year, when the L.A. run of *The King and I* ended, Yul, very weak and barely able to walk, left for Germany. In Hanover he entered the Silbersee Clinic under the care of Dr. Hans Nieper, an oncologist, whose controversial unorthodox methods were frowned upon by other German experts. Yul had always been a believer in homeopathy and alternative therapies and was eager to meet Dr. Nieper (to whom he had been referred by friend and cancer patient Edie Goetz, daughter of producer Louis B. Mayer). Nieper prescribed for him a diet based on enzymes and vitamins extracted from fruits and vegetables. After several days of the alternative treatment, Yul flew on a private jet to Normandy, where he spent Christmas and New Year's Day in his manor before going back to America.

In early 1984, Dr. Richard Silver, Yul's oncologist, noticed an extraordinary recession in his patience's cancer. The good news prompted Yul to resume the tour right away (by now it had been renamed *The Kind and I: The Farewell Tour*). To celebrate the occasion, a party was organized at Studio 54, where Yul falsely announced to the press his victory over the cancer and his comeback. In March he made a brief appearance as part of *The Night of 100 Stars* at Radio City Music Hall. It was a show that reunited many Hollywood stars in which he merely took an elegant bow before the audience to the tune of a melody from *The King and I*.

Baltimore, Kansas City, Cincinnati, St. Louis, Vancouver, Portland,

Milwaukee, Toronto, Boston, Cleveland, Chicago and Washington were the venues where *The Farewell Tour* was performed, always in sold-out theaters.

In each city, Yul visited a hospital to bring comfort to patients with cancer, telling them of his own personal experience and encouraging them to fiercely fight the illness.

During his treatment, Yul met a ten-year-old cancer patient, Todd, who was bald due to the radiation side effects. The boy did not know who Yul Brynner was, but Yul invited him to his show and gave him two first-row tickets so that Todd, whose vision was impaired, could put his hand on the railing of the orchestra pit and feel the vibrations. The boy was thrilled. The following day, Yul said to the youngster, "You don't even know how I look like. Feel my head. See, I'm a star and I'm bald. It's not so bad being bald." At that, the boy laughed—for the first time in a long while.[22]

Yul's illness did not change his routine: Besides the show, long hours of makeup kept him busy most of the day. In between tour stops he tried to see his children, with whom he was always very caring.

In January 1985, after a two-and-a-half-year tour, *The King and I: The Farewell Tour* arrived on Broadway. Yul rented a luxurious three-bedroom Trump Tower apartment where he lived until he bought and moved into a co-op apartment at United Nations Plaza. On opening night he partially lost his voice due to a mild cold; the reviewers were sympathetic. After the performance, Yul attended a party in his honor at the Hard Rock Café, where Rock was one the managers. During his New York stay, Yul was seen on many TV shows where he talked candidly about his cancer battle and at the same time promoted his show, which sold out until May. "How are you going to turn off what you think and feel, lying down and waiting for the radiation to take effect?" Yul asked on CBS-TV's *60 Minutes*. "It's much easier to go in front of 2,500 people and have standing ovations at the end of a show eight times a week."[23]

Suddenly, excruciating back pain returned to afflict him, forcing him to travel in a wheelchair or in his bodyguards' arms. One day, in a hallway of the Memorial Sloan-Kettering Cancer Center in New York, Yul met renowned cancer surgeon Dr. William Cahan. (Yul was first introduced to Cahan during the original run of *The King and I* in the early 1950s when Cahan was the son-in-law of Brynner's co-star

Gertrude Lawrence.) Cahan later reminisced, "When you saw him up on the stage with his bare chest, he looked indestructible. But he smoked four or five packs a day. I used to tell him the same thing I told everybody, 'For God's sake, cut it out.'" With a smile like a mischievous boy, Yul would respond, "Don't worry, Bill. They'll never get me."[24]

Thirty-six years later, Yul was in a wheelchair on his way to radiation therapy for spinal metastases from his lung cancer. After chatting a few minutes with Dr. Cahan, Yul looked at him, shook his head and said, "Why the hell didn't I listen to you?"[25] That was the last time Dr. Cahan saw his friend alive.

Yul would stand or walk only in some rare public occasions and on stage; however, his movements were so slow and awkward that he often had to skip his "The Puzzlement" solo. Actress Mary Beth Peil, who was playing Mrs. Anna, had to hold and lead him during the famous scene of the Polka dance. Peil later commented, "I had no idea really at that time that he was sick or just how sick he was. Most of the time I was working with him, he was very ill, and he was aware of it. When you're in touch with your own mortality, you look at your life and the people around you in a different way. He had just entered into his final marriage and he was very happy in both his personal and his professional life."[26]

Peil never forgot what the stage manager told her when she first started rehearsing the role: "Everything will be fine with Yul, but there are two things that you have to remember: Never look him in the eye, and never touch him." These two strange rules struck the actress as impossible to obey since she had to talk, dance and sing with him the entire show. On the day of the first meeting with Yul, Peil was very nervous, but he gently embraced her, looked into her eyes and said, "Welcome to the family."[27] The actress felt completely relieved and realized that what they told her about Yul was part of a myth built around his reputation of being a difficult and perfectionist artist feared by many. She never experienced any problem working with him and he always showed her great professional generosity. For her performance as Mrs. Anna, Peil won a Tony Award in June; Yul received a special career award.

Day by day Yul's health deteriorated; Rock Brynner remembered that for those who knew about his illness, it was very painful watching him on stage. The audience members, however, who every night filled the theater, gave him a standing ovation acclaiming his performance.

Once again *The King and I* was a big moneymaker, grossing $520,920 in just one week. At the end of May, Yul missed some performances because of a severe throat and ear infection.

June 30, 1985, was announced as his farewell performance as the king of Siam after 4633 performances. The extraordinary event was covered by all the media. Yul told *The New York Times*, "I want to satisfy my need for a good quality of life that is not supplied by the show any more. I want to catch up on friendships, on concerts and paintings I've missed. I want to renew myself."[28] He also said that he didn't want to risk disappointing his fans.[29]

Yul Brynner in a publicity shot for the 1984 revival of *The King and I.*

President Ronald Regan, New York's Governor Mario Cuomo and New York City Mayor Ed Koch all sent Yul letters of congratulations on the occasion of the farewell performance. On July 14, after he signed a new will before his lawyer, Yul, despite the terrible pain that did not let him sleep and forced him to take painkillers with hallucinatory side effects, flew to Los Angeles to visit friend Edie Goetz, who was also dying of cancer. He later went to France, where he spent the entire summer taking his last photographs. Six months later he returned to New York, visibly emaciated and frequently sedated. His cousin Irena regularly visited him, but his wife Kathy was the only one always by his side.

In September, Yul was admitted into the emergency room after the left side of his body was hit by a thrombosis. The hospitalization was hushed up and he was registered under the false name of Robby Lee (the hospital staff was instructed not to reveal his real identity). The doctors determined that the lung cancer had metastasized and spread to the spinal cord. A week later, the press got the news and began speculating about his illness. Yul's agent Robert Lantz denied the rumors of the hospitalization, claiming that Yul was at his home in Normandy, but reporters besieged the Cornell Hospital in New York and forced Lantz to admit that Yul was undergoing treatment for bacterial meningitis; Lantz said that the doctors were very optimistic about a speedy and full recovery. The truth was that Yul was in and out of a coma. His wife was beside him all the time, holding his hand and sleeping in a room in the hospital. Only his children and Irena were allowed to visit him. After a paparazzo was able to snatch a photograph of Yul dying in bed, a couple of bodyguards were hired and stationed outside his room. Mia, Melody and Rock were constant visitors.

On October 10, 1985, at one A.M., after a month in the hospital, unconscious Yul Brynner died. Kathy, Rock and Victoria were at his bedside. Yul died in a regal, way never complaining nor showing a moment of weakness. During his illness, he always demonstrated great dignity and enormous physical strength. Claire Bloom wrote in her memoir, "He died as he lived. A gallant and indomitable spirit."[30] That night, Broadway theaters dimmed their lights in his memory.

Yul died peacefully, surrounded by caring and affectionate loved ones. A few weeks later that atmosphere of apparent serenity suddenly changed at the reading of his will. In a 14-page document, Yul left Kathy Lee all his estate, including the New York apartment, the house in Normandy together with furniture, paintings, jewels and a collection of rare fine wines. He left his son Rock some stock he owned in the restaurant chain Hard Rock Café and $50,000. He left Victoria $50,000 and a $100,000 trust; $25,000 went to his illegitimate daughter Lark. The will also provided for the future of Mia and Melody by setting up a trust for them and designating them as heirs if Kathy Lee were to die. Considering the fact that just in his last tour Yul had earned $5 million, the children felt disinherited and disappointed. In 1987, Yul's third wife Jacqueline sued Kathy Lee, claiming that she was the beneficiary of a life insurance payment Yul had signed when he was still married to her; Kathy Lee maintained that her husband had changed it to her name. According to some friends, the battle ended after a few months when Jacqueline simply gave up her claim. The attorneys of Mia and Melody won a settlement from the estate of almost $500,000.[31]

On January 30, 1986, Kathy Lee organized a memorial service for

Yul at the Schubert Theatre. The audience included friends, members of the theater community and fans, but no relatives or members of the family. Standing across the stage of the theater from a giant photograph of Yul, dozens of speakers remembered his life, off-stage and on, and the experiences they personally shared with him. New York Mayor Ed Koch said he was astonished that Yul could have been so short and yet have "filled the room and filled the stage."[32] A few weeks later, Yul's widow arranged for a religious cer-

Yul Brynner in an undated publicity shot.

emony in Vladivostock, Yul's birth town, without notifying any of his children. To fulfill his last wish, Yul's body was cremated and the ashes were dispersed in a secret location.

In February 1986, American audiences were shocked by a 30-second television commercial aired by the major networks. An eerie voice-over announced, "Ladies and gentlemen, the late Yul Brynner." Suddenly, the TV screen showed a close-up of Yul — bald-pated and steely-eyed — boldly saying into the camera, "Now that I'm gone, I tell you: Don't smoke. Whatever you do, just don't smoke. If I could take back that smoking, we wouldn't be talking about any cancer. I'm convinced of that."[33]

The message was sponsored by the American Cancer Society and was periodically broadcast for over a month. The reaction was immediate as hundreds of viewers called the Cancer Society praising the efficacy of the Brynner ad. The impact was so intense that Israeli and Spanish television networks also planned to air the commercial. The clip had been shot in January 1985, during an appearance on ABC-TV's *Good Morning America*, when Yul seized the opportunity to leave a message to be broadcast posthumously.

In 1996, Victoria Brynner published a beautiful book illustrated with many of Yul's photographs. To publicize the book, an exhibition with some of the photographs was held at the Academy of Motion Picture Arts and Sciences in Los Angeles. It was a important tribute that publicly acknowledged Yul as a photographer and showed (through his pictures) his artistic sensibility, his passion for work, his love of family and colleagues, and his compassion for the less fortunate. That same year, the media reported that Yul's ashes were secretly buried in a small cemetery near the remote Russian Orthodox monastery of Saint Michael de Bois Aubry in the Loire Valley. According to French radio reports, Kathy had moved the ashes from Yul's estate in Normandy after Criquebouef was sold.

Yul's gravesite is marked by a simple stone decorated with a Celtic cross and engraved with the dates of his birth and death. It is situated in a beautiful, solitary, peaceful place and does not attract people's attention — a choice which seems to confirm a traditional tzigan saying that Yul used to repeat: "We are born alone, live alone, die alone."

Filmography

Port of New York

1949. Eagle-Lion. *Director*: Laslo Benedek; *Producer*: Aubrey Schenck; *Screenplay*: Eugene Ling, based on a short story by Arthur Ross and Bert Murray. *Cast*: Scott Brady (Mickey Walters), Yul Brynner (Paul Vicola), Richard Rober (Jim Flannery), K. T. Stevens (Toni Camden), Arthur Blake (Dolley Carney), Lynne Carter (Lili Long), John Kellogg (Lenny), William Challee (Leo Stasser).

The Ten Commandments

1956. Paramount. *Director*: Cecil B. De Mille; *Producer*: Henry Wilcoxon; *Screenplay*: Aeneas MacKenzie, Jesse L. Lasky, Jr., Jack Garriss and Frederic M. Frank. *Cast*: Charlton Heston (Moses), Yul Brynner (Rameses II), Anne Baxter (Nefertiri), Yvonne DeCarlo (Sephora), Edward G. Robinson (Dathan), Debra Paget (Lilia), John Derek (Joshua), Nina Foch (Bithia), John Carradine (Aaron), Vincent Price (Baka), Henry Wilcoxon (Pentaur), Cedric Hardwicke (Sethi), Judith Anderson (Memnet), Douglass Dumbrille (Jannes), H.B. Warner (Amminadab), Francis McDonald (Simon), Tommy Doran (Gershom), Ian Keith (Rameses I), Olive Deering (Miriam), Eugene Mazzola (Rameses' Son).

The King and I

1956. 20th Century Fox. *Director*: Walter Lang; *Producer*: Charles Brackett; *Screenplay*: Ernest Lehman, based on the novel *Anna and the King* by Margaret Landon and on the musical by Richard Rodgers and Oscar Hammerstein. *Cast*: Deborah Kerr (Anna Leonowens), Yul Brynner (King of Siam), Terry Saunders (Lady Thiang), Rita Moreno (Tuptim), Martin Benson (Kralahome), Alan Mowbray (British Ambassador), Geoffrey Toone (Edward Ramsay), Leonard Strong (Interpreter).

Anastasia

1956. 20th Century Fox. *Director*: Anatole Litvak; *Producer*: Buddy Adler; *Screenplay*: Arthur Laurents, based on the play by Marcelle Maurette, adapted in English by Guy Bolton. *Cast*: Ingrid Bergman (Anna Anderson/Anastasia), Yul Brynner (Bounine), Helen Hayes (Empress Marie), Akim Tamiroff (Chernov), Martita Hunt (Baroness Von Livenbaum), Ivan Desny (Prince Paul), Sacha Piteoff (Petrovin), Felix Aylmer (Russian Chamberlain), Karel Stepanek (Vadlos), Ina de la Haye (Marusla).

The Brothers Karamazov

1958. Avon/MGM. *Director*: Richard Brooks; *Producer*: Pandro S. Berman; *Screenplay*: Richard Brooks, based on the novel *The Brothers Karamazov* by Fyodor Dostoyevsky. *Cast*: Yul Brynner (Dmitrij Karamazov), Maria Schell (Grusnenka), Claire Bloom (Katya), Lee J. Cobb (Fëdor Karamazov), Richard Basehart (Ivan Karamazov), Albert Salmi (Smerdjakov), William Shatner (Alexei Karamazov), Judith Evelyn (Mme. Anna Hohlakov).

The Buccaneer

1958. Paramount. *Director*: Anthony Quinn; *Producer*: Henry Wilcoxon; *Screenplay*: Jesse L. Lasky, Jr., Bernice Mosk, Harold Lamb, Edwin Justus Mayer and J. Gardner Sullivan, based on Jeanie Macpherson's adaptation of the book *Lafitte the Pirate* by Lyle Saxon. *Cast*: Yul Brynner (Jean Lafitte), Charlton Heston (Gen. Andrew Jackson), Claire Bloom (Bonnie Brown), Charles Boyer (Dominique You), Inger Stevens (Annette Clairborne), E.G. Marshall (Governor Clairborne), Lorne Greene (Mercier).

The Journey

1959. Alby/MGM. *Director* and *Producer*: Anatole Litvak; *Screenplay*: George Tabori. *Cast*: Yul Brynner (Major Surov), Deborah Kerr (Lady Diana Ashmore), Jason Robards, Jr. (Paul Kedes), Anouk Aimée (Eva), Robert Morley (Hugh Deverill), E.G. Marshall (Harold Rhinelander), Ron Howard (Billy Rhinelander), Anne Jackson (Margie Rhinelander), David Kossoff (Simon Avron), Marie Daems (Francoise Hafouli).

The Sound and the Fury

1959. 20th Century Fox. *Director*: Martin Ritt; *Producer*: Jerry Wald; *Screenplay*: Irving Ravetch and Harriet Frank, Jr., based on the novel by William Faulkner. *Cast*: Yul Brynner (Jason), Joanne Woodward (Quentin), Françoise Rosay (Mrs. Compson), Margaret Leighton (Caddy), Ethel Waters (Dilsey), Jack Warden (Ben), Albert Dekker (Earl Snopes), Stephen Perry (Luster), Stuart Whitman (Charles Bush).

Solomon and Sheba

1959. United Artists. *Director*: King Vidor; *Producer*: Ted Richmond; *Screenplay*; Anthony Veiller, Paul Dudley and George Bruce, based on a story by Crane Wilbur. *Cast*: Yul Brynner (Solomon), Gina Lollobrigida (Sheba), George Sanders (Adonijah), Marisa Pavan (Abishang), Harry Andrews (Baltor), John Crawford (Joab), Finlay Currie (David), David Farrar (Pharaoh), Maruchi Fresno (Bethsheba).

Le Testament d'Orphée (The Testament of Orpheus)

1959. Pagode. *Director and Screenplay*: Jean Cocteau; *Producer*: Jean Thulliter. *Cast:* Jean Cocteau (Jean Cocteau), Maria Casarès (Princess), Jean Marais (Oedipus), Claudine Oger (Pallas Athens), Yul Brynner (Usher), Nicole Courcel, Lucia Bosé, Luis Dominguin, François Périer, Pablo Picasso, Brigitte Bardot, Francoise Sagan, Roger Vadim, Charles Aznavour (extras).

Once More, with Feeling

1960. Columbia Pictures/Stanley Donen Films. *Director and Producer*: Stanley Donen; *Screenplay*: Harry Kurnitz, based on his play. *Cast*: Kay Kendall (Dolly Fabian), Yul Brynner (Victor Fabian), Geoffrey Toone (Dr. Hilliard), Gregory Ratoff (Maxwell Archer), Maxwell Shaw (Gendel), Mervyn Johns (Mr. Wilburn, Jr.), Martin Benson (Bardini), C. S. Stuart (Manning), Shirley Ann Field (Angela Hopper).

Surprise Package

1960. Columbia Pictures/Stanley Donen Films. *Director and Producer*: Stanley Donen; *Screenplay*: Harry Kurnitz, based on the novel *A Gift* *from the Boys* by Art Buchwald. *Cast:* Yul Brynner (Nico March), Mitzi Gaynor (Gabby Rogers), Noël Coward (King Pavel II), Eric Pohlmann (Stefan Miralis), George Coulouris (Dr. Hugo Palmer), Lyndon Brook (Stavrin), Bill Nagy (Johnny Stettina).

The Magnificent Seven

1960. United Artists. *Director and Producer:* John Sturges; *Screenplay:* William Roberts, based on the film *The Seven Samurai* by Akira Kurosawa. *Cast:* Yul Brynner (Chris), Steve McQueen (Vin), Robert Vaughn (Lee), James Coburn (Britt), Charles Bronson (Bernardo O'Reilly), Horst Buchholz (Chico), Brad Dexter (Harry Luck), Eli Wallach (Calvera), Rosenda Monteros (Petra).

Escape from Zahrain

1962. Paramount. *Director and Producer:* Ronald Neame; *Screenplay:* Robins Estridge, based on the novel *Appointment in Zahrain* by Michael Barrett *Cast:* Yul Brynner (Sharif) Sal Mineo (Ahmed), Madlyn Rhue (Laila), Jack Warden (Huston), Tony Caruso (Tahar), Jay Novello (Hassan), Leonard Strong (Ambulance Driver), James Mason (Johnson).

Taras Bulba

1962. United Artists. *Director:* J. Lee Thompson; *Producer:* Harold Hecht; *Screenplay:* Waldo Salt and Karl Tunberg, based on the novel by Nikolaj Gogol. *Cast:* Tony Curtis (Andrei Bulba) Yul Brynner (Taras Bulba), Christine Kaufmann (Natalia Dubrov), Sam Wanamaker (Filipenko), George Macready (Governor), Vladimir Sokoloff (Stephan), Brad Dexter (Shilo), Guy Rolfe (Prince Grigory).

Kings of the Sun

1963. Lewis J. Rachmil Productions/United Artists. *Director:* J. Lee Thompson; *Producer:* Lewis Rachmil; *Screenplay:* Elliott Arnold and James Webb, based on a stort story by Elliott Arnold. *Cast:* Yul Brynner (Black Eagle), George Chakiris (Balam), Shirley Anne Field (Ixchel),

Richard Basehart (Ah Min), Brad Dexter (Ah Haleb), Barry Morse (Ah Zok), Leo Gordon (Humac Ceel), Armando Silvestre (Isatai), Rudy Solar (Pitz).

Flight from Ashiya

1964. United Artists. *Director:* Michael Anderson; *Producer:* Harold Hecht; *Screenplay:* Elliott Arnold and Waldo Salt, based on the novel by Elliott Arnold. *Cast:* Yul Brynner (Sgt. Mike Takashima), Richard Widmark (Col. Glenn Stevenson), George Chakiris (Lt. John Gregg), Suzy Parker (Lucille Carroll), Shirley Knight (Caroline Gordon), Ekio Taki (Tomiko), Daniele Gaubert (Leila), Joe de Reda (Sgt. Randy Smith), Mitsuhiro Sugiyama (Charlie).

Invitation to a Gunfighter

1964. United Artists. *Director* and *Producer:* Richard Wilson; *Screenplay:* Elizabeth Wilson and Richard Wilson, based on a short story by Hal Goodman and Larry Klein. *Cast:* George Segal (Matt Weaver), Yul Brynner (Jules Gaspart D'Estaing), Janice Rule (Ruth Adams), Pat Hingle (Sam Brewster), Brad Dexter (Kenarsie), Clifford Davis (Crane Adams), Alfred Ryder (Doc Barker), Clarke Gordon (Hickman).

The Saboteur: Code Name — Morituri (AKA Morituri)

1965. 20th Century Fox. *Director:* Bernhard Wicki; *Producer:* Aaron Rosenberg; *Screenplay:* Daniel Taradash, based on the novel *Morituri* by Werner Joerg Luedecke. *Cast:* Marlon Brando (Robert Crain), Yul Brynner (Capt. Mueller), Trevor Howard (Col. Statter), Janet Margolin (Esther), Martin Benrath (Kruse), Max Haufler (Branner), William Redfield (Baldwin), Rainer Penkert (Milkereit).

Cast a Giant Shadow

1966. United Artists. *Director and Producer:* Melville Shavelson; *Screenplay:* Melville Shavelson, based on a novel by Ted Berkman. *Cast:* Kirk Douglas (Col. David Marcus), Senta Berger (Magda Simon), James Donald (Safir), Yul Brynner (Asher Goren), Frank Sinatra (Vince), Angie

Dickinson (Emma Marcus), Luther Adler (Jacob Zion), Haym Topol (Abou Ibn Kader), John Wayne (Gen. Mike Randolph).

The Poppy Is Also a Flower (AKA The Opium Connection; Danger Grows Wild)

1966. Telsun Foundation. *Director*: Terence Young; *Producer*: Eulan Lloyd; *Screenplay*: Jo Eisinger, based on a story idea by Ian Fleming. *Cast*: Senta Berger (Nightclub Entertainer), Stephen Boyd (Benson), Yul Brynner (Col. Salem), Angie Dickinson (Linda), Hugh Griffith (Tribal Chief) Rita Hayworth (Monique), Omar Sharif (Dr. Rad), Amedeo Nazzari (Captain Dinonno), Marcello Mastroianni (Inspector Mosca), Trevor Howard (Lincoln), Eli Wallach (Locamo), Anthony Quayle (Capt. Moore), Jack Hawkins (Gen. Bahar).

Return of the Magnificent Seven

1966. Mirisen Corporation/United Artists. *Director*: Burt Kennedy; *Producer*: Ted Richmond; *Screenplay*: Larry Cohen. *Cast*: Yul Brynner (Chris), Robert Fuller (Vin), Elisa Montes (Petra), Warren Oates (Colbee), Emilio Fernandez (Lorea), Claude Akins (Frank), Fernando Rey (Priest), Julian Mateos (Chico), Jordan Christopher (Manuel), Rudy Acosta (Lopez), Virgilio Texeira (Luis).

Triple Cross

1967. Cinerope Films/Warner Brothers. *Director*: Terence Young; *Producer*: Jacques-Paul Bertrand; *Screenplay*: Rene Hardy and William Marchant, based on the novel *The Eddie Chapman Story* by Frank Owen. *Cast*: Christopher Plummer (Eddie Chapman), Romy Schneider (Countess), Trevor Howard (Gentleman), Yul Brynner (Baron von Grunen), Gert Fröbe (Col. Steinhager), Claudine Auger (Paulette), Jean-Claude Barco (Major von Leeb), Frank Letterman (Hans), Harry Meyen (Lt. Keller).

The Long Duel

1967. Paramount. *Director and Producer*: Ken Annakin; *Screenplay*: Peter Yeldham, based on a novel by Ranveer Singh. *Cast*: Yul Brynner (Sultan), Trevor Howard (Freddy Young), Charlotte Rampling (Jane Stafford), Harry Andrews (Superintendent Stafford), Andrew Keir (Gungarem), Antonio Ruiz (Munnu), Virginia North (Champa), Imogen Hassall (Tara), Patrick Newell (Colonel).

The Double Man

1967. Albion/Warner Brothers. *Director:* Franklin J. Schaffner; *Producer:* Hal E. Chester; *Screenplay:* Frank Tarloff and Alfred Hayes, based on the novel *Legacy of a Spy* by Henry S. Maxfield. *Cast:* Yul Brynner (Dan Slater/Kalmar), Britt Ekland (Gina Ericson), Clive Revill (Frank Whealty), Moira Lister (Mrs. Carrington), Lloyd Nolan (Bill Edwards), Brandon Brady (Gregori), David Healy (Halstead), George Mikell (Max Gruner), Anton Diffring (Berthold).

Villa Rides

1968. Paramount. *Director:* Buzz Kulik; *Producer:* Ted Richmond; *Screenplay:* Robert Towne and Sam Peckinpah, based on the novel *Pancho Villa* by William Douglas Lansford. *Cast:* Yul Brynner (Pancho Villa), Robert Mitchum (Lee Arnold), Charles Bronson (Fierro), Herbert Lom (Generale Huerta), Fernando Rey (Fuentes), Maria Grazia Buccella (Fina), Frank Wolff (Ramirez), Alexander Knox (Presidente Madero), Diana Lorys (Emilita), Jill Ireland (Girl in the Restaurant), Regina de Julian (Lupita).

The Battle on the River Neretva

1968. Bosna Film/Commonwealth United/Eichberg Film/IFC Films/Jadran Film. *Director and Producer:* Veljko Bulajic; *Screenplay:* Ratko Djurovic, Stevo Bulajic, Ugo Pirro, Alfred Weidenmann and Veliko Bulajic. *Cast:* Sergej Bondarcuk (Martin), Yul Brynner (Vlado), Sylva Koscina (Danica), Curt Jürgens (Gen. Lohring), Orson Welles (Chetnik Senator), Franco Nero (Capt. Michael Riva), Hardy Kruger (Col. Kranzer), Milena Dravic (Nada).

The File of the Golden Goose

1969. Carolan-Dador/United Artists. *Director:* Sam Wanamaker; *Producer:* David Rose; *Screenplay:* John C. Higgins and James B. Gordon, based on a story by John C. Higgins. Cast: Yul Brynner (Peter Novak), Charles Gray (Nick Harrison), Edward Woodward (Peter Thompson), John Barrie (Sloane), Adrienne Corri (Tina), Bernard Archerd (Collins), Ivor Dean (Reynolds), Anthony Jakobs (Firenos).

The Madwoman of Chaillot

1969. Seven Arts/Warner Brothers. *Director*: Bryan Forbes; *Producer*: Ely Landau; *Screenplay*: Edward Archalt, based on a novel by Jean Giraudoux. *Cast*: Katharine Hepburn (Countess Aurelia), Margaret Leighton (Constance), Giulietta Masina (Gabrielle), Charles Boyer (Broker), Danny Kaye (Ragman), Yul Brynner (The Chairman), Edith Evans (Josephine), John Gavin (Reverend), Paul Henreid (General), Richard Chamberlain (Roderick), Donald Pleasence (Prospector), Claude Dauphin (Dr. Jadin), Oscar Homolka (The Commissar).

The Picasso Summer

1969. Franco London Films/Warner Brothers. *Director*: Robert Sallin and Serge Bourgignon; *Producer*: Bruce Campbell; *Screenplay*: Douglas Spaulding and Edwin Boyd, based on a short story by Ray Bradbury. *Cast*: Albert Finney (George Smith), Yvette Mimieux (Alice Smith), Theo Marcuse (Guest), Jim Connelly (Artist), Louis Miguel Dominguin, Yul Brynner (Extras).

The Magic Christian

1970. Commonwealth United/Grand Films Limited. Director: Joseph McGrath; *Producer*: Dennis O'Dell; *Screenplay*: Terry Southern, based on his novel. *Cast*: Peter Sellers (Sir Guy Grand), Ringo Starr (Young Grand), Richard Attenborough (Oxford Coach), Christopher Lee (Dracula), Laurence Harvey (Amleto), John Cleese (Director of Sotheby's), Yul Brynner (Female Singer), Roman Polanski (Drunk), Raquel Welch (Female Priest), Patric Cargill (Clerk of Sotheby's), Graham Stark (Waiter).

Indio Black, sai che ti dico sei un gran figlio di ...
(AKA Adios Sabata; The Bounty Hunters)

1970. United Artists. *Director*: Gianfranco Parolini AKA Frank Kramer; *Producer*: Alberto Grimaldi; *Screenplay*: Renato Izzo and Gianfranco

Parolini. *Cast*: Yul Brynner (Sabata), Dean Reed (Ballantine), Pedro Maria Sanchez (Escudo), Gerard Herter (Col. Skimmel), Salvatore Borgese (September), Franco Fantasia (Oceano), Salvatore Billa (Manuel), Gianni Rizzo (Folgen).

Romansa Konjokradice (Romance of a Horsethief)

1971. Allied Artists. National General Pictures. *Director*: Abraham Polonsky; *Producer*: Gene Gutowski; *Screenplay*: David Opatoshu. *Cast*: Yul Brynner (Stoloff), Eli Wallach (Kifke), Jane Birkin (Naomi), Oliver Tobias (Zanvill), Lainie Kazan (Estusha), David Opatoshu (Shloime), Serge Gainsbourg (Sigmund), Alenka Rancic (Sura), Vladimir Bacic (Gruber).

The Light at the Edge of the World

1971. National General Pictures. *Director*: Kevin Billington; *Producer*: Kirk Douglas; *Screenplay*: Tom Rowe and Rachel Billington, based on a novel by Jules Verne. *Cast*: Kirk Douglas (Will Denton), Yul Brynner (Jonathan Kongre), Samantha Eggar (Arabella), Fernando Rey (Capt. Moriz), Renato Salvatori (Montefiore), Massimo Ranieri (Felipe), Aldo Sambrell (Tarcante), Tito Garcia (Emilio).

Catlow

1971. MGM. Filmways Pictures/United Artists. *Director*: Sam Wanamaker; *Producer*: Euan Lloyd; *Screenplay*: J.J. Griffith and Scott Finch, based on a novel by Louis L'Amour. *Cast*: Yul Brynner (Catlow), Richard Crenna (Cowan), Leonard Nimoy (Miller), Daliah Lavi (Rosita), Jo Ann Pflug (Christina), Bessie Love (Mrs. Frost), Jeff Corey (Merridew), Michael Delano (Rio).

Fuzz

1972. Filmways Pictures/United Artists. *Director*: Richard A. Colla; *Producer*: Jack Farren; *Screenplay*: Evan Hunter, based on his novel written under the pseudonym of Ed McBain. *Cast*: Burt Reynolds (Steven Carella), Jack Weston (Meyer Meyer), Yul Brynner (The Deaf Man), Raquel Welch (Eileen McHenry), Tom Skerritt (Bert Kling), Gino Conforti (Painter), Dan Gordon (Anthony La Bresca).

Le Serpent (AKA Night Flight from Moscow)

1973. Euro International Films/Films la Boétie/Rialto Film. *Director and Producer*: Henri Verneuil; *Screenplay*: Giles Perrault and Henri Verneuil, based on the novel *Le 13e Suicide* by Pierre Nord. *Cast*: Yul Brynner (Vlassov), Henry Fonda (Allan Davies), Dirk Bogarde (Philip Boyle), Virna Lisi (Annabel Lee), Philippe Noiret (Lucine Berthon), Farley Granger (Computer Expert), Luigi Diberti (Lefevre).

Westworld

1973. MGM. *Director and Screenplay*: Michael Crichton; *Producer*: Paul Lazarus III. *Cast*: Yul Brynner (Gunslinger), Richard Benjamin (Peter Martin), James Brolin (John Blane), Victoria Shaw (Queen), Dick Van Patten (Banker), Linda Scott (Arlette), Norman Bartold (Medieval Knight), Terry Wilson (Sheriff).

The Ultimate Warrior
(AKA The Barony; The Last Warrior)

1975. Warner Brothers. *Director and Screenplay*: Robert Clouse; *Producer*: Fred Weintraub and Paul Heller. *Cast:* Yul Brynner (Carlson), Max von Sydow (Baron), Joanna Miles (Melinda), William Smith (Carrot), Richard Kelton (Cal), Stephen McHattie (Robert), Lane Bradbury (Barrie).

Futureworld

1975. American International Pictures. *Director*: Richard Heffron; *Producer*: Paul Lazarus III; *Screenplay*: Mayo Simon and George Schenck. *Cast*: Peter Fonda (Chuck Browning), Blythe Danner (Tracy Ballard), Yul Brynner (Gunslinger), Arthur Hill (Duffy), Stuart Margolin (Harry), John P. Ryan (Dr. Schneider).

Con la rabbia agli occhi (AKA Death Rage; Anger in His Eyes; Blood Reckoning)

1976. Giovine. *Director*: Anthony M. Dawson aka Antonio Margheriti; *Producer*: Umberto Lenzi; *Screenplay*: Pier Luigi Andreani and Leila

Bongiorno. *Cast*: Yul Brynner (Peter Marciani), Massimo Ranieri (Angelo), Barbara Bouchet (Annie), Martin Balsam (Commissar), Gianfranco Sbragia, (Gennaro Gallo), Giacomo Furia (Cannavale), Sal Borghese (Vincent).

Stage Appearances

Twelfth Night

December 2–8, **1941**. Comedy by William Shakespeare. *Directors*: Michael Chekhov and George Shdanoff. *Producer*: Michael Chekhov. Little Theatre, New York. *Cast*: Beatrice Straight (Viola), Frank Rader (Sea Captain), Ronald Bennett (Sebastian), Charles Barnett (Second Sea Captain), John Flynn (Orsino), Nelson Harrell (Curio), Lester Bacharach (Valentine), Ford Rainey (Sir Toby Belch), Mary Haynsworth (Maria), Hurd Hatfield (Sir Andrew Aguecheek), Alan Harkness (Feste), Sam Schatz (Olivia), Youl Bryner (Fabian).

L'Annonce Faite à Marie

May 20, **1942**. Drama by Paul Claudel. *Director* and *Producer*: Ludmilla Pitoeff. Barbizon Plaza Theatre, New York. *Cast*: Ludmilla Pitoeff (Violaine), Youl Bryner (Pierre de Craon), Varvara Pitoeff (Mara), Francois Denoux (The Father), Mme. Andre Wick (The Mother), Jacques Hury (Youl Bryner), Pierre Claudel (Mayor), George Pitoeff, Jr. (Apprentice).

The Moon Vine

February 11–27, **1943**. Drama by Patricia Coleman. *Director and Producer*: Jack Kirkland. Morosco Theatre, New York. *Cast*: Vera Allen (Mrs. Meade), Grace Coppin (Strother Meade), Kate McComb (Lucy Telfar), Youl Bryner (André), Will Geer (Uncle Yancey Sylvaine), Agnes Scott Yost (Mrs Sylvaine), Haila Stoddard (Mariah Meade), Phyllis Tyler (Miss Francie Taylor), Biddy Fleet (Nic), Elmer Snowden (Pic).

The House in Paris

January 17, **1944**. Drama by E. Mawby Green and Edward Allen Feilbert, based on a novel by Elizabeth Bowen. *Director*: W.M. Harris, Jr. *Pro-

ducer: H. Clay Blaney. Royal Alexandra Theatre, Toronto. *Cast*: Cavada Humphrey (Naomi Fisher), Pauline Robinson (Henrietta), Alastair Kyle (Leopold), Ludmilla Pitoëff (Madame Fisher), Velma Royton (Marietta), Youl Bryner (Max Ebbart), Barbara Kent (Karen Michaels), Isham Constable (Roy Forrester).

Lute Song

February 6–June 8, **1946.** Musical by Sidney Howard and Will Irwin, based on the Chinese drama *Pi-Po-Ki* by Kao-Tong-Kia and Mao-Tseo. *Director*: John Houseman. *Producer*: Michael Meyerberg. Plymouth Theatre, New York. *Cast*: Mary Martin (Tchao-Ou-Niang, the Wife), Yul Brynner (Tsai-Yong), Augustin Duncan (Tsai, the Father), Mildred Dunnock (Madame Tsai, the Mother), McKay Norris (Prince Nieou), Helen Craig (Princess Nieou-Chi), Nancy Davis (Si-Tchun), Ralph Clanton (Imperial Chamberlain).

Dark Eyes

March 24, **1948.** Comedy by Elena Miramova, written in collaboration with Eugenie Leontovich. *Director* and *Producer*: Charles Goldner. Strand Theatre, London. *Cast*: Bill Staughton (Larry Field), Norris Smith (Willoughby), May Carey (Grandmother Field), Gladys Taylor (Pearl), Genine Graham (Helen Field), Yul Brynner (Prince Nikolai Toradje), Dolly Rowles (Natasha Rapakovich), Irina Baronova (Olga Shmilevskya), Edwin Styles (John Field).

The King and I

March 29, **1951.** Musical by Oscar Hammerstein and Richard Rodgers, based on the novel *Anna and the King* by Margaret Landon. *Director*: John van Druten. *Producers*: Oscar Hammerstein and Richard Rodgers. St. James Theatre, New York. *Cast*: Charles Francis (Capt. Orton), Sandy Kennedy (Louis Leonowens), Gertrude Lawrence (Anna Leonowens), Leonard Graves (Interpreter), John Juliana (Kralahome), Yul Brynner (The King), Len Mence (Phra Alack), Doretta Morrow (Tuptim), Dorothy Sarnoff (Lady Thiang), Johnny Stuart (Prince Chulalongkorn), Baayork Lee (Princess Ying Yaowalak), Larry Douglas (Lun Tha), Robin Craven (Sir Edward Ramsay).

Home, Sweet Homer

December 26, 1975–January 4, 1976. Musical by Mich Lee, based on Homer's *Odyssey*. *Director*: Albert Marre. *Producers*: Roger L. Stevens, Martin Feinstein and Alexander Morr. Palace Theatre, New York. *Cast*: Yul Brynner (Ulysses), Joan Diener (Penelope), Russ Thacker (Telemachus), Martin Vidnovic (Antinous), Ian Sullivan (Philokrates), Bill Mackey (Ktesippos), Daniel Brown (Eurymachus), Brian Destazio (Leokritos), Les Freed (Polybos), Diana Davila (Nausikaa), Skev Rodgers (Alkinoos).

The King and I

May 2, 1977–December 30, 1978. Musical by Oscar Hammerstein and Richard Rodgers, based on the novel *Anna and the King* by Margaret Landon. *Director*: Yuriko. *Producers*: Lee Gruber and Shelly Gross. Revival, Uris Theater, New York. *Cast*: Larry Swansen (Capt. Orton), Alan Amick (Louis Leonowens), Constance Towers (Anna Leonowens), Michael Kermoyan (Kralahome), Jae Woo Lee (Interpreter), Yul Brynner (The King), June Angela (Tuptim), Hye-Young-Choi (Lady Thiang), Gene Profanato (Prince Chulalongkorn), Julie Woo (Princess Ying Yaowalak), Martin Vidnovic (Lun Tha), John Michael King (Sir Edward Ramsay).

The King and I

January 7–June 30, 1985. Musical by Oscar Hammerstein and Richard Rodgers, based on the novel *Anna and the King* by Margaret Landon. *Director* and *Producer*: Mitch Leight. Revival, Broadway Theater, New York. *Cast*: Burt Edwards (Capt. Orton), Jeffrey Bryan Davis (Louis Leonowens), Mary Beth Piel (Anna Leonowens), Jonathan Farwell (Kralahome), Jae Woo Lee (Interpreter), Yul Brynner (The King), Patricia Welch (Tuptim), Irma–Estel LaGuerre (Lady Thiang), Araby Abava (Prince Chulalongkorn), Yvette Laura Martin (Princess Ying Yaowalak), Sal Provenza (Lun Tha), Edward Crotty (Sir Edward Ramsay).

Documentaries, Music and Soundtracks, Radio Programs and Television Appearances

Documentaries Narrated by Yul Brynner

Mission to No Man's Land (**1959**), documentary on refugee children in Eastern Europe, BBC-TV, London. Made in collaboration with the United Nations. *Producers:* Stanley Wright and Anatole Litvak; *Screenplay:* Stanley Wright.

Rescue: Yul Brynner (**1960**), documentary by CBS. *Producers:* Gene De Poris, Edward R. Morrow and Fred W. Friendly.

Profile of a Miracle (**1960**), documentary produced in collaboration with the United Nations.

My Friend Nicholas (**1961**), documentary produced in collaboration with the United Nations.

Man is a Man ... (**1962**), documentary produced in collaboration with the United Nations.

Apollo-Soyuz (**1979**), documentary on NASA Apollo-Soyuz's 1975 space mission, distributed by National Audiovisual Center.

Lost to the Revolution (**1980**), documentary about the last years of the Russian Revolution throughout Carl Fabergé jewel's creations. *Director* and *Screenplay:* Tim Forbes.

Music and Soundtracks

The King and I (**1951**) Yul Brynner and Gertrude Lawrence, original Broadway musical soundtrack, Decca LP 9008.

The King and I (**1956**) Yul Brynner and Deborah Kerr, original soundtrack, Capitol Records, W-740.

The Gypsy and I (**1967**) Yul Brynner sings melodies Tziganes with vio-

linist Aliosha Dimitrievitch, Vanguard, VRS 9256. French Version
(**1967**) *Le tzigane et moi*, Gatefold Barclay.
Romance of a Horsethief (**1971**) Original soundtrack by Mort Shuman.
Yul Brynner sings "Soft as the Evening." RCA Victor 49830.

Radio Programs

The Martha Deane Show, WOR-AM Radio, New York.
Army Archerd from Hollywood, Yul Brynner interviewed by Wynn
Keenan, 1964.
Panorama of the Lively Arts: France and Yul Brynner, WRTI Radio, Jan-
uary 12, 1973.

Television Programs

Mr. Jones and His Neighbors, CBS, 1944.
Mr. and Mrs., CBS, 1948
Fireside Theatre, episode: "Friend of a Family," NBC, April 5, 1949.
Studio One, episode: "Flower from a Stranger," CBS, May 25, 1949.
Studio One, episode: "Flower from a Stranger," CBS, February 13, 1950.
Toast of the Town, episode 163, CBS, July 29, 1951.
Toast of the Town, episode 174, CBS, October 14 , 1951.
Toast of the Town, episode 210, CBS, June 22 , 1952.
Omnibus, episode: "A Lodging for the Night," CBS, March 8, 1953.
What's My Line, episode 345, CBS, January 6, 1957.
The World's Greatest Showman, tribute to Cecil B. DeMille, NBC,
December 1, 1963.
Anna and the King, TV series, 13 episodes, CBS, September 1972.
Night of 100 Stars, ABC, March 10, 1985.

Brynner as Director

Studio One, episode: "Concerning a Woman of Sin," CBS, October 31, 1949.
Mr. I. Magination (children program), CBS, 1949.
Actors Studio, episode: "The Timid Guy," CBS, January 24, 1950.
Sure as Fate, CBS, July 4, 1950.
Danger, CBS, September 1950.
Life with Snarky Parker, also producer (puppets show for children), CBS, 1950.
Omnibus, episode: "The Capital of the World," CBS, December 6, 1953.

Notes

Chapter 1

1. Pete Martin, *Pete Martin Calls On ...* (New York: Simon & Schuster, 1962), pp. 347–48.

2. Rock Brynner, *Yul: The Man Who Would Be a King* (New York: Simon & Schuster, 1989), p. 155.

3. Bertil Lintner, *Blood Brothers: The Criminal Underworld of Asia* (New York: Macmillan, 2002), p. 190.

4. Rock Brynner, *op. cit.*, pp. 23–25.

5. Jhan Robbins, *Yul Brynner: The Inscrutable King* (New York: Dodd, Mead & Co., 1987), p. 6–7.

6. Ronald L. Davis, *Yul Brynner: Oral History Project N.85* (Dallas: Southern Methodist University, 1978), pp. 1–2.

7. Rock Brynner, *op. cit.*, pp. 25–27.

Chapter 2

1. Michael Parkinson, *Selected Interviews from the Television Series* (London: Elm Tree Books, 1975), p. 96.

2. *Ibid.*

3. Ronald L. Davis, *op. cit.*, p. 4.

4. "At 17, I Was an Acrobatic Clown in a Circus," *Asbury Park Press*, August 19, 1977, sec. D, p. 20.

5. Ronald L. Davis, *op. cit.*, p. 6.

6. Michael Chekhov, *To the Actor: On the Technique of Acting* (New York: Harper & Row, 1953), p. ix.

7. Ronald L. Davis, *op. cit.*, pp. 7–8.

8. Rock Brynner, *op. cit.*, p. 30.

9. Gene Feldman, *Yul Brynner. The Man Who Was King*, 1995, videocassette.

10. Ronald L. Davis, *op. cit.*, p. 9.

11. "Yul Brynner," *Motion Picture*, June 1957, p. 67.

12. Rock Brynner, *op. cit.*, pp. 33–34.

13. Brooks Atkinson, *New York Times*, December 3, 1941, sec. 2, p. 32.

14. Earl Wilson, "Brynner Confesses Baring All, " *New York Post*, April 27, 1977.

15. Richard G. Hubler, "Yul Brynner Jacks of All Mimes," *Coronet*, July 1957, p. 133.

16. Mary Braggiotti, "Mad Life," *New York Post*, July 3, 1949, sec. M, p. 2.

17. *New York Sun*, February 12, 1943.

18. Augustus Bridle, "Caucasian Pitoëff Stages Debut Here," *Toronto Star*, January 18, 1944, p. 4.

19. Jhan Robbins, *op. cit.*, p. 27.

20. Nantas Salvataggio, "Il calvo che piaceva alle donne," *Il corriere della sera*, October 11, 1985, p. 23.

21. Cameron Shipp, "Self-Made Mystery Man," *Redbook Magazine*, May 19, 1957, p. 32.

22. Pete Martin, *op. cit.*, pp. 345–46.

23. "Yul Brynner–Golden Egghead," *Newsweek*, May 19, 1958, p. 100.

24. Cameron Shipp, *op. cit.*, p. 96.

25. John Houseman, *Front and Center* (New York: Simon & Schuster, 1979), pp. 164–65.

26. Nancy Reagan, *Nancy* (New York: Morrow, 1980), p. 71.

27. John Houseman, *op. cit.*, p. 172.

28. *Ibid.*, pp. 172–73.

29. Ronald L. Davis, *op. cit.*, pp. 14–15.

30. Howard Barnes, "The Theater: Fifteen Century Contributes to Broadway," *Herald Tribune*, February 17, 1946, p. 12.

31. Jhan Robbins, *op. cit.*, p. 32.

32. Vincent Hartnett, "Disputes Brynner," *The American Legion Magazine*, August 1953.

33. Gearld Clarke, *Get Happy: The Life of Judy Garland* (New York: Random House, 2000), pp. 233–34.

34. Irene Thirer, "Screen Views," *New York Post*, April 17, 1952, p. 32.

Chapter 3

1. Pete Martin, " I Call on Yul," *The Sunday Evening Post*, November 22, 1958, p. 84.

2. Gene Feldman, *Yul Brynner. The Man Who Was King*, 1995, videocassette.

3. Joyce Haber, "Sensitive, Strong and Well in His Skin," *Los Angeles Times*, August 10, 1975, p. 31.

4. Alvin H. Marill, "Yul Brynner," *Films in Review*, October 1979, Vol. XXI, No. 8, pp. 460–61.

5. Carlton Jackson, *Picking Up the Tab: The Life and Movies of Martin Ritt* (Bowling Green, OH: Bowling Green Stare University Popular Press, 1994), p. 25.

6. Carol Channing, *Just Lucky I Guess* (New York: Simon & Schuster, 2002), pp. 23–24.

7. *Ibid.*, pp. 24–25.

8. T. M. Pryor, "Port of New York," *The New York Times*, February 3, 1950, sec. 2, p. 29.

9. Ralph Blumenthal, *The Stork Club: America's Most Famous Nightspot and the Lost World of Café Society* (New York: Little, Brown and Company, 2001), p. 156.

10. Frank R. Cunningham, *Sidney Lumet: Film and Literary Vision* (Lexington: University of Kentucky Press, 1991), p. 17.

Chapter 4

1. Richard Rodgers, *Musical Stages: An Autobiography* (New York: Random House, 1975), p. 270.

2. Hugh Fordin, *Getting to Know Him: A Biography of Oscar Hammerstein II* (New York: The Ungar Publishing Company, 1977), p. 296.

3. Patrick Garland, *The Incomparable Rex: A Memoir of Rex Harrison in the 1980's* (New York: Macmillan, 1998), p. 15.

4. Richard Rodgers, *op. cit.*, pp. 271–72.

5. Pete Martin, *Pete Martin Calls on ...* (New York: Simon & Schuster, 1962), p. 344.

6. Mary Martin, *My Heart Belongs* (New York: Morrow, 1976) p. 122.

7. Ronald L. Davis, *Yul Brynner: Oral History Project. N.85* (Dallas: Southern Methodist University, 1978), p. 22.

8. Richard Stoddard Aldrich, *Gertrude Lawrence as Mrs. A: An Intimate Biography of the Greatest Star* (New York: Greystone Press, 1954), pp. 362–63.

9. Joyce Haber, "Sensitive, Strong and Well in His Skin," *Los Angeles Times*, August 10, 1975, p. 31.

10. Ronald L. Davis, *op. cit.*, p. 23.

11. *Ibid.*

12. *Ibid.*, p. 24.

13. Irene Sharaff, *Broadway & Hollywood* (New York: Van Nostrand Reinhold Company, 1976), p. 82.

14. Rick Du Brow, "Bald in Western," *Newark Evening News*, May 1, 1960.

15. Otis L. Guernsey, Jr., "The King and I," *Herald Tribune*, March 30, 1950.

16. Rock Brynner, *Yul: The Man Who Would Be a King* (New York: Simon & Schuster, 1989), pp. 57–58.

17. Michael Parkinson, *Selected Interviews from the Television Series* (London: Elm Tree Books, 1975), p. 97.

18. Irene Sharaff, *op. cit.*, p. 92.

19. H. Paul Jeffers, *Sal Mineo: His Life, Murder, and Mystery* (New York: Carroll & Graf, 2000), pp. 9–10.

20. *Ibid.*

21. *Ibid.*, p. 11.

22. *Ibid.*, p. 12.

23. *Ibid.*, p. 14.

24. Myrna Katz Frommer and Harvey Frommer, *It Happened on Broadway* (New York: Harcourt Brace & Company, 1998), p. 111.

25. Hy Gardner, *Coast to Coast.*

26. Cameron Shipp, "Self-Made Mystery Man," *Redbook Magazine*, May 19, 1958, p. 97.

27. *Ibid.*

28. Michael Parkinson, *op. cit.*, p. 97.

29. Ronald L. Davis, *op. cit.*, pp. 28–29.

30. Jhan Robbins, *Yul Brynner: The Inscrutable King* (New York: Dodd, Mead & Company, 1987), p. 52.

Chapter 5

1. Maria Riva, *Marlene Dietrich* (London: Bloomsbury, 1992), p. 617.
2. Rock Brynner, *op. cit.*, p. 61–62.
3. Maria Riva, *op. cit.*, p. 621.
4. *Ibid.*, p. 650.
5. Ean Wood, *Dietrich: A Biography* (London: Sanctuary, 2002), p. 275.
6. Don Ross, "Backstage with the King of Siam," *New York Herald Tribune*, September 2, 1951, sec. 4, p. 12.
7. Virginia Brynner, "The King and I," *Good Housekeeping*, July 1955, p. 53.
8. Charles Castle, *Joan Crawford: The Raging Star* (London: New English Library, 1977), p. 132.
9. Christina Crawford, *Mommie Dearest* (New York: William Morrow and Company, 1978), pp. 67–68.
10. Jane Ellen Wayne, *Crawford's Men* (New York: Prentice Hall, 1988), p. 185.
11. "Yul Brynner's Nose Hurt in Stage Mishap," *Los Angeles Times*, June 21, 1954.
12. Cameron Shipp, *op. cit.*, p. 32.
13. Joel Sayre, "Yul Brynner: Why Do Women Find Him Irresistible," *Collier's*, July 6, 1956, p. 33.
14. Rock Brynner, *op. cit.*, p. 75.

Chapter 6

1. Michael Parkinson, *op. cit.*, p. 97.
2. Cecil B. DeMille, *The Autobiography of Cecil B. DeMille* (New York: Garland Publishing, 1985), p. 416.
3. Henry Wilcoxon, *Lionheart in Hollywood: The Autobiography of Henry Wilcoxon* (Metuchen, NJ: The Scarecrow Press, 1991), p. 307.
4. Ronald B. Davis, *op. cit.*, p. 38.
5. Charlton Heston, *In the Arena* (New York: Simon & Schuster, 1995), p. 344.
6. *Ibid.*, p. 342.
7. Katherine Orrison, *Written in Stone: Making DeMille's Epic The Ten Commandments*, (Lanham, MD: Vestal Press, 1999), p. 121–22.
8. Anne Baxter, *Intermission: A True Tale* (New York: G.P. Putnam, 1976), p. 314.
9. "Yul Brynner's Candid Camera Covers *The Ten Commandments*," *Collier's*, September 14, 1956, p. 92.
10. *Ibid.*
11. Yul Brynner, *Yul Brynner on Life and Acting*, sound recording (North Hollywood: Center for Cassette Studies, 1974).
12. Hedda Hopper, "You'll Love Yul!," *Chicago Tribune Magazine*, August 28, 1955, p. 18.
13. Cecil B. DeMille, *op. cit.*, p. 416.
14. Pete Martin, *op. cit.*, p. 350.
15. Maria Riva, *op. cit.*, p. 691.
16. Donald Spoto, *Blue Angel: The Life of Marlene Dietrich* (New York: Cooper Square Press, 2000), p. 225.
17. Rock Brynner, *op. cit.*, p. 90.

Chapter 7

1. Erik Braun, *Deborah Kerr* (New York: St. Martin's Press, 1977), p. 153.
2. "Yul Brynner — Golden Egged," *op. cit.*, p.103.
3. Gene Feldman, *op. cit.*
4. Herbert Whittaker, "Deborah Kerr's Mind Is Made Up — Broadway Is Out," *Globe and Mail*, December 17, 1973.
5. Erik Braun, *op. cit.*, p. 154.
6. Joel Sayre, *op. cit.*, p. 38.
7. Geoffrey Block, *The Richard Rodgers Reader* (New York: Oxford University Press, 2002), p. 102.
8. Bosley Crowther, *New York Times*, June 29, 1956, sec. 6, p. 15.
9. Ronald L. Davis, *op. cit.*, pp. 31–32.
10. Robert Cushman and Stacey Endress, *Hollywood at Your Feet* (Los Angeles: Pomegrate Press, 1992), p. 257.
11. Helen Hayes, *My Life in Three Acts* (New York: Harcourt, Brace & Jovanovich, 1990), p. 189.
12. Ingrid Bergman, *My Story* (New York: Delacorte Press, 1980), p. 333.
13. Rock Brynner, *op. cit.*, p. 95.
14. Maria Riva, *op. cit.* p. 674.
15. "Yul Brynner — Golden Egghead," *op. cit.*, p. 102.
16. Bosley Crowther, *The New York Times*, December 14, 1956, sec. 6, p. 35.
17. Ingrid Bergman, *op. cit.*, p. 339.
18. Kermit Joyce, "Yul Brynner Academy Award Faker," *QJ*, September 1956.

19. *Tonight Show*, NBC, September 23, 1983.

20. Richard Brooks, "On Bringing the 'Karamazovs' to the Screen."

21. Patrick Brion, *Richard Brooks* (Paris: Chêne, 1986), p. 135.

22. Pete Martin, *op. cit.*, p. 341.

23. Claire Bloom, *Leaving a Doll's House* (New York: Little, Brown and Company, 1996), pp. 98–99.

24. Oriana Fallaci, *I 7 peccati di Hollywood* (Milano: Longanesi, 1958), pp. 189–91.

25. *Ibid.*

26. Peter Guralnick, *Last Train to Memphis: The Rise of Elvis Presley* (New York: Little, Brown and Company, 1994), p. 418.

27. "Flatly Deny Catcalls at Cannes for *Karamazov*," *Variety*, May 21, 1956.

28. Bosley Crowther, *The New York Times*, February 21, 1958, sec. 2, p. 18.

29. Hedda Hopper, "What's a Million to Yul?," *Chicago Sunday Tribune Magazine*, November 24, 1957.

30. Patrick McGilligan, *Alfred Hitchcock: A Life in the Darkness and Light* (New York: ReganBooks, 2004), p. 568.

31. Natasha Fraser Cavassoni, *op. cit.*, p. 215.

32. Henry Wilcoxon, *op. cit.*, p. 322.

33. Jesse L. Lasky, Jr., *Whatever Happened to Hollywood?* (New York: Funk & Wagnalls, 1975), p. 324.

34. *Ibid.*, p. 325

35. *Ibid.*

36. Anthony Quinn, *One Man Tango* (New York: HarperCollins, 1995), p. 263.

37. Edith Head, *The Dress Doctor* (New York: Little, Brown and Company, 1959), p. 152.

38. Charlton Heston, *op. cit.*, p. 177.

39. Claire Bloom, *op. cit.*, p. 99.

40. Joe Hyams, "Yul Brynner Is Also a Skilled Photographer," *Herald Tribune*, 1957.

41. Charles Higham, *Cecil B. DeMille* (New York: Da Capo Press, 1973), p. 311.

42. "Anthony Quinn," *Film and Filming*, February 1970, p. 9.

Chapter 8

1. Sheridan Morley, *Robert: My Father* (London: Weindenfeld and Nicolson, 1993), p. 144.

2. Russ Bradley, "It's Never Dull With Yul," *Sunday News*, August 10, 1958, p. 77.

3. *Ibid.*

4. Beverly Gray, *Ron Howard: From Mayberry to the Moon ... and Beyond* (Nashville: Rutledge Hill Press, 2003), p. 10.

5. Dorothy Roe, "Yul's Wife Does Research," *Baltimore Sun*, December 15, 1958.

6. Louella Parsons, "Yul Lets His Hair Down," *Los Angeles Examiner*, November 26, 1958, p. 33.

7. Kirk Douglas, *The Ragman's Son* (New York: Simon & Schuster, 1988), pp. 304–05.

8. *Ibid.*

9. Carlton Jackson, *op. cit.*, p. 48.

10. Joe Morella and Edward Z. Epstein, *Paul and Joanne: A Biography of Paul Newman and Joanne Woodward* (New York: Delacorte Press, 1988), p. 75.

11. Jerry Wald, "From Faulkner to Film," *Saturday Review*, 1959, p. 42.

12. Gabriel Miller, *Martin Ritt: Interviews* (Jackson: University Press of Mississippi, 2002), p. 116.

13. Luis Canales, *Imperial Gina: The Strictly Unauthorized Biography of Gina Lollobrigida* (Brookline Village, MA: Branden Publishing, 1990), p. 124.

14. George Sanders, "Memoirs of a Cad," *Good Housekeeping*, April 1960, pp. 63–64.

15. Nancy Dowd and David Shepard, *King Vidor* (Meteuchen, NJ: The Scarecrow Press, 1988), p. 275.

16. Jean-Pierre Aumont, *Dis-moi d'abord que tu m'aimes* (Paris: Flammarion, 1986), pp. 155–56.

17. Luis Canales, *op. cit.*, p. 125.

18. Godfrey Morgan, "A Spectacle Is Saved," *Picturegoer*, March 7, 1959, p. 9.

19. Raymond Durgnat and Scott Simmon, *King Vidor, American* (Berkley: University of California Press, 1988), p. 301.

20. Rock Brynner, *op. cit.*, p. 117.

21. Joe Hyams, "Yul Brynner Reveals

Himself as Philatelist," *Los Angeles Times*, April 19, 1959.

22. Yul Brynner, *Bringing Forth the Children* (New York: McGraw Hill, 1960), p. 3.

23. Alvin H. Marill, "Yul Brynner," *Films in Review*, October 1970, Vol. xxi, No. 8, p. 466.

24. Samuel G. Freedman, "When An Actor Is Taken Captive by a Single Role," *The New York Times*, December 23, 1984, p. 5.

25. Joseph Andrew Camper, *Stanley Donen* (Metuchen, NJ: The Scarecrow Press, 1983), p. 151.

26. Eve Golden, *The Brief, Madcap Life of Kay Kendall* (Lexington: University of Kentucky Press, 2002), p. 143.

27. *Ibid.*, p.145

28. Suzanne Jill Levine, *Manuel Puig and the Spider Woman. His Life and Fictions* (New York: Farrar Straus Giroux, 2000), p. 122.

29. *Ibid.*, p.113

30. Louella Parsons, "Yul Brynner — Man of Mystery," *Los Angeles Examiner*, November 29, 1959.

31. Joseph Andrew Camper, *op. cit.*, p. 155.

32. Jhan Robbins, *op. cit.*, p. 80.

33. Joseph Andrew Camper, *op. cit.*, p. 157.

34. Gene Feldman, *op. cit.*

35. *Ibid.*

Chapter 9

1. Anthony Quinn, *op. cit.*, p. 263.

2. "Quinn Sues Brynner on 'Magnificent 7,'" *Los Angeles Times*, February 9, 1960.

3. Michael Parkinson, *op. cit.*, p. 98.

4. Christopher Sandford, *McQueen: The Biography* (New York: HarperCollins Entertainment, 2001), p. 109.

5. Marshall Terrill, *Steve McQueen: Portrait of an American Rebel* (New York: Donald I. Fine, 1993), p. 62.

6. John Woodforde, *The History of Vanity* (New York: St. Martin's Press, 1992), p. xxiv.

7. Malachy McCoy, *Steve McQueen.*

The Unauthorized Biography (Chicago: Henry Regnery Company, 1974), p. 87.

8. Marshall Terrill, *op. cit.*, p. 62.

9. Gene Feldman, *op. cit.*

10. "Brynner Glad He Took Year's Absence From Movie-Making," *The Morning Telegraph*, July 15, 1961.

11. Eugene Archer, *The New York Times*, July 12, 1962, sec. 3, p. 19.

12. Ronald Neame, *Straight from the Horse's Mouth's* (Lanham, MD: The Scarecrow Press, 2003), p. 176.

13. Paul H. Jeffers, *op. cit.*, pp. 106–07.

14. Edwin Miller, *Seventeen Interviews: Film Stars and Superstars* (New York: Macmillan, 1970), p. 102.

15. Tony Curis, *Tony Curtis. The Autobiography* (New York: Morrow, 1993), pp. 204–05.

16. Gene Feldman, *op. cit.*

17. Ray Falk, "On a Japanese Flight," *The New York Times*, October 19, 1962.

18. Howard Thompson, *The New York Times*, April 23, 1964, sec. 1, p. 34.

19. Yul Brynner, *Yul Brynner on Life and Acting*, sound recording (North Hollywood: Center for Cassette Studies, 1974).

20. "Yul Brynner Starts School for Youngsters," *Citizen News*, December 17, 1962.

Chapter 10

1. Philip K. Scheuer, "Yul Brynner's Only for 'Must' Movies," *Los Angeles Times*, May 14, 1963.

2. Stanley Kramer, *A Mad, Mad, Mad, Mad World* (New York: Harcourt, Brace & Company, 1997), p. 231.

3. Allen Eyles, "Invitation to a Gunfighter," *Films and Filming*, July 1965.

4. Julia Hantopol Hirsh, *The Sound of Music: The Making of America's Favorite Movie* (Chicago: Contemporary Books, 1993), p. 53.

5. Peter Manso, *Marlon Brando. The Biography* (New York: Hyperion, 1994), p. 581.

6. Marlon Brando, *Songs My Mother Taught Me* (New York: Random House, 1994), pp. 307–09.

7. Sally Quinn, "The King Sails Back," *Los Angeles Times*, June 8, 1975, p. 64.

8. Peter Manso, *op. cit.*, pp. 582–83.

9. Jhan Robbins, *op. cit.*, p. 91.

10. Melville Shavelson, *How to Make a Jewish Movie* (Englewood Cliffs, NJ: Prentice-Hall, 1971), pp. 56–57.

11. *Ibid.*, p. 196.

12. Zinn Arthur, *Shooting Superstars* (Chicago: Artique Press, 1990), p. 70.

13. Melville Shavelson, *op. cit.*, p. 196.

14. Mia Farrow, *What Falls Away* (New York: Nan A. Telese, 1997), p. 96.

15. George Jacobs, *Mr. S. My Life with Frank Sinatra* (New York: HarperEntertainment, 2003), p. 226.

16. "Brynner Gives Up His U.S. Passport for Family's Sake," *The New York Times*, June 22, 1965.

17. Tony Williams, *Larry Cohen: The Radical Allegories of an Independent Filmmaker* (Jefferson, NC: McFarland & Company, 1997) p. 297.

18. *Ibid.*, p. 298.

19. Michael Munn, *Trevor Howard: The Man and His Films* (Chelsea, MI: Scarborough House, 1990), pp. 109–10.

20. Michael Munn, *Hollywood Rogues* (London: Robson Books, 1992), p. 133.

21. Michael Munn, *Trevor Howard, op. cit.*, p. 111.

22. Britt Ekland, *True Britt* (Englewood Cliffs, NJ: Prentice-Hall, 1980), p. 80.

23. Patrick McGilligan, *Tender Comrades: A Backstory of the Hollywood Black List* (New York: St. Martin's Press, 1997), p. 653.

24. Graham Stark, *Stark Naked: The Autobiography of Graham Stark* (London: Sanctuary, 2003), pp. 115–16.

25. *Ibid.*, p.116.

Chapter 11

1. Marshall Fine, *Bloody Sam: The Life and Films of Sam Peckinpah* (New York: Donald I. Fine, 1991), p. 111.

2. *Ibid.*

3. Mark Litwak, *Reel Power: The Struggle for Influence and Success in the New Hollywood* (New York: Morrow, 1986), p. 158.

4. Lee Server, *Robert Mitchum. Baby I Don't Care* (New York: St. Martin's Press, 2001), pp. 418–19.

5. Rock Brynner, *op. cit.*, p. 174.

6. Wes Herschensohn, *Resurrection in Cannes: The Making of The Picasso Summer* (Cranbury, NJ: A.S. Barnes and Company, 1979), pp. 246–47.

7. Yul Brynner, *Yul Brynner on Life and Acting*, sound recording (North Hollywood: Center for Cassette Studies, 1974).

8. Anne Edwards, *A Remarkable Woman: A Biography of Katharine Hepburn* (New York: Morrow, 1989), p. 338.

9. Carroll Harrison, "Star Almost Killed," *Los Angeles Herald-Examiner*, January 10, 1969.

10. Halsey Raines, " 'Indelible' Yul in Yugoslavia," *Hollywood Citizen-News*, January 14, 1969.

11. Ed Sanders, *The Family: The Manson Group and His Aftermath* (New York: Dutton, 1971), p. 334.

12. Paul Krassner, *Confessions of a Raving, Unconfined Nut* (New York: Simon & Schuster, 1993), p. 197.

13. Rock Brynner, *op. cit.*, pp 178–79.

14. Gene Feldman, *op. cit.*

15. Anita Pereire and Gabrielle van Zuylen, *Gardens of France* (New York: Harmony Books, 1983), p. 80.

16. Susan Rogers, "Yul Brynner Finally Found Life of Peace," *The Chronicle Herald*, August 7, 1972.

17. Kirk Douglas, *op. cit.*, p. 411.

18. C. Thurlow, *Sexo, surrealismo, Dalí yo. Las memorias de Carlos Lozano* (Barcelona: RBA Libros, 2001), p. 157.

19. Gilles Verlant, *Gainsbourg* (Paris: Albin Michael, 2000), p. 418.

20. Jhan Robbins, *op. cit.*, pp. 99–100.

21. Nancy Holmes, "The Music Would Go Waroomph, and We Would Start to Dance," *TV Guide*, September 16, 1972, p. 29.

22. Jhan Robbins, *op. cit.*, p. 103.

23. David Hemmings, *Blow-Up and Other Exaggerations* (London: Robson Books, 2004), p. 271.

24. Dirk Bogarde, *An Orderly Man* (New York: Knopf, 1983), p. 147.

Chapter 12

1. Stuart Kaminsky, "Westworld," *Cinefantastique*, 1973.
2. Paul N. Lazarus III, *The Movie Producer* (New York: Barnes & Noble Books, 1985), p. 123.
3. Giovanni Mongini, *Storia del cinema di fantascienza 2* (Roma: Fanucci, 1977), p,. 286.
4. Hazel Mosley, "Arts & Pleasures," *Women's Wear Daily*, March 15, 1976, p. 11.
5. Massimo Ranieri, interview with the author, New York, New York, November 25, 2004.
6. Kathryn Leigh Scott, *The Bunny Years* (New York: Henry Holt, 1990), p. 16
7. "The Brynners," *The Vancouver Sun*, April 11, 1975.
8. "Yul Brynner," *The Vancouver Sun*, April 23, 1975.
9. Yul Brynner, *Yul Brynner on Life and Acting*, sound recording (North Hollywood: Center for Cassette Studies, 1974).
10. Sally Quinn, *op. cit.*, p. 50.
11. William Glover, "Brynner Continues *Odyssey* to Stage," *Vancouver Sun*, January 6, 1975.
12. Sally Quinn, *op. cit.*, p. 50.
13. "Plaza Settles Brynner's Stomach," *New York Magazine*, June 18, 1979.
14. Maria Riva, *op. cit.*, p. 750.
15. Ken Mandelbaum, *Not Since Carrie* (New York: St. Martin's Press, 1991), p. 32.
16. Patricia O' Haire, "Sailing to Broadway," *Daily News*, November 20, 1975.
17. *Ibid.*
18. Louis Calta, "After Year's Tour, 'Homer' Dies Quickly on Broadway," *The New York Times*, January 8, 1976, p. 28.
19. "Announcement," *The Hollywood Reporter*, August 13, 1976.

Chapter 13

1. Roderick Mann, "Actor with an Appetite Fit for a King," *Los Angeles Times*, July 7, 1978, p. 49.
2. John Brady, *The Craft of the Screenwriter* (New York: Touchstone, 1981), p. 208.
3. Stephen M. Silverman, *Public Spectacles* (New York: Dutton, 1981), p. 56.
4. Dennis McGovern and Deborah Grace Winer, *Sing Out Louise!* (New York: Schirmer Books, 1996), pp. 168–69.
5. *Ibid.*, p. 171.
6. Charles Mitchner, "Long Live the King," *Newsweek*, May 16, 1977, p. 103.
7. Samuel G. Freedman, "When an Actor Is Taken Captive by a Single Role," *The New York Times*, December 23, 1984, p. 5.
8. Stephen M. Silverman, *op. cit.*, p. 55.
9. Carol Channing, *op. cit.*, p. 26.
10. "Brynner Student Mourns," *The Provinces*, October 11, 1985.
11. Samuel G. Freedman, *op. cit.*, p. 5.
12. Rock Brynner, *op. cit.*, p. 218.
13. *Ibid.*, p. 199.
14. J. Parrott, *Los Angeles Times*, April 12, 1978.
15. Jane F. Lane, "Jacqueline de la Chaume Being Herself," *W Magazine*, January 27, 1987, p. 36.
16. "Born to Be King," *Globe*, October 29, 1985, p. 37.
17. Robert T. Sommers, *Golf Anecdotes* (New York: Oxford University Press, 1995), p. 287.
18. Yul Brynner and Susan Reed, *The Yul Brynner Cookbook* (New York: Stein and Day, 1983).
19. Army Archerd, "Just for Variety," *Variety*, September 14, 1983.
20. Gene Feldman, *op. cit.*
21. Cindy Adams, "The Strange Case of Yul Brynner's Cancer," *Good Housekeeping*, November 1985, p. 68.
22. *Ibid.*, p. 70.
23. Angela Fox Dunn, "Yul Brynner, Gypsy King," *The Province*, October 20, 1985, p. 5.
24. Bob Herbert, "Reduced to Dust," *The New York Times*, May 12, 1997, sec. A, p. 15.
25. William G. Cahan, *No Stranger to Tears* (New York: Random House, 1992), p. 233.
26. Dennis McGovern and Deborah Grace Winer, *op. cit.*, p. 168.

27. *Ibid.*

28. Nan Robertson, "Farewell Performance for Brynner in 'King and I,'" *The New York Times*, July 1, 1985, sec. C, p. 11.

29. "Con Yul Brynner il cinema perde un simpatico eroe," *Il Corriere della sera*, October 11, 1985, p. 23.

30. Claire Bloom, *op. cit.*, p. 101.

31. Stephen M. Silverman, *Where There's a Will* ... (New York: Harper-Collins, 1991), p. 32.

32. Nan Robertson, "Brynner's Friends Reminisce at Actor's Memorial Service," *The New York Times*, July 1, 1985, sec. B, p. 6.

33. "Yul's Warning from the Grave," *The Province*, February 20, 1986, p. 24.

Bibliography

Aldrich Stoddard, Richard. *Gertrude Lawrence as Mrs. A.* New York: Greystone Press, 1954.

Arthur, Zinn. *Shooting Superstars.* Chicago: Artique Press, 1990.

Aumont Jean-Pierre. *Dis-moi d'abord que tu m'aimes.* Paris: Flammarion, 1986.

_____. *Sun and Shadow.* New York: Norton, 1977.

Aylesworth, Thomas G. *Broadway to Hollywood: Musicals from Stage to Screen.* New York: Gallery Books, 1985.

Bacall, Lauren. *Now.* New York: Knopf, 1994.

Bach, Steven. *Marlene Dietrich: Life and Legend.* New York: Da Capo Press, 2000.

Barraciu, Angelo. *Gina Lollobrigida. Una vita che sa di leggenda.* Saluzzo: Edizioni Vitalita,1968.

Baxter, Anne. *Intermission: A True Tale.* New York: Putman, 1976.

Berg, Chuck, and Tom Erskine. *The Encyclopedia of Orson Welles.* New York: Facts on File, 2003.

Bergman, Ingrid, and Alan Burgess. *La mia storia.* Milan: Mondadori, 1981.

Bernstein, Walter. *Inside Out. A Memoir of the Blacklist.* New York: Knopf, 1996.

Block, Geoffrey. *The Richard Rodgers Reader.* New York: Oxford University Press, 2002.

Bloom, Claire. *Leaving a Doll's House.* Boston: Little, Brown and Company, 1996.

Blum, Daniel. *Great Stars of the American Stage.* New York: Greenberg, 1952.

Blumenthal, Ralph. *Stork Club.* Boston: Little, Brown and Company, 2001.

Bogarde, Dirk. *An Orderly Man.* New York: Knopf, 1983.

Brady, John. *The Craft of the Screenwriter.* New York: Touchstone, 1981.

Brando, Marlon. *Songs My Mother Taught Me.* New York: Random House, 1994.

Braun, Eric. *Deborah Kerr.* New York: St. Martin's Press, 1977.

Brincourt, Marc. *On Set and Off Guard.* London: Thames and Hudson, 2002.

Brion, Patrick. *Richard Brooks.* Paris: Chene, 1986.

Brown, May Wale. *Reel Life on Hollywood Movie Sets.* Riverside, CA: Ariadne Press, 1995.

Brown, Peter Harry, and Pat H. Broeske. *Down at the End of Lonely Street.* New York: Dutton, 1997.

Brynner, Rock. *Yul. The Man Who Would Be King.* New York: Simon & Schuster, 1989.

Brynner, Victoria. *Yul Brynner: Photographer.* New York: Abrams, 1996.

Brynner, Yul, and Susan Reed. *Yul Brynner Cookbook.* New York: Stein and Day, 1983.

Buhle, Paul, and Dave Wagner. *A Very Dangerous Citizen*. Berkeley: University of California Press, 2001.

Burkart, Jeff, and Bruce Stuart. *Hollywood's First Choices*. New York: Crown Trade, 1994.

Cahan,William G. . *No Stranger to Tears: A Surgeon's Story*. New York: Random House, 1992.

Camper, Joseph Andrew. *Stanley Donen*. Metuchen, NJ: The Scarecrow Press, 1983.

Canales, Luis. *Imperial Gina: The Strictly Unauthorized of Gina Lollobrigida*. Boston: Braden Publishing Company, 1990.

Carney, Ray. *Cassavetes on Cassavetes*. New York: Faber and Faber, 2001.

Castle, Charles. *Joan Crawford: The Raging Star*. London: New English Library, 1977.

_____. *Noel*. New York: Doubleday, 1972.

Channing, Carol. *Just Lucky I Guess*. New York: Simon & Schuster, 2002.

Chekhov, Michael. *To the Actor: On the Technique of Acting*. New York: Harper & Row, 1953.

Clarke, Gerald. *Get Happy: The Life of Judy Garland*. New York: Random House, 2000.

Clergue, Lucien. *Jean Cocteau and the Testament of Orpheus*. New York: Viking Studio, 2001.

Clooney, Rosemary. *Girl Singer: An Autobiography*. New York: Random House, 1999.

Cohan, Steven. *Masked Men: Masculinity and the Movies in the Fifties*. Bloomington: Indiana University Press, 1997.

Comizio, Ermanno. *Vidor*. Firenze: La Nuova Italia, 1986.

Crawford, Christina. *Mammina Cara*. Milano: Mondatori, 1979.

Cunningham, Frank R. *Film and Literary Vision*. Lexington: The University Press of Kentucky, 1991.

Curtis, Tony, and Barry Paris. *Tony Curtis: The Autobiography*. New York: Morrow, 1993.

Cushman, Robert, and Stacey Endress. *Hollywood at Your Feet*. Los Angeles: Pomegrate Press, 1992.

DeMille, Cecil B., and Donald Hayne. *The Autobiography of Cecil B. DeMille*. New York: Garland Publishing, 1985.

Douglas, Kirk. *Climbing the Mountain*. New York: Simon & Schuster, 1997.

_____. *The Ragman's Son: An Autobiography*. New York: Simon & Schuster, 1998.

Dowd, Nancy, and David Shepard. *King Vidor*. Metuchen, NJ: The Scarecrow Press, 1988.

Dunaway, Faye. *Looking for Gatsby: My Life*. New York: Simon & Schuster, 1995.

Durgnat, Raymond, and Scott Simmon. *King Vidor. American*. Berkeley: University of California Press, 1988.

Edgerton, Robert B. *Warriors of the Rising Sun*. New York: Norton, 1997.

Edward, Anne. *A Remarkable Woman: A Biography of Katharine Hepburn*. New York: Morrow, 1989.

Ekland, Britt. *True Britt*. Englewood Cliffs, NJ: Prentice-Hall, 1980.

Ellero, Roberto. *Martin Ritt*. Firenze: La Nuova Italia, 1990.

Ewen, David. *American Musical Theater*. New York: Holt, Rinehart and Winston, 1970.

_____. *The Story of America's Musical Theater*. Philadelphia: Chilton Books Co., 1968.

Fallaci, Oriana. *I 7 peccati di Hollywood*. Milano: Longanesi, 1958.

Farrow, Mia. *What Falls Away*. New York: Nan A. Talese, 1997.

Fehl, Fred. *On Broadway*. Austin: University of Texas Press, 1978.

Fine, Marshall. *Bloody Sam: The Life and the Films of Sam Peckinpah*. New York: Donald I. Fine, 1991.

Fisher, Clive. *Noel Coward*. New York: St. Martin's Press, 1992.

Fleischer, Richard. *Just Tell Me When to Cry*. New York: Carroll & Graf, 1993.

Fonda, Peter. *Don't Tell Dad*. New York: Hyperion, 1998.

Fordin, Hugh. *Getting to Know Him: A Biography of Oscar Hammerstein II*. New York: The Ungar Publishing Company, 1977.

Fowler, Karin, J. *Anne Baxter. A Bio-Bibliography*. Westport, CT: Greenwood Press, 1991.

Fraser Cavassoni, Natasha. *Sam Spiegel*. New York: Simon & Schuster, 2003.

Frommer Katz, Myrna, and Harvey Frommer. *It Happened on Broadway*. New York: Harcourt, Brace & Company, 1998.

Galbraith IV, Stuart. *The Emperor and the Wolf*. New York: Faber and Faber, 2001.

Garland, Patrick. *The Incomparable Rex Harrison*. New York: Macmillan, 1998.

Godfrey, Lionel. *Paul Newman. Superstar*. New York: St. Martin's Press, 1978.

Golden, Eve. *The Brief, Madcap Life of Kay Kendall*. Lexington: University of Kentucky Press, 2002.

Gordon, Mel. *The Stanislavsky Technique*: New York: Applause, 1987.

Gray, Beverly. *Ron Howard. From Mayberry to the Moon ... and Beyond*. Nashville: Rutledge Hill Press, 2003.

Green, Stanley. *The Rodgers and Hammerstein Story*. New York: Da Capo Press, 1963.

Guralnick, Peter. *Last Train to Memphis*. Boston: Little, Brown and Company, 1994.

Guttmacher, Peter. *Legendary Westerns*. New York: Metro Books, 1995.

Hadleigh, Boze. *Hollywood and Whine*. New York: Birch Lane Press, 1998.

_____. *Hollywood Babble On*. New York: Birch Lane Press, 1994.

Haining, Peter. *Raquel Welch. Sex Symbol to Superstar*. New York: St. Martin's Press, 1984.

Harrison, Rex. . *Rex: The Autobiography of Rex Harrison*. New York: Morrow, 1975.

Hayes, Helen. *My Life in Three Acts*. New York: Harcourt, Brace & Jovanovich, 1990.

Head, Edith. *The Dress Doctor*. Boston: Little, Brown and Company, 1959.

Hemmings, David. *Blow-Up and Other Exaggerations*. London: Robson Books, 2004.

Herschensohn, Wes. *Resurrection in Cannes. The Making of the Picasso Summer*. Cranbury, NJ: A.S. Barnes and Co., 1979.

Heston, Charlton. *Charlton Heston's Hollywood*. New York: G.T. Publishing, 1998.

_____. *In the Arena: An Autobiography*. New York: Simon & Schuster, 1995.

Higham, Charles. *Cecil B. De Mille*. New York: Da Capo Press, 1973.

_____. *Orson Welles*. New York: St. Martin's Press, 1985.

Hirsh Antopol, Julia. *The Sound of Music. The Making of America's Favorite Movie*. Chicago: Contemporary Books, 1993.

Hoare, Philip. *Noel Coward — A Biography*. London: Sinclair Stevenson, 1995.

Holston, Kim. *Richard Widmark. A Bio-Bibliography*. Westport, CT: Greenwood Press, 1990.

Houseman, John. *Front and Center*. New York: Simon & Schuster, 1979.

_____. *Unfinished Business. A Memoir*. London: Chatto & Windus, 1986.

Hyland, William G. . *Richard Rodgers*. New Haven, CT: Yale University Press, 1998.

Jackson, Carlton. *Picking Up the Tab. The Life and Movies of Martin Ritt*. Bowling Green, OH: Bowling Green State University Popular Press, 1994.

Jacobs, George. *Mr. S. My Life with Frank Sinatra*. New York: Harper Entertainment, 2003.

Jeffers, Paul H. *Sal Mineo: His Life, Murder, and Mystery*. New York: Carroll & Graf, 2000.

Keith, Slim. *Slim. Memories of a Rich and Imperfect Life*. New York: Simon & Schuster, 1990.

Knight, Vivienne. *Trevor Howard. A Gentleman and a Player*. New York: Beaufort Books, 1987.

Kramer, Stanley. *A Mad, Mad, Mad, Mad World*. New York: Harcourt Brace & Company, 1997.

Krassner, Paul. *Confessions of a Raving, Unconfined Nut: Misadventures in the Counter Culture*. New York: Simon & Schuster, 1993.

Lasky, Jesse L. *Whatever Happened to Hollywood?* New York: Funk & Wagnalls, 1975.

Lawrence, Greg. *Dance with Demon: The Life of Jerome Robbins*. New York: Putnam, 2001.

Lazarus III, Paul N. *The Movie Producer*. New York: Barnes and Noble, 1985.

Leamer, Laurence. *As Time Goes By: The Life of Ingrid Bergman*. New York: Harper & Row, 1986.

Leigh, Janet. *There Really Was a Hollywood*. New York: Doubleday, 1984.

Levine, Suzanne Jill. *Manuel Puig and the Spider Woman. His Life and Fictions*. New York: Farrar Straus Giroux, 2000.

Lintner, Bertil. *Blood Brothers*. New York: Macmillan, 2002.

Litwak, Mark. *Reel Power*. New York: Morrow, 1996.

Lyons, Arthur. *Death on the Cheap*. New York: Da Capo Press, 2000.

Mandelbaum, Ken. *Not Since Carrie*. New York: St. Martin's Press, 1991.

Manso, Peter. *Brando: The Biography*. New York: Hyperion, 1994.

Martin, Mary. *My Heart Belongs*. New York: Morrow, 1976.

Martin, Pete. *Pete Martin Calls On....* New York: Simon & Schuster, 1962.

McCoy, Malachy. *Steve McQueen*. Chicago: Henry Regnery Company, 1974.

McGillian, Patrick. *Alfred Hitchcock: A Life in the Darkness and Light*. New York: Regan Books, 2003.

_____. *Tender Comrades: A Backstory of the Hollywood Black List*. New York: St. Martin's Press, 1997.

McGovern, Tennis, and Deborah Grace Winer. *Sing Out, Louise!*. New York: Schirmer Books, 1996.

Medved, Harry. *The Fifty Worst Films of All Time*. New York: Fawcett, 1978.

Mellen, Joan. *Big Bad Wolves. Masculinity in the American Film*. New York: Pantheon, 1977.

Miller, Edwin. *Seventeen Interviews: Film Stars and Superstars*. New York: Macmillan, 1970.

Miller, Gabriel. *Martin Ritt Interviews*. Jackson: University Press of Mississippi, 2002.

Moix, Terenci. *Mis inmortales del cine Hollywood. años 50*. Barcelona: Planeta, 2001.

Mongini, Giovanni. *Storia del cinema di fantascienza. Volume secondo*. Roma: Fanucci, 1977.

Mordden, Ethan. *Rodgers & Hammerstein*. New York: Abrams, 1992.

Morella, Joe, and Edward Z. Epstein. *Paul and Joanne: A Biography of Paul Newman and Joanne Woodward*. New York: Delacorte Press, 1988.

Morley, Sheridan. *Gertrude Lawrence*. New York: McGraw-Hill, 1981.

_____. *The Private Life of Noel and Gertie*. London: Oberon Press, 1999.

_____. *Robert: My Father*. London: Weidenfeld and Nicolson, 1993.

Munn, Michael. *Charlton Heston*. New York: St. Martin's Press, 1986.

_____. *Hollywood Rogues*. London: Robson Books, 1991.

_____. *Trevor Howard: The Man and His Films*. Chelsea, MI: Scarborough House, 1990.

Nolan, Frederick. *The Sound of Their Music: The Story of Rodgers and Hammerstein*. New York: Applause, 2002.

Orrison, Katherine. *Written in Stone*. Lanham, MD: Vestal Press, 1999.

Owings, Alison. *Hey. Waitress. The USA from the Other Side of the Tray*. Berkeley: University of California Press, 2002.

Parish, James Robert, and Michael R. Pitts. *The Great Western Pictures*. Metuchen, NJ: The Scarecrow Press, 1976.

Parkinson, Michael. *Selected Interviews from the Television Series*. London: Elm Tree Books, 1975.

Pasciuto, Bernard. *La double mort de Romy*. Paris: Albin Michael, 2002.

Payn, Graham, and Sheridan Morley. *The Noel Coward Diaries*. New York: Da Capo Press, 1982.

Pererire, Anita, and Gabrielle Van Zuylen. *Gardens of France*. New York: Harmony Books, 1983.

Pettigrew, Terence. *Trevor Howard: A Personal Biography*. London: Peter Owen, 2001.

Pitts, Michael R. *Charles Bronson*. Jefferson, NC: McFarland, 1999.

Ponzi, Maurizio. *The Films of Gina Lollobrigida*. Secaucus, NJ: Citadel Press, 1998.

Power, Romina. *Cercando Mio Padre*. Roma: Gremese Editore, 1998.

Quinn, Anthony. *One Man Tango*. New York: HarperCollins, 1995.

Quirk, Lawrence J. *The Films of Ingrid Bergman*. Secaucus, NJ: Citadel Press, 1970.

Reagan, Nancy. *Nancy Reagan*. New York: Morrow, 1980.

Riva, Maria. *Marlene Dietrich*. London: Bloomsbury, 1992.

Robbins, Jhan. *Yul Brynner: The Inscrutable King*. New York: Dodd, Mead & Co., 1987.

Roberts, Jerry. *Robert Mitchum. A Bio-Bibliography*. Westport, CT: Greenwood Press, 1992.

Rodgers, Richard. *Musical Stages: An Autobiography*. New York: Random House, 1975.

Sanders, Ed. *The Family: The Manson Group and Its Aftermath*. New York: Dutton, 1971.

Sanders, George. *Memoirs of a Professional Cad*. Metuchen, NJ: The Scarecrow Press, 1992.

Sandford, Christopher. *McQueen. The Biography*. New York: HarperCollins Entertainment, 2001.

Schickel, Richard. *Brando. A Life in Our Times*. New York: Athenaum, 1991.

Secrest, Meryle. *Somewhere for Me: A Biography of Richard Rodgers*. New York: Knopf, 2001.

Server, Lee. *Robert Mitchum: Baby, I Don't Care*. New York: St. Martin's Press, 2001.

Sharaff, Irene. *Broadway & Hollywood*. New York: Van Nostrand Reinholt Co., 1976.

Shavelson, Melville. *How to Make a Jewish Movie*. Englewood Cliffs, NJ: Prentice-Hall, 1974.

Sheedy, Helen. *Margo. The Life and Theatre of Margo Jones*. Dallas: Southern Methodist University Press, 1989.

Silverman, Stephen M. *Dancing on the Ceiling*. New York: Knopf, 1996.

_____. *Public Spectacles*. New York: Dutton, 1981.

_____. *Where There's a Will....* New York: HarperCollins, 1991.

Simon, John. *Movie Into Film*. New York: The Dial Press, 1971.

Smith, Cecil. *Musical Comedy in America*. New York: Theatre Arts Books, 1950.

Sommert, Robert T. *Golf Anecdotes*. New York: Oxford University Press, 1995.

Spiegel, Penina. *McQueen: The Untold Story of a Bad Boy in Hollywood*. New York: Doubleday, 1986.

Spoto, Donald. *Blue Angel. The Life of Marlene Dietrich*. New York: Cooper Square Press, 2002.

_____. *Notorious. La vita di Ingrid Bergman*. Torino: Lindau, 2000.

Stark, Graham. *Stark Naked: The Autobiography of Graham Stark*. London: Sanctuary, 2003.

Suntree, Susan. *Rita Moreno*. New York: Chelsea House Publishers, 1993.

Suskin, Steven. *More Opening Nights on Broadway*. New York: Schirmer Books, 1997.

Sweeney, Kevin. *Henry Fonda. A Bio-Bibliography*. Westport, CT: Greenwood Press, 1992.

Tapert, Annette. *The Power of Style*. New York: Crown, 1994.

Tashman, George. *I Love You Clark Gable, Etc.: Male Sex Symbols of the Silver Screen*. Richmond, CA: Brombacher Books, 1976.

Teichmann, Howard. *Fonda: My Life*. New York: New American Library, 1981.

Terrill, Marshal. *Steve McQueen. A Portrait of an American Rebel*. New York: Donald I. Fine, 1993.

Thomas, Tony. *The Films of Henry Fonda*. Secaucus, NJ: Citadel Press, 1983.

_____. *The Films of Kirk Douglas*. Secaucus, NJ: Citadel Press, 1972.

Thurlow, Clifford. *Sex Surrealism. Dali and Me*. Penryn, Cornwall: Razor Books, 2000.

Tims, Hilton. *Erich Maria Remarque. The Last Romantic*. New York: Carroll & Graf, 2003.

Van Der Beets Richard. *George Sanders: An Exhausted Life*. London: Madison Books, 1990.

Verlant, Gilles. *Gainsbourg*. Paris: Albin Michel, 2000.

Wade, Don. *And Then Jack Said to Arnie....* Lincolnwood, IL: Contemporary Books, 1991.

Walzer, Alexander. *Fatal Charm: The Life of Rex Harrison*. New York: St. Martin's Press, 1992.

Wander, Bonanno Margaret. *Angela Lansbury: A Biography*. New York: St. Martin's Press, 1987.

Warner, Denis, and Peggy Warner. *The Tide at Sunrise*. London: Frank Cass, 2002.

Wayne, Jane Ellen. *Crawford's Men*. New York: Prentice Hall, 1988.

_____. *The Golden Girls of MGM*. New York: Carroll & Graf, 2003.

_____. *Marilyn's Men*. New York: St. Martin's Press, 1992.

Weddle, David. *If They Move ... Kill 'Em!* New York: Grove Press, 1994.

Welles, Orson, and Peter Bogdanovich. *This Is Orson Welles*. New York: Harper-Collins, 1992.

Wells, Lawrence Mary. *A Big Life in Advertising*. New York: Knopf, 2002.

Wilcoxon, Henry. *Lionheart: The Autobiography of Henry Wilcoxon*. Metuchen, NJ: The Scarecrow Press, 1991.

Williams, Tony. *Larry Cohen: The Radical Allegories of an Independent Filmmaker*. Jefferson, NC: McFarland, 1999.

Wood, Ean. *Dietrich: A Biography*. London: Sanctuary, 2002.

Woodforde, John. *The History of Vanity*. New York: St. Martin's Press, 1992.

Zollo, Paul. *Hollywood Remembered*. New York: Cooper Square Press, 2002.

Index

Ace in the Hole 94
Adams, Cindy 154
Adios Sabata 131
Adler, Buddy 60
Aimée, Anouk 76
Aimez vous Brahms? 98
Alton, John 66
Anastasia 1, 60–64, 75, 113
Anderson, Michael 105, 106
Anna and the King of Siam 31
Annakin, Ken 120
L'Annonce Faite à Marie 17
Antonioni, Michelangelo 133
Arnold, Elliott 105
Arthur, Zinn 113
Attenborough, Richard 127
Aumont, Jean Pierre 82–83

Bacall, Lauren 144
Balsam, Martin 139
Bancroft, Anne 26, 39
Barnes, Howard 22
Bartley, Tony 76
Basehart, Richard 68
The Battle on the River Neretva 127–128
Baur, Harry 101
Baxter, Anne 51–52
Beatty, Warren 75, 128
A Beautiful Mind 76
Bedeck, Lazlo 28–29
Ben-Gurion, David 114
Benjamin, Robert 136
Berger, Senta 113
Bergman, Ingrid 60–64, 98
Berman, Pandro S. 65
Bernarhard, Wicki 112
Bernstein, Elmer 98, 118
Bernstein, Walter 94
Bertrand, Paul 118
Birkin, Jane 131–132

Blagovidova, Marousia 5–6, 7, 8, 14–15, 17–18
Blagovidova, Vera 5–6, 13
Bloom, Claire 65, 68–69, 72, 73, 158
Blow-Up 133
Bogarde, Dirk 135
Bolton, Guy 60
Bonnie and Clyde 123
Bosé, Lucia 89, 125
Bowen, Elizabeth 18
Boyer, Charles 72
Brackett, Charles 56, 57
Brando, Marlon 23, 56, 65, 110–112
Bronson, Charles 94, 96, 97, 100, 124, 125
Brooks, Richard 65–66, 69, 70, 75
The Brothers Karamazov 65–70, 71, 105
Bruner, Johannes 4
Bruner, Julius 5
Bryner, Boris 5–6, 14, 28
Bryner, Felix 5
Bryner, Irena 157, 158
Bryner, Vera 5, 7, 8, 14, 20, 23, 122
Brynner, Melody 140–141, 158
Brynner, Mia 140–141, 158
Brynner, Rock (Rocky) 4, 23–24, 25–26, 28, 42, 44, 48, 55, 62, 78, 85, 92, 104, 113–114, 122, 129, 130, 140–141, 145–146, 150, 155, 156, 158
Brynner, Victoria 14, 92, 107, 117, 140–141, 153, 158, 160
The Buccaneer 70, 75
Buccella, Maria Grazia 124
Bucholtz, Horst 94, 97, 100
Buchwald, Art 89
Bulajic, Veljko 128

Cahan, William 155–156
Camille 13
Cardinale, Claudia 104
Caron, Leslie 104
Carousel 30

195

Carpenter, Constance 41
Cassidy, Claudia 22
Cast a Giant Shadow 112–116, 130
Catlow 132
Chakiris, George 105, 109
Chamberlain, Richard 126
Chandler, Jeff 50
Channing, Carol 28, 149
Chapman, Eddie 118
Chau, Richard 149–150
Chekhov, Michael 12–13, 14, 15, 16, 47, 51, 144
Chester, Hal 121
Claudel, Paul 17
Cleese, John 127
Cleopatra 53
Cobb, Lee 65, 68
Coburn, James 94, 97, 100
Cocteau, Jean 69, 88–89, 125, 129
Cohen, Larry 116, 117, 118
Colette 88
Cooper, Gary 17, 81
Coppola, Francis Ford 137
Cotten, Joseph 87
Coward, Noël 30, 32, 90, 127
Cox, Wally 110
Crawford, Cristina 46–47
Crawford, Joan 44–46
Crichton, Michael 136–137
Crowther, Bosley 59
Cuomo, Mario 157
Curtis, Tony 101, 102, 103–104

Dalí, Gala 131
Dalí, Salvador 26, 131
Danger 26, 29
Danner, Blythe 138, 139
Dark Eyes 25
Darrieux, Danielle 101
Davis, Nancy 21
Dawson, Anthony *see* Margheriti, Antonio
Dean, James 26, 38
Death of a Salesman 29
Death Rage 139–140
De Croisset, Francis 129
De Croisset, Philippe 129
De Mille, Cecil Blount 48, 49–55, 70–74, 110
De Mille, Katherine 72
de Sica, Vittorio 127
Deval, Jacques 44
De Villfranco, Edgardo 97

Dexter, Anthony 50, 97, 109
Dexter, Brad 94, 100
Dickinson, Angie 113, 116
Diener, Joan 141–142
Dietrich, Marlene 42–44, 55, 62, 142–143
Dimitrievitch, Aliosha 8, 122
Dimitrievitch, Ivan 8
Dimitrievitch, Marukha 8
Dimitrievitch, Valentina 8
Dominguín, Luis Miguel 89, 125, 145
Donen, Stanley 86–88, 89–91, 98
The Double Man 120–122
Douglas, Kirk 78–79, 113, 114, 130–131, 139
Drake, Alfred 32
Dunne, Irene 30

Eggar, Samantha 133
Ekberg, Anita 122
Ekland, Britt 120–121
Elliot, Cass 128–129
Epstein, Philip G. 65
Escape from Zahrain 39, 100–101
Eyles, Allen 109

Falk, Peter 117
Fallaci, Oriana 68, 69
Farrow, Mia 114, 140
Faulkner, William 79
Fearnly, John 33–34
Fellini, Federico 126
Ferrer, José 32
Ferrer, Mel 50
The File of the Golden Goose 128
Finney, Albert 125
Fischer, Eddie 100
Fisher, Carol 142
Five Miles to Midnight 110
Fleming, Ian 116
Flight from Ashiya 104–106
Fonda, Henry 134, 135, 151
Fonda, Peter 138
Forbes, Bryan 126
Forsythe, John 26
Francis, Arlene 87
Frank, Harriett 79
Frankenheimer, John 26
Funny Face 87
Futureworld 137–138
Fuzz 133

Gainsbourg, Charlotte 132
Gainsbourg, Serge 131, 132

Garbo, Greta 69
Garland, Judy 23
Gavin, John 126, 145
Gaynor, Mitzi 90–91
Gelbert, Larry 133
Gielgud, John 70
Gilmore, Virginia 17, 18, 19, 20, 23–24, 25–26, 27, 28, 42, 43–44, 48, 62, 75, 85, 92, 110
The Gladiators 78
The Godfather 137
Goetz, Edie 154, 157
Gogol, Nikolai 101
Good Morning America 159
Graham, Martha 145
Granger, Farley 135
Granger, Steward 50
Grant, Gary 70
Gravas, Costa 128
Graziano, Rocky 23
Grimaldi, Alberto 131
Gross, Shelly 144
Gruber, Lee 144
Guernsey, Otis L., Jr. 36
Guinness, Alec 70
The Guns of Navarone 101
Guns of the Magnificent Seven 118

Haas, Dolly 22, 25
Hammerstein, Dorothy 30
Hammerstein, Oscar 30–31, 32, 34–35, 58
Harrison, Rex 30, 31–32, 37, 87
Harvey, Laurence 127
Havelock Allan, Anthony 75
Hawkins, Jack 116
Hayes, Helen 62
Haynes, Alfred 121
Hayward, Leland 31
Hayworth, Rita 116
Head, Edith 72
Hecht, Harold 101, 105, 106
Heffron, Richard 138
Hefner, Hugh 140
Hemingway, Ernest 55
Hemmings, David 133–134
Hepburn, Audrey 50
Hepburn, Katharine 126, 127
Heston, Charlton 26, 51, 54, 72, 73, 81
High Noon 108
Hitchcock, Alfred 70
Holden, William 50, 70, 81

Holtzmann, Fanny 30
Home Sweet Homer 141, 142–144
Hopper, Hedda 52–53
The House in Paris 18
Houseman, John 20, 21
Howard, Ron 76–77
Howard, Trevor 116, 118–119
Huber von Windisch, Maria 4
Hughes, Howard 98
Hunt, Martita 63
Huston, John 126

Indiscreet 87
Invitation to a Gunfighter 108–109, 112
Ireland, Jill 124

Jackson, Anne 76
Jacobs, George 114
Jacobson, Max 50
Journey 75–78, 80, 86
Julius, J. 65
Julius Caesar 127

Kaplan, Leo 93–94
Karlin, Miriam 127
Kaufmann, Christine 103–104
Kaye, Danny 126
Kazan, Elia 23
Kelly, Gene 87
Kelly, Grace 26, 116
Kendall, Kay 87–89
Kennedy, Burt 118
Kermoyan, Michael 146
Kerr, Deborah 56–59, 60, 75–76, 77, 145
The King and I 1, 13, 29, 30–41, 42, 43, 44–45, 47, 48, 49, 50, 53, 56–60, 64, 65, 93, 110, 113, 114, 127, 128, 143, 144, 145–153, 154, 155–157
Kings of the Sun 108, 109, 111
Kleiner, Doris 92, 97–98, 100, 101, 104, 117, 122, 125, 129
Knight, Shirley 105
Koch, Ed 157, 159
Koestler, Arthur 78
Kornakova, Katya 14, 28
Koscina, Silva 127
Kramer, Stanley 108, 109
Krasna, Norman 98
Krassner, Paul 128
Krim, Arthur 78
Kruger, Hardy 127
Kulik, Buzz 124
Kunitz, Harry 87

Kurkutova, Natalya 5
Kurnitz, Harry 87
Kurosawa, Akira 93

The Lady in the Car with Glasses and a Gun 133
L'Amour, Louis 132
Lancaster, Burt 101
Landau, Ely 126
Landon, Margaret 30
Lang, Walter 57–58
Lantz, Robert 152, 158
Lasky, Jessie, Jr. 71–72
The Last Warrior 139
Laurents, Arthur 61
Lawrence, Gertrude 30–31, 33–36, 40–41, 152, 156
Lawrence of Arabia 70
Lawson, Don 23, 37, 38, 44, 48, 85, 97
Lazarus, Paul, III 137
Lear, Amanda 131
Lee, Christopher 127
Lee, Kathy 152, 153, 157, 158–159, 160
Lee, Ronald 39
Lehman, Ernest 56, 146
Leigh, Janet 104
Leigh, Mitch 142, 151
Leigh, Vivien 56
Leighton, Margaret 79
Lemmon, Jack 26
Leone, Sergio 98, 123
Leontovich, Eugenie 25
Let's Make Love 98
The Light at the Edge of the World 130–131, 133, 139
Lindley, Margaret 17
Litvak, Anatole 60, 75, 77–78, 86, 98, 110
Lloyd, Eulan 116
Logan, Joshua 31
Lollobrigida, Gina 81, 82, 83, 95
The Long Duel 118–119
The Long Hot Summer 79
The Longest Day 118
Loren, Sophia 110
Love Story 141
Lozano, Carlos 131
Lumet, Sidney 26, 29
Lute Song 7, 20–24, 25, 33
Lux Theatre of the Air 49

Macbeth 127
Macdonald, Carey 32

The Madwoman of Chaillot 126–127
The Magic Christian 127
Magnani, Anna 64, 72, 75
The Magnificent Seven 1, 92, 93–98, 115, 132, 136
The Magnificent Seven Ride! 118
Mann, Abby 72
Mann, Thomas 19
Marais, Jean 88
Marceau, Marcel 88
March, Fredric 70
Marette, Marcelle 60
Margheriti, Antonio 139, 140
Marre, Albert 141–142
Martin, Mary 20, 21–22, 33
Martin, Pete 3, 19
Masina, Giulietta 126–127
Mason, James 70, 100–101
Mastroianni, Marcello 116
Matthau, Walter 26
Mayer, Louis B. 154
Mazzola, Eugene 51–52
McDonald, Joseph 105
McQueen, Steve 94–97, 100, 116
Mercouri, Melina 104
Mermaid with Oranges 133–134
Miller, Arthur 65
Mineo, Sal 38–39, 100–101, 114
Miner, Worthington 25
Minnelli, Vincent 23, 58
Miramova, Elena 25
Mission to No Man's Land 86
Mr. and Mrs. 26
Mr. Jones and His Neighbors 19
Mitchum, Robert 124–125
Miyagawa, Kazuo 105
Monroe, Marilyn 55, 65, 98
Montand, Yves 98
The Moon Vine 18
Morarth, Inge 86
Moreheim, Lou 93
Moreno, Rita 57
Morgan, Hamilton 27
Morison, Patricia 133
Morley, Robert 76
Myerberg, Michael 20, 21, 24

Nantas, Salvataggio 19
Neame, Roland 39, 101
Nero, Franco 127
A New Kind of Love 50
Newell, Patrick 118–119
Newman, Paul 79

Newman, Walter 94
Nielsen, Leslie 26, 38
Nieper, Hans 154
The Night of 100 Stars 154
Niven, David 110
Nixon, Marnie 58
Noiret, Philippe 134, 135
North by Northwest 70
Novak, Kim 70

Odyssey see *Home Sweet Homer*
Oklahoma! 30, 32
Olivier, Laurence 64, 70
Omnibus 26, 39
On the Town 87
Once More, with Feeling 87–89
Opium 129
Orphée 88
O'Sullivan, Maureen 144
Othello 144

Parker, Suzy 105
Parsons, Louella 18, 23, 88
Pascal, Gabriel 70
Pavan, Marisa 82
Peck, Gregory 98
Peckinpah, Sam 123–124
Peil, Mary Beth 156
Perkins, Anthony 98, 110
Picasso Jacqueline 89
Picasso, Pablo 88, 89, 125
The Picasso Summer 125
Pinza, Ezio 32
Pitoëff, Georges 13, 69
Pitoëff, Ludmilla 13, 17, 18, 69
Pitoëff, Sacha 62
Platt Lynes, George 16
Plummer, Christopher 118, 119
Polanski, Roman 127
Polonsky, Abraham 131, 132
Pool, Sherman see Gilmore,
   Virginia
The Poppy Is Also a Flower 116,
   118
Port of New York 28–29
Porter, Cole 30
Power, Tyrone 80–81, 82
Presley, Elvis 69–70
The Pride of the Yankees 17
Private Lives 30
Puig, Manuel 88

Quinn, Anthony 72, 73, 74, 93–94

Ranieri, Massimo 139–140
Rashmon 105
Ravetch, Irving 79
Reagan, Ronald 21, 157
Rebel Without a Cause 38
Redfield, William 110
Reed, Susan 152
Rennie, Michael 50
Rescue: Yul Brynner 86
Return of the Seven 117–118
Rey, Fernando 124
Reynolds, Burt 133
Richard III 64
Richmond, Ted 81, 123
Ritt, Martin 26–27, 78, 79–80
Riva, Maria 42–44
Robards, Jason 75
Robbins, Jerome 31
Roberts, William 94
Rodgers, Richard 30–31, 32, 34–35, 58
Romance of a Horsethief 131–132
Rossellini, Roberto 60
Rudnick, Paul 153
Rule, Janice 109

The Saboteur: Code Name — Morituri
   110–112, 118
Sabrina 56
Sagan, Françoise 98
Saint, Eve Marie 70
Salmi, Albert 65
Salt, Waldo 101, 105
Sanders, George 82
Le Sang d'un poet 88
Savalas, Telly 117
Scharaff, Irene 31, 35–36, 58
Schary, Dore 65
Schell, Maria 65, 66
Schlipp, Paul Arthur 47
Schneider, Romy 118
Scott, Raymond 21
Segal, Erich 141, 142
Segal, George 109
Sellers, Peter 121, 122, 127, 128–129
The Serpent 134–135
Seven Brides for Seven Brothers 87
The Seven Samurai 93
Sharif, Omar 116
Shary, Dore 65
Shatner, William 65
Shavelson, Melville 112–113
Shdanoff, George 15, 144
Shore, Dinah 56

Silver, Richard 154
Sinatra, Frank 95, 113, 114
Singin' in the Rain 87
Small, Edward 81
Solomon and Sheba 80–85, 92
Soto, Manuel 97
The Sound and the Fury 79–81, 118
The Sound of Music 109–110
South Pacific 30, 31, 33
Spartacus 78, 130
Spiegel, Sam 70
Splash 76
Stark, Graham 121–122
Starlight Theatre 26–27
Starr, Ringo 127
Stevens, Inger 72, 73
Stevens, Roger 141
Stoddard, Sheila 21
The Stork Club Show 29
Strauss, Helen 30
Studio One 26, 73
Sturges, John 93, 94, 95
Sullivan, Ed 63
Surprise Package 89–91
Sweet Smell of Success 56

Tabori, George 75
Taki, Eiko 105
Tamiroff, Akim 61
Taradash, Daniel 111
Taras Bulba 101–104, 105–106, 128
Tarloff, Frank 121
Tate, Sharon 128–129
Taylor, Elizabeth 100
Taylor, Robert 81
The Ten Commandments 49–55, 64
Le Testament d'Orphée 88–89, 125
Texeira, Virgilio 81
Thang, Mai Long 7
Thion de la Chaume, Jacqueline 129–130, 133, 140, 141–142, 151, 152, 185
Thompson, Lee J. 101, 102–103, 108
Those Endearing Young Charms 18
Those Magnificent Men in Their Flying Machines 118
Tilden, Frankie 78
Tolo, Marilu 132
Tolstoj, Andrei 66
The Tonight Show 64
Towers, Costance 145, 146
Towne, Robert 123

Triple Cross 118
Truman, Bess 36
Truckline Café 23, 110
Tunberg, Karl 101
Turner, Lana 79
Twelfth Night 15, 22
20,000 Leagues Under the Sea 130

The Ultimate Warrior 139
Utgesu Monogatari 105

Van Druten, John 31, 32–33
Vaughn, Robert 94, 100
Verne, Jules 130
Vidor, King 81, 84, 108
Viertel, Peter 76
The Vikings 78
Villa, Pancho 123
Villa Rides 123–125, 126
Von Sydow, Max 139

Wald, Jerry 79
Wallach, Eli 94, 131, 132
Wanamaker, Sam 128
Wanted: Dead or Alive 95
Warhol, Andy 16
Wayne, John 113
Welch, Raquel 127, 133
Welles, Orson 127
Westworld 1, 98, 136–137, 138
White Nights 65
Widmark, Richard 103, 105
Wilcoxon, Henry 70–71
The Wild Bunch 123
Wild Is the Wind 72
The Wild One 29
Wilder, Billy 50
Wilding, Michael 50
Wise, Robert 109–110
The Wizard of Oz
Wood, Natalie 38
Woodward, Joanne 79, 80
The World's Greatest Showman 110
Wright, Stanley 86

Young, Terence 118
The Yul Brynner Cookbook 152
Yuriko 145

Z 128